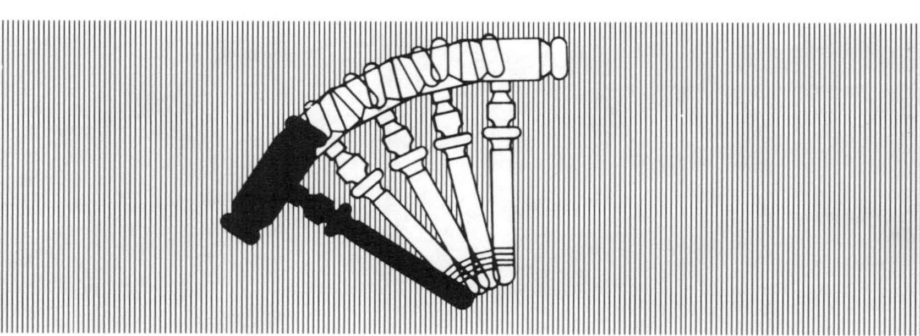

WILLS, TRUSTS, & ESTATES

William M. McGovern
Professor of Law
University of California, Los Angeles

Editor: *Cases and Materials on Wills, Trusts and Future Interests: An Introduction to Estate Planning*
Co-author: *Wills, Trusts & Estates* (with S. Kurtz and J. Rein)

NORMAN S. GOLDENBERG
Senior Editor

PETER TENEN
Managing Editor

CASENOTES PUBLISHING CO., INC.
1640 Fifth Street, Suite 208
Santa Monica, CA 90401
(310) 395-6500

Third Edition, 2000
First Printing, 2000

ISBN 0-87457-183-9

With the introduction of *Casenote Law Outlines,* Casenotes Publishing Company brings a new approach to the legal study outline. Of course, we have sought out only nationally recognized authorities in their respective fields to author the outlines. Most of the authors are editors of widely used casebooks. All have published extensively in respected legal journals, and some have written treatises cited by courts across the nation in opinions deciding important legal issues on which the authors have recommended what the "last word" on those issues should be.

What is truly novel about the *Casenote Law Outlines* concept is that each outline does not fit into a cookie-cutter mold. While each author has been given a carefully developed format as a framework for the outline, the format is purposefully flexible. The student will therefore find that all outlines are not alike. Instead, each professor has used an approach appropriate to the subject matter. An outline on Evidence cannot be written in the same manner as one on Constitutional Law or Contracts or Torts, etc. Accordingly, the student will find similar features in each *Casenote Law Outline,* but they may be handled in radically different ways by each author. We believe that in this way the law student will be rewarded with the most effective study aid possible. And because we are strongly committed to keeping our publications up to date, *Casenote Law Outlines* are the most current study aids on the market.

For added studying convenience, the *Casenote Law Outlines* series and the *Casenote Legal Briefs* are being coordinated. Many titles in the *Casenote Legal Briefs* series have already been cross-referenced to the appropriate title in the *Casenote Law Outlines* series, and more cross-referenced titles are being released on a regular basis. A tag at the end of most briefs will quickly direct the student to the section in the appropriate *Casenote Law Outline* where further discussion of the rule of law in question can be found.

We continually seek law student and law professor feedback regarding the effectiveness of our publications. As you use *Casenote Law Outlines,* please do not hesitate to write or call us if you have constructive criticism or simply would like to tell us you are pleased with the approach and design of the publication.

Best of luck in your studies.

CASENOTES PUBLISHING CO., INC.

CASENOTE LAW OUTLINES — SUPPLEMENT REQUEST FORM

Casenotes Publishing Co., Inc. prides itself on producing the most current legal study outlines available. Sometimes between major revisions, the authors of the outline series will issue supplements to update their respective outlines to reflect any recent changes in the law. Certain areas of the law change more quickly than others, and thus some outlines may be supplemented, while others may not be supplemented at all.

In order to determine whether or not you should send this supplement request form to us, first check the printing date that appears by the subject name below. If this outline is less than one year old, it is highly unlikely that there will be a supplement for it. If it is older, you may wish to write, telephone, or fax us for current information. You might also check to see whether a supplement has been included with your *Casenote Law Outline* or has been provided to your bookstore. If it is necessary to order the supplement directly from us, it will be supplied without charge, but we do insist that you send a stamped, self-addressed return envelope. If you request a supplement for an outline that does not have one, you will receive the latest *Casenotes* catalogue.

If you wish to request a supplement for this outline:

#5220, WILLS, TRUSTS, & ESTATES by McGovern ▶ (Third Edition, 2000)
(First Printing, 2000)

please follow the instructions below.

TO OBTAIN YOUR COMPLIMENTARY SUPPLEMENT(S), *YOU MUST FOLLOW THESE INSTRUCTIONS PRECISELY* IN ORDER FOR YOUR REQUEST TO BE ACKNOWLEDGED.

1. **REMOVE AND SEND THIS ENTIRE REQUEST FORM:** You *must* send this *original* page, which acts as your proof of purchase and provides the information regarding which supplements, if any, you need. The request form is only valid for any supplement for the outline in which it appears. *No photocopied or written requests will be honored.*

2. **SEND A STAMPED, SELF-ADDRESSED, FULL-SIZE (9" x 12") ENVELOPE:** *Affix enough postage to cover at least 3 oz.* We regret that we absolutely cannot fill and/or acknowledge requests unaccompanied by a stamped, self-addressed envelope.

3. **MULTIPLE SUPPLEMENT REQUESTS:** If you are sending supplement requests for two or more different *Casenote Law Outlines,* we suggest you send a return envelope for each subject requested. If you send only one envelope, your order may not be filled immediately should any supplement you requested still be in production. In that case, your order will not be filled until it can be filled completely, *i.e.,* until all supplements you have requested are published.

4. **PLEASE GIVE US THE FOLLOWING INFORMATION:**

Name: ______________________ **Telephone:** (   ) ____ - ____

Address: ______________________ **Apt.:** ______

City: ______________ **State:** ________ **Zip:** ______

Name of law school you attend: ______________________

Name and location of bookstore where you purchased this *Casenote Law Outline:* ______

____

Any comments regarding *Casenote Law Outlines?* ______________________

____

CASENOTES PUBLISHING CO., INC., 1640 Fifth Street, Suite 208, Santa Monica, CA 90401
TELEPHONE (310) 395-6500

INTRODUCTION

In most law schools today, the former separate courses in Wills and Trusts have been merged into one offering, which has various titles. This merger makes good sense since many wills create trusts, and living trusts are often used as will substitutes. The administration of estates and trusts raises similar problems. This outline therefore covers both wills and trusts, as well as other devices commonly used to transmit property at death, such as joint tenancy.

Much of the law in this area is statutory. In every state the property of a person who dies intestate (having no valid will) is distributed to persons designated by a statute that specifies very clearly who gets what. No outline can describe the law of every state. This one focuses on the Uniform Probate Code, which has been adopted in about fourteen states and has influenced the law in many others, but it also refers to other state statutes so the reader can be familiar with other views, for on some points the UPC represents a minority position.

Because state laws differ, this outline discusses the rules governing choice of law. Since state laws change from time to time, it also discusses the retroactive effect of changes in the law. A statute does not provide the answer to a problem if the statute is unconstitutional. In recent years a few state statutes have been held invalid by courts, particularly those dealing with children born out of wedlock or which make indefensible distinctions between the sexes.

The rules of law for wills and trusts are often phrased in abstract terms which are not common in ordinary discourse, *e.g.,* was this a "class gift"? Should distribution be *per capita* or *per stirpes*? One of the principal tasks of a lawyer is to see what these rules mean for a particular client. This outline prepares you for this task by providing concrete illustrations, most of them drawn from actual cases.

The examples are omitted from the capsule outline in order to keep it within manageable size, but the capsule outline is closely coordinated with the full outline. If you find something in the capsule which is puzzling to you because you have forgotten the context of the rule, use the paragraph number to find a fuller discussion of the same point in the main outline. Similar references in the answers to the sample examination will help you to review and prepare for your own examinations.

All of the topics discussed in this outline are covered in greater detail in a hornbook written by Sheldon Kurtz, Jan Rein, and me. The organization of the hornbook is similar to, but not identical with, this outline; with the table of contents and index you can find your way easily from one to the other. This outline, unlike the hornbook, does not cover future interests or taxation, but it does occasionally refer to income, estate and gift taxes because trusts are very often used to save taxes.

Many students approach the study of wills and trusts with distaste, perhaps because they connect it with the antiquated rules often covered in first-year property courses, like the Rule in Shelley's Case. However, the modern law of wills and trusts has very little to do with the hangovers from feudalism which you may (or may not) remember. It has to do with death and property, matters which are still very much with us today.

Medical science has improved life expectancy, but it has not made us immortal. Most law students are too young to have seriously contemplated their own death, and few have accumulated substantial amounts of property. Therefore, you may find it hard to "relate to" the subject, but it affects many persons who have no other contact with the law. Many lay attitudes about the law and lawyers are shaped by exposure to the legal system when a spouse or relative dies. Try to get a "feel" for the issues raised in this outline by thinking of them in the context of your own family.

Most students enter the legal profession, in part at least, to help other people. Lawyers who practice in this area can provide a lot of this help, not in the form of correcting social injustices, but in helping individual clients plan their estates so as to do the most good for the persons they want to benefit. By and large, persons can dispose of their property as they wish. Because of inadequate counseling, many persons fail to take advantage of this freedom. Most of the cases used as examples in this outline represent mistakes which could easily have been avoided. Often it was a lawyer who made the mistake. Lawyers are increasingly being sued for failing to draft wills properly. But lawyers who do the job right often report on the satisfaction which this provides. I hope that you will find the subject interesting and that this outline will help you to understand it.

In this second edition, many cases are cited or used as examples. Also, the newest version of the Uniform Probate Code is frequently cited. Where the differences between this and earlier versions are substantial, I have added the date (1990) to the citation to highlight this fact. It remains to be seen how many states will adopt these changes. As the UPC is further revised, the original goal of promoting uniformity seems more and more unattainable.

TC

TABLE OF CONTENTS

INTRODUCTION IN-1

TABLE OF CONTENTS TC-1

CAPSULE OUTLINE CO-2

CHAPTER 1: INTESTATE SUCCESSION

I. Choice of Law 1-2
II. Surviving Spouse 1-3
III. Relatives 1-4
IV. Wrongful Death 1-9
V. Disadvantages of Intestacy 1-9

CHAPTER 2: COMMON PROBLEMS IN WILLS AND INTESTACY

I. Claims by Remoter Issue 2-2
II. Lapse 2-3
III. Shares 2-8
IV. Children Born Out of Wedlock 2-9
V. Adoption 2-13
VI. Spouses 2-16
VII. Misconduct 2-18
VIII. Advancements 2-20
IX. Disclaimer 2-22

CHAPTER 3: LIMITATIONS ON THE RIGHT OF DISPOSITION

I. Protection of Children 3-2
II. Protection of the Spouse 3-7
III. Elective Share 3-7
IV. Community Property 3-10
V. Choice of Law 3-13
VI. Omitted Spouse 3-14
VII. Waiver 3-16
VIII. Other Limitations 3-17

CHAPTER 4: FORMAL REQUIREMENTS

I. Wills 4-2
II. Gifts 4-9
III. Trusts 4-13
IV. Joint Tenancy 4-17
V. Payable-on-death Contracts 4-18

CHAPTER 5: REVOCATION

I. Wills 5-2
II. Gifts 5-7
III. Trusts 5-8
IV. Insurance 5-9
V. Joint Tenancy 5-9
VI. Change of Circumstances 5-11

CHAPTER 6: EXTRINSIC EVIDENCE

I. Mistake of Fact 6-2
II. Mistake as to Contents 6-3
III. Ambiguity 6-4
IV. Constructive Trusts 6-5
V. Incorporation by Reference and Pour-over Wills 6-6
VI. Bank Accounts 6-8
VII. Other *Inter Vivos* Transfers 6-9

CHAPTER 7: INCAPACITY AND UNDUE INFLUENCE

I. Incapacity 7-2
II. Undue Influence 7-4
III. *Inter Vivos* Transfers 7-5
IV. Ethical Problems 7-7

CHAPTER 8: CONTRACTS TO MAKE WILLS

I. Formal Requirements 8-2
II. Remedies 8-4
III. Disadvantages of Contractual Wills 8-5

CHAPTER 9: ADEMPTION AND ABATEMENT

I. Ademption 9-2
II. Abatement 9-5
III. Payment of Taxes 9-7

CHAPTER 10: PURPOSES OF TRUSTS

I. Historical Uses of Trusts 10-2
II. Avoiding Probate 10-2
III. Tax Advantages of Trusts 10-4
IV. Management of Property 10-7
V. Discretionary Trusts 10-8
VI. Modification of Trusts 10-10
VII. Charitable Trusts 10-13

CHAPTER 11: RIGHTS OF CREDITORS

I. Fraudulent Conveyances 11-2
II. Joint Tenancy 11-2
III. Insurance 11-4
IV. Trusts 11-5
V. Spendthrift Provisions 11-6
VI. Claims against Probate Estate 11-9
VII. Liability of Beneficiaries, Heirs and Devisees 11-12

CHAPTER 12: PROBATE AND ADMINISTRATION

I. Probate 12-2
II. Necessity for Administration 12-5
III. Ancillary Administration 12-6
IV. Choice of Fiduciary 12-6
V. Fees and Other Costs 12-10
VI. Sales by Fiduciaries 12-13
VII. Investments 12-14
VIII. Self-dealing 12-17
IX. Remedies against Fiduciaries 12-19
X. Allocations between Principal and Income 12-22
XI. Distribution 12-24

EXAM PREPARATION

Exam Preparation EP-2

GLOSSARY

Glossary of Legal Terms and Phrases G-2

TABLES OF AUTHORITIES

Tables of Authorities (including Tables of Cases and Code Sections) TA-2

CROSS-REFERENCE CHART CR-2

INDEX ID-2

LAW

OUTLINES

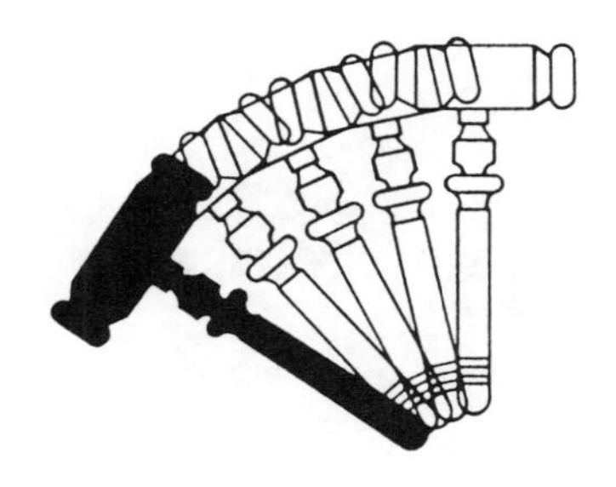

WILLS, TRUSTS, & ESTATES

CAPSULE OUTLINE

I. Intestate Succession CO-2

II. Common Problems in Wills and Intestacy CO-4

III. Limitations on the Right of Disposition CO-10

IV. Formal Requirements CO-14

V. Revocation CO-19

VI. Extrinsic Evidence CO-22

VII. Incapacity and Undue Influence CO-25

VIII. Contracts to Make Wills CO-27

IX. Ademption and Abatement CO-28

X. Purposes of Trusts CO-30

XI. Rights of Creditors; Spendthrift Trusts CO-34

XII. Probate and Administration CO-37

CHAPTER 1

CO

CHAPTER 1: INTESTATE SUCCESSION

I. CHOICE OF LAW

A. Each state has its own statute governing intestate succession. (#1.1)

1. Land is governed by the law of the state where it is situated. (#1.2)

2. Personal property is governed by the law of the state in which the decedent was domiciled at death. (#1.3)

3. A will can choose the governing law, *e.g.*, a devise "to my heirs as determined under the law of New York." (#1.5)

B. Time

1. The intestate succession statute which was in effect when the decedent died controls. (#1.6)

2. A devise to "heirs" should specify the time that the relevant law is to be determined, *e.g.*, "to my heirs as determined under the laws of the state of New York as of the date of my death." (#1.7)

II. SURVIVING SPOUSE

A. Virtually all states have eliminated the historical distinction between widows and widowers. (#1.10)

B. When the intestate is survived by a spouse and issue, most statutes give the spouse a fraction of the estate. In a few states, the surviving spouse gets everything. (#1.11)

1. In some states, the spouse's share depends upon the number of children. The UPC reduces the spouse's share if the spouse or the intestate has children by another marriage. (#1.12)

2. In most community property states, when a spouse dies intestate the other spouse inherits all the community property. (#1.14)

3. The longer a marriage lasts, the more community property is likely to exist. In separate property states, the length of the marriage is irrelevant. (#1.15)

C. The spouse gets a larger share, often all the estate, if the intestate has no surviving issue or other close relatives. (#1.16)

III. RELATIVES

A. Whatever does not go to the surviving spouse goes to the issue of the decedent. (#1.17)

B. **Remoter Issue**

1. More remote issue do not get a share if their parents are living. (#1.18)

2. If one of the decedent's children predeceases her, the dead child's children take his share by representation. (#1.19)

C. **If a person's only surviving issue are grandchildren, in many states the grandchildren take an equal share because they are all in the same degree of kinship to the decedent. In other states, the grandchildren would take by representation or *per stirpes*. (#1.20)**

D. **In most states, the decedent's parents take everything if there are no issue. In some states, parents share with siblings. (#1.23)**

E. **If there are no issue or parents, the property goes to the issue of the parents. (#1.24)**

1. Half-brothers and half-sisters usually take the same share as whole brothers and sisters, but in a few states they get a smaller share. (#1.25)

2. Many states limit representation among collateral relatives. (#1.26)

F. **If a decedent is not survived by issue, parents or issue of parents, the grandparents or their issue (uncles, aunts, first cousins) take. (#1.28)**

1. In some states, the estate is divided equally between the paternal grandparents or their issue and the maternal grandparents or their issue. (#1.29)

G. **Many states allow any relative, however remote, to inherit if there is no closer relative of the decedent. The UPC does not allow relatives more remote than issue of grandparents to inherit. (#1.30)**

H. **In most states, relatives of the decedent's spouse do not inherit from the decedent. But in some states, they do in some cases. (#1.33)**

I. **If there are no heirs, the property of a person who dies intestate escheats to the state. (#1.36)**

IV. **WRONGFUL DEATH**

A. **The intestacy statutes are often the basis for dividing damages for wrongful death, but in many states the wrongful death statute departs from the intestacy rules. (#l.38)**

V. **DISADVANTAGES OF INTESTACY**

A. **The intestacy statutes are general rules which may be inappropriate in a particular case. (#1.40)**

B. Intestacy statutes often give a share to persons who are legally incompetent, such as minor children. (#1.41)

C. Often intestacy statutes divide property among several persons. This may make it hard to manage or sell the property. (#1.43)

D. Most statutes provide only for the decedent's spouse and blood relatives. The decedent may prefer to have the property go to a friend or a charity. (#1.44)

CHAPTER 2

CHAPTER 2: COMMON PROBLEMS IN WILLS AND INTESTACY

I. CLAIMS BY REMOTER ISSUE

A. A devise to "issue" or "descendants" is usually construed to include only children and the descendants of any deceased child. (#2.1)

B. A devise to "children" does not usually include grandchildren, even the children of a deceased child. (#2.4)

II. LAPSE

A. A devisee must survive the testator in order to take under a will. (#2.5)

B. Antilapse Statutes

1. Nearly all states have antilapse statutes. In most states, they give the share of a deceased devisee to her issue. (#2.6)

2. Most antilapse statutes apply only if the devisee is a relative of the testator, but some are broader. (#2.7)

3. The antilapse statutes do not apply if the will otherwise provides. (#2.8)

4. A devise "to John or his issue" produces the same result as an antilapse statute. (#2.9)

5. Some courts do not apply the antilapse statute to class gifts, but many do. The UPC even covers persons who were dead when the will was executed, but some statutes only cover class members who died after the execution of the will. (#2.10)

C. If the Statute Does Not Apply

1. Property sometimes passes intestate as a result of a lapse. (#2.12)

2. Class gifts are divided among the other members of the class if the antilapse statute does not apply. (#2.13)

3. Even without a class designation, a will can produce the same result by appropriate language, such as "to John and Mary or the survivor." (#2.14)

4. If a will says "I leave the residue of my estate to *X* and *Y*" and *X* predeceases the testator without issue, the UPC gives *X*'s share to *Y* just as if it were a class gift. In some states, *X*'s share would pass intestate. (#2.15)

D. Nonprobate property

1. Most insurance policies expressly require the beneficiary to survive the insured. A condition of survival is sometimes, but not always, implied in a living trust. (#2.16)

2. By their terms, most antilapse statutes apply only to wills, but the UPC also applies to will substitutes like a living trust. (#2.17)

3. If an insurance policy does not designate an alternate beneficiary, and no antilapse statute applies, the proceeds are paid to the insured's probate estate if the beneficiary fails to survive. (#2.18)

E. Future Interests

1. When a will creates an interest, for example, in "my wife for life, remainder to my children" and a child survives the testator but predeceases the wife, many courts hold that the child's interest is "vested" and passes to the child's estate. (#2.20)

2. The UPC extends the idea of the antilapse statute to future interests so that the child's interest in the foregoing example would pass directly to the child's issue or would fail if the child had no surviving issue. (#2.21)

3. When a future interest is given to "heirs," it often makes a difference when the heirs are determined. The UPC determines them as of the time when the interest becomes possessory. Thus in a devise "to my wife for life, remainder to my heirs," the heirs are determined as of the wife's death, and not at the testator's death. (#2.22)

F. Nearly all states have adopted a Uniform Simultaneous Death Act (USDA). (#2.23)

1. Under the USDA, a devisee or an heir is treated as if he predeceased if the order of deaths cannot be proved. If a person survives the decedent, even if only by a fraction of a second, the statute in its original version did not apply. But the UPC requires a devisee to survive by 120 hours unless the will provides otherwise. A will can override the presumption that the testator survived. (#2.24)

2. If the insured and the beneficiary die simultaneously, the insured is presumed to have survived. If two persons holding property in joint tenancy die simultaneously, the property is equally divided between the two estates. (#2.25)

III. SHARES

A. The term "equally" is ambiguous and has been variously interpreted. (#2.27)

B. The words "*per stirpes*" or "by representation" are also subject to conflicting interpretations. (#2.28)

C. A devise to persons who are all in the same generation, like "grandchildren," is construed to give each person an equal share. (#2.29)

D. Devises to "heirs" are usually interpreted to incorporate by reference the intestacy statutes in determining shares. The UPC also follows the intestacy statutes in dividing among "issue." (#2.30-.31)

IV. CHILDREN BORN OUT OF WEDLOCK

A. Historically, a child born out of wedlock did not inherit from his parents nor did they inherit from the child. A devise "to children" was presumed not to include children born out of wedlock. (#2.32)

B. Absolute bars against inheritance by children born out of wedlock are unconstitutional, but problems in proving paternity justify some limitations on inheritance from or by the father. (#2.33)

C. Terms such as "bastard" and "illegitimate" have fallen out of favor, but a provision in a will for "lawful" issue may exclude children born out of wedlock. (#2.36-.37)

D. Many states have adopted a Uniform Parentage Act, which, under the UPC, controls succession as well as other issues. (#2.39)

1. Most states treat a child as born in wedlock even if the parents' marriage was invalid or took place after the birth of the child. (#2.40-.41)

2. Even without any marriage, under the UPA a man is presumed the father of a child whom he receives into his home and holds out as his child. (#2.42)

3. Even without any presumption, paternity can be proved as a fact. Conversely, even if paternity is presumed, the presumption is usually rebuttable. For example, the mother's husband is presumed to be the father, but he can prove otherwise. However, claims or denials of paternity may be barred by the passage of time. (#2.43-.44)

4. When a child is conceived artificially, the mother's husband is deemed the father and not the donor of the semen. (#2.45)

E. All states allow a child to inherit from the mother, since proof of maternity is rarely a problem. (#2.46)

1. Claims to inherit from or by an unmarried father or his relatives are more

problematic. The UPC bars claims by any parent who has refused to support or acknowledge the child. (#2.47)

F. In construing terms like "children" in a will or other instrument, the UPC and many courts use the intestacy rules as a guide to intent. But an express intent to exclude children born out of wedlock will be respected. (#2.48-.49)

1. In construing wills, some courts apply the law in effect when the testator died to determine intent. This may bar children born out of wedlock. (#2.50)

V. ADOPTION

A. Originally, adoptees could not inherit or take under a will of a "stranger to the adoption." (#2.54)

1. Most states reject the stranger-to-the-adoption idea today. (#2.55)

2. In construing devises to "children" and the like, courts often follow the intestacy statutes, but not if the will shows a contrary intention. (#2.56)

3. In construing older wills, some courts exclude adoptees on the ground that the law in effect at the testator's death controls. (#2.57)

B. Adults

1. Most states permit the adoption of an adult, but some courts refuse to recognize such an adoption in construing a will. The UPC recognizes it only if the adopter raised the adoptee from an early age. (#2.58-59)

C. Biological Relatives

1. In some states an adopted child continues to inherit from biological relatives, but under the UPC, the tie between them is severed unless the adoption is by a stepparent. These rules apply also to gifts in an instrument to "children" and the like, unless the instrument otherwise provides. (#2.60-.61).

2. The UPC limits the rights of parents who have consented to an adoption by others from inheriting from the child. (#2.63)

D. Equitable Adoption: Courts sometimes treat a child who has been raised by foster parents as having been "equitably adopted" and thus entitled to inherit from them. However, the foster parents are not permitted to inherit from the child by virtue of an equitable adoption. (#2.64-.65)

E. Stepchildren normally do not inherit from their stepparents, and a devise to "children" does not usually include them. But in some states, they inherit in the absence of other heirs. (#2.66-.67)

F. **Courts usually recognize an adoption which took place in another state, but not if it offends the public policy of the forum. (#2.68)**

VI. SPOUSES

A. **"Spouses" have rights under the intestacy statutes as well as an elective share, *etc.*, so the legality of a marriage may be important. However, a devise to "my wife Mary" is effective even if the testator was not legally married to Mary. (#2.70-.71)**

B. **If John marries Mary when he is already married to Sally, the marriage is invalid, but Mary may acquire rights as a "putative spouse" if she married John in good faith. (#2.72)**

C. **Common Law Marriage**

1. If a couple live together without a marriage ceremony, some states treat them as married on the theory that a marriage only requires consent, and their conduct shows consent. (#2.76)

2. Such a "common law " marriage which was contracted in a state where they are valid will be recognized in other states. (#2.77)

D. **Parties who cohabit without a legal marriage may acquire rights on the basis of an express or implied contract, but this does not usually include a right to inherit. (#2.79)**

E. **A marriage may be invalidated for lack of capacity, but this may be impossible after one of the spouses has died. (#2.80)**

F. **A divorce terminates the spousal relationship when it is final. Even an invalid divorce may work an "estoppel" to claim that a marriage was in effect. (#2.81-.82).**

VII. MISCONDUCT

A. **Some states bar a spouse who abandoned a decedent from sharing in the estate, but many do not. (#2.83)**

B. **Homicide**

1. Most states today have statutes which bar inheritance by someone who killed the decedent. (#2.87)

2. The UPC bars anyone who "feloniously and intentionally kills the decedent," but some statutes bar only those who are guilty of murder. (#2.88)

3. Some courts hold that the bar operates only if the killer is convicted, but the UPC allows a court to determine guilt in the absence of a conviction. (#2.89)

4. If the killer is disqualified, the property passes as if she had predeceased the decedent. (#2.90)

5. If the killer and victim owned property in joint tenancy, one-half of it goes to the estate of each. (#2.91)

6. The killer's own property is not affected by the assumption that the killer died before the victim. (#2.92)

7. Third parties, like insurance companies who pay benefits without notice of the crime, are protected from liability. (#2.93)

VIII. ADVANCEMENTS

A. If an intestate gave property to one child as an "advancement," the law may take the gift into account in dividing the estate. (#2.94)

1. If the donee received more than her share of the intestate's property, she is not required to return this excess unless the transfer was a loan. (#2.95)

2. The UPC applies the idea of advancements to all heirs, but in some states, it affects only issue of the intestate. (#2.96)

B. In many states, gifts of a substantial amount to a child are presumed to be advancements, but under the UPC a gift is an advancement only if so declared in a writing. (#2.100)

C. Relationship to Wills

1. If a person dies with a valid will, the doctrine of advancements has no place. (#2.101)

2. Gifts made after the will is executed may be treated as a satisfaction of devises in the will, but under the UPC a gift satisfies a devise only if this intention is stated in writing. (#2.102)

IX. DISCLAIMER

A. Reasons for Disclaimer

1. Usually an heir or devisee disclaims property in order to save taxes. A qualified disclaimer is not a taxable gift. (#2.102)

2. An heir or devisee may also disclaim in order that his family receives property rather than his creditors. In most states, a disclaimer is not subject to challenge by creditors. (#2.105)

B. Requirements for Disclaimer

1. A disclaimer must be in writing, but it requires no consideration, unlike

the release or assignment of an expectancy by a prospective heir while the ancestor is still alive. (#2.106)

2. Under Int. Rev. Code § 2518(b)(2), the disclaimer must be made within nine months. (#2.107)

C. Disclaimers by Fiduciaries. Many states allow fiduciaries to disclaim on behalf of those they represent, but such a disclaimer may be disallowed if it is not in the best interest of the person represented. (#2.108-.109)

D. Disclaimed property passes as if the disclaimant had predeceased the testator. This can accelerate future interests following a disclaimed life interest. (#2.110-.11)

CHAPTER 3

CHAPTER 3: LIMITATIONS ON THE RIGHT OF DISPOSITION

I. PROTECTION OF CHILDREN

A. Children receive very little protection in American law from being disinherited. (#3.1)

B. Policy

1. **Parents must support their minor children, but any share such children receive from the parents' estate would have to be managed by a guardian. (#3.4)**

2. **A fixed share would have the same disadvantages as the intestacy laws; a discretionary one would require litigation to establish the appropriate share. (#3.5)**

C. In Louisiana, a person with children must leave them a portion of the estate even though the children are adults. (#3.6)

D. Courts often hold that the support obligation of a parent ends when the parent dies. (#3.9)

E. In order to support the decedent's family during administration, they receive a "family allowance" from the estate. (#3.10)

1. The family allowance takes precedence over claims of the decedent's creditors and the provisions of the will. (#3.11)

2. Trial courts have discretion in fixing the allowance. The UPC allows the personal representative to fix it, subject to court review. (#3.12)

3. Many states have a homestead exemption, which also protects the spouse and minor children from disinheritance and from claims of the decedent's creditors. (#3.15)

F. Nearly all states have "pretermitted heir" statutes. They are designed to protect children from being disinherited through oversight. (#3.16)

1. The UPC version applies only to children who are born after the execution of the parent's will. In some states, the statute covers all children. (#3.17)

2. The UPC only covers children, but many statutes provide for all issue. (#3.18)

3. An intention to disinherit a child expressed in the will bars any claim, but evidence outside the will showing an intent to disinherit may not be admissible. However, the UPC bars any child to whom the testator gave property in lieu of a devise in the will. (#3.20)

4. Most statutes give a pretermitted child his intestate share. (#3.21)

5. The statutes do not apply to nonprobate property, such as life insurance payable to a designated beneficiary. (#3.22)

II. PROTECTION OF THE SPOUSE

A. Almost all states protect spouses against disinheritance. (#3.23)

B. Traditionally widows got dower, and widowers got curtesy. (#3.23)

1. Dower and curtesy only covered land. Most modern statutes give the spouse a share of personal property as well. (#3.25)

2. Many states have abolished dower and curtesy. (#3.26)

III. ELECTIVE SHARE

A. In most states today, a surviving spouse can elect to take a share of the decedent's property regardless of the decedent's will. (#3.27)

1. The elective share is a fraction which does not vary depending on the size of the estate. Under the UPC, but not in most states, the fraction depends upon the length of the marriage. (#3.28-.29)

2. In most states, the elective share does not depend upon need; a spouse with ample resources can claim it. However, the UPC dictates otherwise. (#3.30)

B. The elective share is taken from the estate *after* creditors' claims, unlike the family allowance. (#3.31)

C. Some modern elective share statutes only cover the decedent's probate estate. (#3.32)

1. The UPC, however, allows the spouse one-third of the "augmented estate." This includes assets which the decedent transferred during life if the transfer was will-like. (#3.33)

2. Even without such legislation, some courts allow a surviving spouse to attack such transfers as "illusory" or "fraudulent." (#3.34-.35)

3. ERISA, a federal statute, prevents a spouse from being cut out of pension benefits. (#3.36)

4. The UPC exempts transfers for which the decedent received full consideration. (#3.37)

5. In some states a spouse can even upset transfers made prior to a marriage as "fraudulent." (#3.38)

C. Other Benefits Given to Spouse

1. The spouse must elect between the elective share and the benefits provided by the decedent's will. (#3.39)

2. The UPC also charges the spouse with any benefits received from the decedent by gift or a will substitute. (#3.40)

D. A spouse has a limited period in which to elect. (#3.41)

E. A conservator can claim the elective share for an incompetent spouse, but not a personal representative if the spouse dies before making the election. (#3.43-.45)

IV. COMMUNITY PROPERTY

A. In the eight community property states, one-half of the community property belongs to each spouse. A disinherited spouse can claim one-half of the community property but has no rights in the testator's separate property if the decedent leaves it to another person. (#3.46)

B. All property acquired during the marriage by gainful activity is community property. (#3.49)

1. All property is presumed to be community, even if title is held in the name of only one spouse. (#3.50)

2. Property can be proved to be separate by tracing. (#3.51)

3. When community property is commingled with separate property in acquiring an asset, some states simply reimburse the community for its contribution. Others give the community a pro rata share of the asset. (#3.53)

4. Parties can "transmute" separate property into community by agreement, *e.g.*, by putting the other spouse's name on the title. (#3.54)

C. Each spouse owns a share of the community property, whereas the elective share is only an expectancy until one spouse dies. (#3.56)

1. A spouse can usually set aside transfers of community property made by the other spouse during life. However, each spouse has "managerial" rights over community property, and in some states, a spouse can even make gifts of community property. (#3.57)

2. Community property rights do not depend on which spouse dies first, in contrast to the elective share. (#3.59)

3. A spouse does not have to elect between community property and property devised to the spouse by the decedent unless the will purports to dispose of both halves of the community property. (#3.60)

V. CHOICE OF LAW

A. The law of the situs traditionally governs land, but there is a trend to make domicile the controlling factor. (#3.61-.62)

B. Personal Property

1. Personal property is governed by the law of the decedent's domicile. (#3.63)

2. If a couple is domiciled in a community property state when the property is acquired, it remains community property if they later move to a separate property state. Conversely, property acquired while a couple is domiciled in a separate property state remains separate if they move to a community property state. But California treats such property as "quasi-community property." (#3.64)

C. A will cannot reduce the elective share by designating the law of another state. (#3.65)

D. Federal law supersedes community property claims with respect to certain property, such as pensions. (#3.67)

VI. OMITTED SPOUSE

A. Many states give a spouse who is not mentioned in a will an intestate share of the testator's estate if the marriage occurred after the will was executed. This is often larger than the elective share, but it does not cover nonprobate assets. (#3.68-.69)

1. Under the UPC, an omitted spouse has no claim against property devised to a child of the testator. (#3.71)

B. Proof of Contrary Intent

1. The omitted spouse's claim is subject to a contrary provision in the will, but a devise to a person whom the testator later marries does not bar the devisee. (#3.74)

2. Under the UPC, the claim may be barred if the will was made in contemplation of the marriage or if the spouse received property outside the will. (#3.75)

VII. WAIVER

CO

A. The UPC excludes from the augmented estate any property transferred with the written consent of the surviving spouse. (#3.76)

B. Parties may turn community property into separate by agreement, which in some states must be in writing. (#3.77)

C. The right of a spouse to an elective share may be waived by a written contract. (#3.78).

D. Such a waiver is unenforceable if it was not voluntarily made, or if it is "unconscionable" and there was not adequate disclosure of the other spouse's property. (#3.81-.83) Additional requirements are imposed for a waiver of the spouse's rights to pension benefits under ERISA. (#3.84)

VIII. OTHER LIMITATIONS

A. A few states limit devises to charity in a will executed shortly before the testator's death. Most states that once had such statutes have repealed them, and a few courts have held them to be unconstitutional. (#3.86)

B. A direction in a will that property be destroyed may be unenforceable as contrary to public policy. (#3.88) Devises that encourage divorce have also been held to violate public policy, but more recent cases have undercut this rule. (#3.89)

C. Many cases refuse to give effect to a disinheritance clause in a will which fails to give the property to others, but under the UPC, the disinherited heirs are treated as if they had disclaimed. (#3.90-.91)

CHAPTER 4

CHAPTER 4: FORMAL REQUIREMENTS

I. WILLS

A. History

1. The Statute of Frauds required that wills be signed and attested by three witnesses. The Wills Act of 1837 reduced the number of witnesses to two but required that wills be signed at the end. (#4.1)

2. Most American statutes are based either on the Wills Act or the Statute of Frauds. (#4.2)

B. Policy

1. Formalities provide reliable evidence of intent, safeguard against rash

dispositions, and enable courts to distinguish manifestations of testamentary intent from casual statements. (#4.3)

2. There is a trend to relax these formal requirements. The UPC and some courts permit wills when there was substantial compliance with the requirements. (#4.4)

CO

3. However, the trend to dispense with formalities has not been carried as far for wills as for contracts because the testator is unavailable to rebut false claims as to intent when a will is probated. (#4.5)

C. All states require that wills be signed. (#4.6)

1. Initials or an "X" are sufficient. (#4.7)

2. Someone else may sign for the testator if he signs in the testator's presence and by his direction. (#4.8)

3. Some statutes require that the will be signed "at the end." Others do not. (#4.9)

D. Witnesses

1. Nearly all states require two witnesses. (#4.10)

2. In many states, a devise to the witness of a will is void, but a devise to an extra witness is allowed. The devise is also valid if the witness would take just as much if the will were not probated, *e.g.,* because he is the testator's heir. The UPC abolishes the bar against interested witnesses. (#4.12)

E. What Witnesses See

1. Normally the witnesses see the testator sign the will, but it suffices if they see the testator acknowledge a signature previously made. (#4.13)

2. Some statutes require the testator to tell the witnesses that this is his will and request them to sign it. (#4.14)

3. In most states, a testator may sign the will before one witness and later acknowledge her signature before another, but some require that all the witnesses be present at the same time. (#4.15)

F. In most states, the witnesses must sign the will in the presence of the testator. The UPC merely requires that they sign the will "within a reasonable time." (#4.16)

G. The witnesses usually sign an "attestation clause" which recites that the proper formalities were observed. Such a clause has several advantages. (#4.18)

1. Sometimes the witnesses deny that the requirements for proper execution were satisfied. (#4.19)

2. In many states, if the witnesses sign an affidavit, the will can be probated without having them appear in court (#4.20)

H. The UPC allows "holographic" (unwitnessed) wills if they are in the testator's handwriting. Not all states allow them. (#4.23)

1. A handwritten will provides an extensive specimen of the testator's handwriting, but the absence of witnesses may cause doubt as to whether the writing was intended to be a will. (#4.24-.25)

2. Since witnesses are not available to establish the date of a holograph, some states require that they be dated. (#4.26)

3. Many writings have been denied probate as holographs because the paper on which they were written contained some printed matter. The UPC only requires that the material portions of the will be in the testator's handwriting. (#4.27)

I. The UPC does not allow oral wills, but some states do in very unusual situations. (#4.28)

J. Choice of Law

1. Traditionally, the law of the situs governed land, and the law of the testator's domicile governed personal property. (#4.29)

2. Under many statutes, a will is formally valid if it complies either with the law of the place of execution or of the place of the testator's domicile at death or at the time of execution. (#4.30)

K. Lawyers who draft wills which fail to comply with formal requirements may be liable to the intended beneficiaries. Most states now reject the traditional view that a lawyer is not liable to the intended beneficiary because there is no "privity" between them. (#4.32-.33)

II. GIFTS

A. The formalities required for *inter vivos* gifts are less stringent than those required for wills. Courts sometimes hold that a gift was testamentary and invalid for failure to comply with the formalities prescribed for wills, but such decisions are increasingly rare. (#4.35-.36)

1. All states require a signed writing to convey land. But an oral gift of land may be effective on an estoppel theory. (#4.38)

2. Most personal property of substantial value is in the form of claims against an institution, *e.g.*, a bank account. Failure to comply with the rules of the institution governing transfer may make a gift invalid, but some courts say such rules merely protect the institution from liability if it has acted without notice of the transfer. (#4.39)

C. Delivery

1. An effective gift usually requires delivery, but delivery can be only symbolic. (#4.40-.41)

2. If the intended donee is already in possession of property, delivery is unnecessary. (#4.42)

3. The donor can keep the property but deliver a writing to the donee indicating donative intent. (#4.43)

4. Delivery can be made to a third person for the donee. (#4.44)

5. Registration of property in the name of the donee may be a substitute for delivery. (#4.45)

D. Consideration

1. Deeds usually recite a consideration, but this is not necessary for validity. (#4.47)

2. Promises require consideration (or some substitute therefor like promissory estoppel). The distinction between a gift and a promise turns on (a) whether the donor's words indicated a present transfer, and (b) on whether the transfer involved property or only an "expectancy." (#4.48)

E. An unrecorded deed may be invalid as to some third persons but valid as to the parties themselves. (#4.49)

1. Recording creates a presumption that a deed was delivered. (#4.50)

III. TRUSTS

A. Trusts are either created by will (testamentary trusts) or *inter vivos* (often called living trusts). A testamentary trust must comply with the formalities prescribed for wills. (#4.51)

B. Most American states require that trusts of land be in writing. (#4.52)

1. The term of the trust can be pieced together from several writings. The writing need not have created the trust. (#4.53)

2. The trustee may waive the defense of lack of a writing by failing to raise it or by admitting the existence of the trust. (#4.54)

3. The writing requirement does not apply to trusts of personal property or to constructive and resulting trusts. (#4.55-.56)

C. A settlor can declare himself trustee of property without delivering anything to the beneficiary. But delivery is necessary if someone other than the settlor is the trustee. (#4.57-.58)

D. Custodianships for minors under the Uniform Transfers to Minors Act are much like trusts. When property is registered in a form which mentions the Act, no delivery is needed. (#4.59-.61)

E. No consideration is necessary to create a trust, but language indicating an intent to create a trust in the future is enforceable only if supported by consideration. Also, without a "res," a trust fails. (#4.62)

F. Attempts to enforce a trust sometimes fail because the settlor did not use appropriate language, but a "trust" can be created even though the word was not used. (#4.63)

1. When *A* transfers property to *B* with a statement indicating how *B* is to use the property, no trust is created if the suggestion was merely precatory. (#4.64)

2. Language may impose an enforceable obligation without creating a trust. One who gets property subject to a "charge" can keep it after he fulfills the charge, unlike a trustee. (#4.65)

F. Trusts in which the settlor reserves a life estate and a power to revoke may be challenged as testamentary, but the modern cases uphold such trusts if the settlor has signed a formal writing since this fulfills the policy behind the formalities for wills. (#4.66-.67)

1. Many persons open bank accounts "as trustee" for someone else, without indicating what the terms of the trust are. Such trusts are effective to make the account pass to the designated person when the depositor dies. (#4.68)

2. Often the owner of an insurance policy designates a trustee as the beneficiary. Many cases have upheld such trusts. (#4.69)

3. Today revocable living trusts are widely used to avoid probate. (#4.70)

G. Failure to designate a trustee does not invalidate a trust. Nor does a trust fail if the designated trustee is unwilling or unable to serve unless the settlor would not have wanted the trust without the designated trustee. (#4.71)

H. Some trusts have been held invalid for failure to designate beneficiaries. (#4.72)

1. Under the Restatement of Trusts, however, a gift may be upheld as a power of appointment in the "trustee." (#4.73)

2. The beneficiaries of a trust do not have to be named. Often a trust is created for the settlor's "issue," for example. (#4.75)

IV. JOINT TENANCY

A. Joint tenancy is not subject to the formal requirements for wills even

though it operates to transfer property at death to the surviving joint tenant. (#4.76)

B. **Historically, a gift "to *A* and *B*" was presumed to make them joint tenants, but many statutes change this presumption to tenancy in common. When a tenant in common dies, her share passes to her estate. (#4.77)**

1. Under the UPC, a bank account payable to two or more persons is a joint account even if there is no mention of a right of survivorship. (#4.79)

C. **In most states, a joint account can be created without any writing. (#4.80)**

D. **Historically, a person who wanted to put land which he owned into joint tenancy first had to deliver it to a straw man. Many states dispense with this formality, and no delivery is required to create a joint bank account. (#4.81-.82)**

E. **The contents of the joint safe deposit box do not become the property of the surviving tenant. (#4.83)**

V. PAYABLE-ON-DEATH CONTRACTS

A. **Designation of the beneficiary of an insurance policy or a pension plan is valid even though it does not comply with the formal requirements prescribed for wills. (#4.84)**

B. **Other Interests**

1. The UPC validates bank accounts which provide that at the death of the depositor the funds shall pass to a beneficiary. A similar rule applies to securities. (#4.84-.5)

2. Where there is no institutional setting for the transaction, validity is more doubtful. (#4.86)

CHAPTER 5: REVOCATION

I. WILLS

A. **Physical Act**

1. A will can be revoked by being torn or canceled. Total destruction of the will is not necessary. (#5.1)

2. Unless the act is done with the intent to revoke, the will is not revoked. (#5.2)

3. The physical act can be performed by another person, but only if it is done in the testator's presence. (#5.3)

4. Most states allow partial revocation by physical act, but some do not. A testator cannot add words to a will after signing it. (#5.4)

5. If an executed copy of a will was in the testator's possession and after his death the will cannot be found or is mutilated, courts presume that the testator intended to revoke it. This presumption can be rebutted by any evidence. (#5.5-.6)

6. Even if a missing will was not destroyed with the intent to revoke it, proof of its contents may be impossible. (#5.7)

B. A will can also be revoked by a subsequent instrument which is executed with the formalities prescribed for wills. (#5.9)

1. A holograph can revoke an attested will. (#5.10)

2. The subsequent instrument need not contain dispositive provisions. (#5.11)

3. The later instrument can revoke the earlier will by inconsistency, but if there is no express provision for revocation, courts try to reconcile the two instruments. (#5.11)

C. Revival

1. Suppose that a testator executes will 1 then executes will 2, which revokes will 1, then destroys will 2. Most states presume that the testator does not intend thereby to revive will 1. The UPC allows testimony that the testator did so intend, but in some states, will 1 would have to be re-executed. (#5.14)

2. A codicil may revive a revoked will by "republishing" it. (#5.15)

D. Dependent Relative Revocation

1. If a testator revokes a will under the mistaken assumption that a new will is valid, courts may find that the revocation was "dependent" on the validity of the new will. (#5.16)

2. Dependent relative revocation is sometimes confused with revival, but they may produce different results. Most states have statutes governing revival, but dependent relative revocation is a common law concept. (#5.18)

E. In most states if a testator divorces after executing a will, any devise to the former spouse is revoked. Separation without a divorce does not bar a spouse, but the spouse may be barred by the terms of a separation agreement. (#5.19)

1. The UPC extends this rule to devises to relatives of the former spouse, such as stepchildren.

2. Extrinsic evidence cannot be used to show a different intent.

3. Other changes in the testator's circumstances, such as an increase or decrease in wealth, cannot be used to infer an intent to revoke the will. (#5.20)

II. GIFTS

A. Ordinarily gifts, unlike wills, cannot be revoked. (#5.21)

B. Exceptions

1. Gifts "*causa mortis*" (in contemplation of death) are revocable. (#5.23)

2. A donor can recover a conditional gift if the condition is not satisfied. The gift of an engagement ring is usually held to be conditional on the marriage taking place. (#5.24)

III. TRUSTS

A. In most states, a living trust is irrevocable unless the trust instrument reserves a power to revoke. (#5.25)

1. Bank account trusts are presumed to be revocable. (#5.26)

2. If the settlor intended a revocable trust but the power to revoke was omitted by mistake, the settlor can have the trust reformed. (#5.26)

3. A settlor who creates a trust because of a material mistake of fact can rescind it. (#5.27)

B. Most trusts which reserve a power of revocation specify how it shall be exercised. Failure to comply with the prescribed method causes the revocation to fail. (#5.29)

IV. INSURANCE

A. Most insurance policies allow the insured to change the beneficiary, unless the insured has transferred ownership of the policy. (#5.31-.32)

B. Insurance policies generally state that a change of beneficiary is effective only when the insurer receives written notice, but "substantial compliance" with this requirement suffices. (#5.34)

V. JOINT TENANCY

A. Joint bank accounts belong to the parties in proportion to their contributions, unless there is clear evidence of a different intent. But when a person puts stock into joint tenancy, courts may find that a present gift was intended. (#5.37-.39)

B. A person who puts land into joint tenancy is presumed to intend a gift to the other party, but any party to a joint tenancy can "sever" it, turning it into a tenancy in common. (#5.40-.41)

1. When a husband and wife hold as tenants by the entirety, neither spouse can sever as long as the marriage exists. Tenancy by the entirety no longer exists in many states. (#5.42)

CO

C. A joint tenancy cannot be severed by will. However, a will which purports to dispose of property in joint tenancy puts the other tenant to an election if the will also devises other property to him. (#5.43-.44)

VI. CHANGE OF CIRCUMSTANCES

A. In most states, when a testator marries or has a child after executing a will, the child or spouse gets a share of the estate, but this does not extend to assets outside the probate estate. (#5.46)

B. In most states divorce has no effect on assets outside the probate estate, but the UPC now extends the rule for wills to all instruments. (#5.47-.49)

1. When spouses hold property in joint tenancy, a divorce usually severs the joint tenancy. (#5.50)

CHAPTER 6

CHAPTER 6: EXTRINSIC EVIDENCE

I. MISTAKE OF FACT

A. Evidence that a testator was laboring under a mistake of fact does not bar probate of a will unless the mistake was induced by fraud. (#6.1-.3)

II. MISTAKE AS TO CONTENTS

A. In contrast to contracts, courts have not traditionally reformed wills to correct mistakes, but the Restatement of Property now authorizes this. Courts delete words which were included in a will by mistake. (#6.4-.6)

III. AMBIGUITY

A. Courts admit extrinsic evidence to resolve a latent ambiguity in a will. (#6.7)

1. Courts may correct a mistake in describing an asset on the ground that a devise of property which the testator does not own is ambiguous. (#6.8)

2. When no legatee meets the description in the will, extrinsic evidence can show that someone else was intended. (#6.9)

3. Some courts regard a term like "children" as ambiguous when, for example, a claim is made by an adopted child. (#6.10)

B. Some courts do not allow extrinsic evidence when the ambiguity is "patent," *i.e.,* apparent on reading the will alone. There is no policy reason for this distinction, and many states reject it. (#6.11)

C. **Some courts allow evidence of the circumstances surrounding the testator, but not of alleged statements by the testator on the ground that they may be misremembered or misreported by witnesses. (#6.12-.13)**

IV. CONSTRUCTIVE TRUSTS

A. **If a devisee promised the testator to give the property to someone else, the promise will be enforced by imposing a constructive trust on the devisee. (#6.16)**

1. Sometimes the will indicates that the devisee is not to keep the property but does not reveal the terms of the trust. Here, there is no risk of unjust enrichment since there will be a resulting trust to the estate if the terms of the trust cannot be proved. Nevertheless, Restatement (Second) of Trusts gives the intended beneficiary the property, but not all courts agree. (#6.17)

2. No trust is imposed if the testator's intent was not communicated to the devisee while the testator was alive. (#6.18)

3. Out of respect for the policy behind the requirement that wills be in writing, courts require that the evidence of the promise be clear and convincing. (#6.19)

B. **If a person by force or fraud prevents a testator from making a will, courts impose a constructive trust for the benefit of the intended legatee. (#6.20)**

V. INCORPORATION BY REFERENCE AND POUR-OVER WILLS

A. **A will can incorporate a document by reference. This allows the document to be probated even though it is not signed or attested. (#6.21)**

1. Incorporation by reference is not limited to papers present when the witness signed the will. (#6.22)

2. The will must clearly identify the writing and manifest an intent to incorporate it. (#6.23)

3. The writing must be in existence when the will was executed. (#6.24)

4. The UPC permits a will to refer to a list of tangible personal property written before or after the execution of the will if it is signed by the testator. (#6.25)

B. **A bequest to a trust is valid, even though the will itself does not contain the terms of the trust, if the terms are set forth in a written instrument. The trust can be amended after the "pour-over" will is executed. (#6.26-.29)**

C. **A will can require resort to facts outside the will if they have significance apart from the will. They can involve events which occur after the will was executed. (#6.31-.32)**

VI. BANK ACCOUNTS

A. A joint bank account does not pass to the surviving party if there is clear and convincing evidence of a different intention. (#6.33)

1. Admissibility of extrinsic evidence does not depend on ambiguity or wrongful conduct warranting a constructive trust. (#6.34)

2. Some statutes make the account "conclusive evidence" of the depositor's intent. (#6.35)

B. Although the relevant intention is at the time the account was created, this can be proved by statements made before and after that time. (#6.37)

VII. OTHER *INTER VIVOS* TRANSFERS

A. Courts often exclude parol evidence when interpreting a written instrument, but deeds and trusts can be reformed to correct mistakes. (#6.38-.39)

1. Some courts require for reformation that the mistake be shared by both the donor and donee. (#6.40)

2. Courts may deny relief if the donor was negligent, e.g., signed the deed without reading it. (#6.41)

3. Courts do not generally give relief for a mistake of fact by the donor. (#6.42)

B. Courts sometimes hold that a deed was not delivered if the person who executed it did not intend to make a gift. (#6.44)

C. When *A* conveys land to *B* with the understanding that *B* is to hold the land for *A* or for a third person, courts may impose a constructive trust on *B* in order to prevent unjust enrichment. (#6.45)

1. When the transfer is by deed, a constructive trust is imposed only in cases of fraud or breach of a confidential relationship. (#6.46)

2. If the grantee never intended to perform, he is guilty of fraud. (#6.47)

3. The term "confidential relationship" has been variously interpreted. (#6.48)

D. When *A* pays for land but title is conveyed to *B*, courts presume that the parties intended that *B* hold the land in trust for *A*, unless *B* is "a wife, child or other natural object" of *A*'s bounty. (#6.50)

1. Evidence is admissible to show the actual intent of the parties. (#6.53)

2. Even if *A* does not actually pay the price but agrees to do so at the time of the purchase, the presumption of a trust arises. (#6.54)

3. Someone who pays part of the price may be awarded part of the land. (#6.53)

E. For reformation or for the imposition of a constructive or resulting trust, the evidence of intent must be clear and convincing. (#6.56)

1. Intent which is not communicated at the time of a transfer is irrelevant, but conduct subsequent to a transfer can be used to show what the parties intended. (#6.58)

2. The statute of limitations does not start to run until the trustee repudiates the trust. (#6.59)

F. Courts sometimes refuse to impose a constructive or resulting trust because of the plaintiff's "unclean hands." (#6.60)

1. The clean hands defense is often rejected in order to avoid unjust enrichment. (#6.61)

2. Trial courts have broad discretion on this issue. (#6.62)

G. Constructive and resulting trusts are enforceable against third persons who derive title from the trustee unless they are bona fide purchasers. (#6.63)

1. Creditors of the trustee can reach the trust property only if, with the beneficiary's knowledge, they extended credit in reliance on the trustee's apparent ownership. (#6.64)

2. If the trustee goes bankrupt, the bankruptcy trustee will hold free of trust. (#6.65)

CHAPTER 7: INCAPACITY AND UNDUE INFLUENCE

CHAPTER 7

I. INCAPACITY

A. In most states, a person must be eighteen years of age or older to make a will. (#7.1)

B. A will is invalid if the testator lacked mental capacity, but a testator who has been adjudicated incompetent may nevertheless have the capacity to make a will. (#7.2-.3)

C. Evidence

1. Most states put the burden on contestants of a will to prove lack of capacity. (#7.4)

2. Both laypersons and experts can testify as to the testator's capacity. Courts give great weight to testimony by the subscribing witnesses. (#7.6)

3. The relevant test for determining capacity is when the will was executed. But

evidence relating to a time before or after execution is admissible if it is not too remote. (#7.7)

D. If the will was the product of an insane delusion, it will not be probated. But if there is some basis for a testator's erroneous belief, it is not an insane delusion. (#7.8-.9)

II. UNDUE INFLUENCE

A. A will may be denied probate because the testator signed under duress or undue influence. If undue influence affects only part of the will, the rest is probated. (#7.11-.12)

1. Influence exerted on the testator is not necessarily "undue." (#7.13)

2. Influence may be undue even if it is exerted by someone who does not benefit from the will. (#7.14)

3. Courts and juries often find undue influence if the will seems "unnatural." (#7.15)

B. Proof

1. The burden of proof of undue influence is on the contestants. (#7.16)

2. Courts may infer undue influence from the circumstances. (#7.17)

C. If a person in a confidential relationship with the testator participated in preparing the will, a presumption of undue influence arises. (#7.19)

1. Certain relationships are deemed confidential by nature, such as attorney/client. Kinship does not necessarily create a confidential relationship; the key factor is dominance by one person over another.

2. The presumption can be rebutted by showing that the testator received independent advice. (#7.21)

III. *INTER VIVOS* TRANSFERS

A. *Inter vivos* conveyances can also be challenged for undue influence or incapacity. (#7.22)

1. In many states, an adjudication of incompetence renders all subsequent gifts invalid. (#7.23)

2. A presumption of undue influence arises from a confidential relationship between the donor and the donee even if the donee did not participate in preparing the donative instrument. (#7.24)

3. Even if a transfer is voidable for incapacity or undue influence, a bona fide purchaser from the donee can retain the property. (#7.25)

B. Gift by Guardians and Agents

1. A conservator cannot make a will for the conservatee but can make gifts of the conservatee's property if a court finds that the conservatee would have done so if competent. (#7.28)

2. Normally a power of attorney does not allow the agent to make gifts, but some powers have been construed to authorize this. (#7.29)

IV. ETHICAL PROBLEMS

A. A lawyer may be disciplined for drafting a will in which the lawyer or relative of the lawyer receives a benefit. (#7.32)

1. The Model Rules of Professional Conduct makes an exception when the lawyer and client are "related" to each other. (#7.35)

2. A lawyer's recommendation of herself as executor or trustee may be unethical under EC § 5-6 of the Code of Professional Responsibility, but the Model Rules have no comparable provision. (#7.36)

B. Since a lawyer's credibility as a witness may be impaired if he also appears as an advocate, a lawyer who expects to be called as a witness should not serve in a will contest. (#7.37)

CHAPTER 8: CONTRACTS TO MAKE WILLS

I. FORMAL REQUIREMENTS

A. Statute

1. Contracts to devise land are covered by the requirement in the Statute of Frauds that contracts to sell land must be in writing. (#8.1)

2. Many states require that all contracts to make a will be in writing and signed. (#8.2)

B. Joint and Mutual Wills

1. Some courts presume that persons who execute a joint will have agreed not to revoke it. UPC is contra. (#8.3)

2. Most courts refuse to infer the existence of a contract from mutual wills, separate wills executed at the same time. (#8.4)

3. Under the UPC, signing a will does not satisfy the requirement of a writing to prove a contract unless the will states the material provisions of the contract or expressly refers to it. (#8.5)

C. Part Performance

1. Part performance can satisfy the sale-of-land provision in the Statute of Frauds, but the UPC contains no part performance exception. (#8.7-.8)

2. Most courts hold that either party to a contract to make a will can repudiate it before there has been any part performance, even if the contract is in writing. (#8.9)

II. REMEDIES

A. Most courts probate a will even if it was executed in breach of a contract on the ground that probate courts have no jurisdiction to enforce contracts. (#8.11)

B. Courts allow suit if the testator repudiates the agreement while he is still living, but the promisee can wait until the promisor dies to sue; only then does the statute of limitations start to run. (#8.12-.13)

C. Courts impose a trust on the property for the benefit of the beneficiary. But if the promise was indefinite, the plaintiff may be restricted to quasi-contractual relief. (#8.14-.15)

D. Third Parties

1. An inter vivos transfer from the promisor may constitute a breach even if the contract by its terms only covered wills. (#8.16)

2. Some courts give the rights of the promisor's spouse precedence over the contract. (#8.17)

III. DISADVANTAGES OF CONTRACTUAL WILLS: Knowledgeable estate planners recommend against the use of contractual wills. A trust is a better way to accomplish the parties' goals.

CHAPTER 9: ADEMPTION AND ABATEMENT

I. ADEMPTION

A. If property which is specifically devised is not in the testator's estate, the devise may be "adeemed." However, where the facts indicate that the testator would not have wanted an ademption, an exception is often made. (#9.1-.2)

1. Ademption applies only to specific devises. A "general" devise can be satisfied with any property. A devise of "100 shares of IBM stock" is usually treated as general, but a devise of "my 100 shares of IBM stock" is specific. (#9.3)

2. If a testator sold property on credit, under the UPC the specific devisee gets any balance of the purchase price owed to the testator at death. (#9.4)

3. A mere "change of form" does not cause ademption. (#9.5)

B. **If a testator ceases to own property for reasons over which he had no control, usually there is no ademption. (#9.6)**

1. Under the UPC, a specific devisee of securities gets securities of another entity owned by the testator as a result of a merger and additional securities of the same entity received by the testator from a stock split. (#9.7-.8)

2. If property is destroyed by accident, the devisee gets any insurance proceeds payable to the testator at death. (#9.9)

3. If the property is sold by a conservator for a testator who has become incompetent, the specific devisee gets a general devise equal to the net proceeds of the sale. (#9.10)

II. ABATEMENT

A. **When the assets in an estate are insufficient to pay all the devises, residuary devises abate before general devises, and general devises abate before specific devises. Within each class, abatement is pro-rata. (#9.15)**

1. Under the UPC, this order of abatement is not followed if it would defeat "the express or implied purpose of the devise." (#9.17)

2. In a few states, devises of personal property abate before devises of land. (#9.18)

3. Legacies to a wife or children are commonly preferred to other legacies in the same class. (#9.19)

4. At common law, if property specifically devised was subject to a mortgage, other assets of the estate were used to pay off the mortgage. But under the UPC a specific devise passes subject to any mortgage without exoneration. (#9.20)

5. Under the UPC the spouse's claim to an elective share is equitably apportioned among all the beneficiaries of the estate. (#9.22)

B. **The UPC allows creditors to reach assets in a multiple party account only if other assets of the estate are insufficient. (#9.23)**

III. PAYMENT OF TAXES

A. **Federal law calls for apportionment of the estate tax as to certain assets such as insurance. Many states require that all beneficiaries of the estate pay a pro-rata share of estate taxes. (#9.25-.26)**

1. Some states distinguish between probate and nonprobate assets; taxes

attributable to the latter are pro-rated, but all taxes attributable to the probate estate come from the residue. (#9.27)

2. These rules can be modified by the terms of the will. (#9.29)

CO

B. If a devise to a spouse or a charity pays a portion of the estate tax, the federal estate tax marital or charitable deduction is reduced. The UPC expressly exempts such devises from paying a share of taxes. (#9.30)

C. Some states impose an inheritance tax. These are almost always apportioned, but a will may provide otherwise. (#9.35)

CHAPTER 10

CHAPTER 10: PURPOSES OF TRUSTS

I. AVOIDING PROBATE

A. Many persons use trusts to avoid administration, which is expensive and time-consuming. (#10.3)

1. In many states, the fees of the executor and the attorney are based on the size of the probate estate. (#10.4)

2. Distribution is much quicker for assets outside the probate estate. (#10.5)

3. Wills are more likely to be contested than nonprobate transfers because notice is usually given to heirs when a will is offered for probate. (#10.6)

4. In some states, the spouse's elective share does not extend to assets outside the probate estate, and creditors cannot reach them. (#10.7)

B. Advantages of Probate

1. Many attorneys charge more for drafting a living trust than for a will. (#10.8)

2. The short time limits for contesting a will do not apply to nonprobate transfers. (#10.9)

C. A living trust is not the only way to avoid probate, but commonly used alternatives like joint tenancy have drawbacks. (#10.10)

1. A surviving joint tenant may be incapable of managing the property, and the assets will be included in the probate and taxable estate of the surviving joint tenant. (#10.11-.12)

2. Joint tenancy may be regarded as a present gift. This can be unfortunate if the parties have a falling out or are subjected to claims of creditors. (#10.13)

II. TAX ADVANTAGES OF TRUSTS

A. A person who owns income-producing property may reduce taxes by

shifting the income to a person in a lower tax bracket. As to spouses, income shifting is unnecessary because they can file a joint return. (#10.14-.15)

1. In order to shift income for tax purposes, the trust must be irrevocable. (#10.17)

2. The trustee of a discretionary trust can distribute income to persons in lower tax brackets. (#10.18)

3. It is not necessary to use a trust to give income-producing property, but if the potential donees are incompetent to handle property, a trust is desirable. (#10.19)

B. Irrevocable trusts are sometimes used to reduce estate taxes. Gifts are taxed at the same rate as transfers at death, but they can save taxes. (#10.20)

1. There is an annual exemption from the gift tax of $10,000 for each donee. (#10.21)

2. A gift is valued as of the date of the gift, so if property appreciates, the gift tax will be lower than an estate tax. (#10.22)

3. If the settlor reserves the income for life or a power to revoke, the trust assets will be taxable in her estate. (#10.23)

C. Bypass trusts allow a beneficiary to enjoy income without having the assets included in his probate or taxable estate. (#10.25)

1. To qualify for the marital deduction, however, the trust assets must be includable in the spouse's estate. (#10.26)

2. Bypass trusts may incur a generation-skipping tax, but there are liberal exemptions. (#10.27)

3. It is not necessary to use a trust in order to bypass an estate, but legal life estates are usually less desirable than a trust. (#10.28)

III. MANAGEMENT OF PROPERTY

A. Trusts are often used to handle property for persons who are incapable of managing it. (#10.29)

B. Alternatives

1. Guardianship is less desirable than a trust because it terminates when a minor comes of age (usually 18). Many persons cannot handle property at that age. An adult can be adjudicated incompetent, but this is an expensive and embarrassing experience. (#10.30)

2. Virtually all states have enacted the Uniform Transfers to Minors Act. Using

this act makes it unnecessary to draft a trust, but the property must be distributed when the minor comes of age. (#10.31)

3. Most states allow durable powers of attorney which continue despite the principal's incapacity. Durable powers can be used in lieu of a trust to avoid a guardianship. (#10.32)

4. The owner of an insurance policy can select an option under which the insurer holds the proceeds when the insured dies, but it is often better to have them paid to a trust. (#10.33)

IV. DISCRETIONARY TRUSTS

A. Judicial Review of Trustees' Decisions

1. Even if the trust instrument gives the trustee "sole discretion," courts review for an abuse of discretion by the trustee, but they usually defer to the trustee's judgment. (#10.36-.37)

2. Some courts hold it improper to consider the beneficiary's other resources in determining her needs. Others disagree, and some approve withholding trust funds from a beneficiary who is receiving public assistance. (#10.38).

3. In determining what is necessary for support, the trustee should take into account the beneficiary's station in life. (#10.39)

4. If the trust instrument contains no standard like "support," judicial review is more limited. (#10.40)

B. If a beneficiary is named trustee or cotrustee of a discretionary trust, some courts do not allow her to make distributions to herself. (#10.41)

1. If a trustee can distribute to herself, the trust assets will be taxable in her estate unless the power is restricted by a standard. (#10.42)

2. If a sole trustee can distribute to herself, she will be taxed on trust income even if it is actually paid to someone else. (#10.43)

VI. MODIFICATION OF TRUSTS

A. Modification of irrevocable trusts requires the consent of the beneficiaries. This is often impossible because some beneficiaries are minors, unborn, or unascertainable. (#10.45)

1. Many courts accept proof that no other beneficiaries will come into being because a person can no longer have children. (#10.46)

2. A provision for the settlor's "heirs" may be construed to give them no interest. (#10.47)

3. A guardian may consent on behalf of minor or unborn beneficiaries, but they have a fiduciary duty to preserve the ward's property. (#10.48)

4. If some beneficiaries want to terminate and others do not, partial termination may be allowed. (#10.49)

B. Even if all the beneficiaries consent, most courts will not terminate a trust if its purposes have not been accomplished. England and a few American states do not follow this rule. (#10.51-.52)

1. A court may find that the purposes of a trust have been accomplished even though the time designated for termination has not arrived. But courts assume that the settlor's purpose would be defeated by termination of a trust that has a spendthrift provision. (#10.53)

2. A trustee's interest in collecting fees is not a valid reason for refusing termination, but a trustee has standing to oppose termination. (#10.54)

3. Since small trusts are uneconomical, some statutes allow them to be terminated prematurely. (#10.56)

VII. CHARITABLE TRUSTS

A. The rules governing charitable trusts differ somewhat from those applicable to private trusts, and they qualify for tax advantages. (#10.57)

B. Charitable purposes include the relief of poverty, advancement of education, religion, health, governmental and other purposes beneficial to the community. (#10.58)

1. Courts treat a trust as charitable even if they do not agree with the settlor's objectives, unless they are too eccentric. (#10.59)

2. A trust may not be charitable if the benefits are confined to too small a group, such as the settlor's descendants. Racial restrictions are valid as a matter of trust law but may cause a loss of any tax deduction, and they violate the Constitution if they involve state action. (#10.60)

3. A trust to promote change in the law is charitable, but one to support a political party is not. (#10.61)

4. Even an institution devoted to a charitable purpose is not charitable if it makes a profit, but charging fees for services does not disqualify a charity. (#10.62)

5. Even if a trust is not charitable, it may be valid as an "honorary" trust, such as a trust to care for a pet or a tomb. Honorary trusts are not exempt from the Rule against Perpetuities and so cannot be perpetual like charitable trusts. (#10.65)

C. The Attorney General has standing to enforce charitable trusts. (#10.66)

1. The settlor has no standing to enforce the trust but can recover the assets if the trust fails. (#10.67)

2. A cotrustee can challenge actions by other trustees. (#10.68)

3. Other persons have no standing to sue unless they have a "special interest." (#10.69)

D. Restrictions in a charitable gift are enforceable, whether or not the gift is in trust. (#10.70)

1. Under the "*cy pres*" power, courts remove restrictions in a charitable gift which have become impracticable. *Cy pres* has also been used when money is left to a charitable organization which goes out of existence, or when the designated purpose has been accomplished. (#10.71)

2. Courts do not apply *cy pres* when the donor intended only to benefit a particular charity as distinguished from a general charitable intent.

CHAPTER 11

CHAPTER 11: RIGHTS OF CREDITORS; SPENDTHRIFT TRUSTS

I. FRAUDULENT CONVEYANCES

A. Creditors of a donor can aside a fraudulent transfer. (#11.1)

II. JOINT TENANCY

A. While Parties Are Alive

1. A joint bank account belongs to the parties in proportion to the amounts each has contributed. (#11.2)

2. When land is put into joint tenancy, creditors of either party can reach the debtor's interest. (#11.3)

3. If spouses hold land in tenancy by the entirety, creditors of one spouse cannot reach it while both spouses are alive. (#11.4)

B. At common law, creditors of a deceased joint tenant cannot reach the property, but the UPC allows them to reach a joint bank account. (#11.5-.6)

III. INSURANCE

A. In many states, insurance policies are totally or partially exempt from claims by creditors of the insured, both during life and after the insured dies. This exemption is lost if the proceeds are paid to the insured's probate estate. (#11.7-.9)

B. Promises made in a divorce settlement that a spouse or child will be the

beneficiary of an insurance policy are enforceable despite the exemption of insurance from creditors. (#11.10)

IV. TRUSTS

A. Creditors of the Settlor

1. If the settlor retains an interest, her creditors can reach it. Even if the trustee has discretion over distributions to the settlor, her creditors can reach the trust. (#11.14-.15)

2. If the settlor only has a power to revoke his trust, his creditors cannot reach the assets at common law, but many states have changed this rule by statute. (#11.16)

3. A person may be deemed the settlor even if a trust was technically created by another person. (#11.17)

B. Creditors of Other Beneficiaries. If the terms of a trust give a trustee discretion to distribute to a beneficiary, ordinary creditors of the beneficiary usually cannot reach this interest. (#11.19)

V. SPENDTHRIFT PROVISIONS

A. In most states the settlor of a trust can restrict creditors of the beneficiaries from reaching their interest by a "spendthrift" provision. (#11.21)

1. England does not allow them, but it allows "protective trusts" under which a beneficiary's interest is forfeited if his creditors try to reach it. (#11.22-.23)

2. Some states allow creditors to reach the income of a spendthrift trust if it exceeds the amount necessary for the support of the beneficiary or they impose a dollar limit on spendthrift trusts. (#11.24)

3. The Bankruptcy Code makes spendthrift trusts effective in bankruptcy if valid under the law of the state. (#11.25)

B. Traditionally, restraints on the alienation of a legal interest were invalid, but the federal Employee Retirement Income Security Act of 1974 (ERISA) makes benefits under most pension plans unassignable. (#11.27-.28)

C. After Payment

1. Creditors can reach money from a spendthrift trust after it has been distributed. (#11.29)

2. When corpus becomes payable, creditors can reach it even before it is distributed. (#11.30)

D. Claims for alimony and child support can be satisfied from a spendthrift trust or pension plan. (#11.31-.33)

E. Creditors who supply necessaries to a beneficiary can get reimbursement despite a spendthrift provision. (#11.34)

F. Tort claimants can reach a spendthrift trust since they did not voluntarily extend credit to the beneficiary, but ERISA makes no exception for tort claims. (#11.35)

G. Spendthrift provisions are invalid with respect to any interest reserved by the settlor. But insurance and pensions may be exempt from creditors even when paid for by the debtor. (#11.39-.40)

H. Most spendthrift provisions also bar the beneficiary from alienating her interest voluntarily. But a timely disclaimer is effective despite a spendthrift provision. (#11.42)

VI. CLAIMS AGAINST PROBATE ESTATE

A. Most claims survive death and can be asserted against the debtor's estate or by the estate of the creditor. (#11.44)

B. If an estate does not have enough assets to pay all claims, the personal representative must pay them in a prescribed order. Claims within each class are paid pro rata. (#11.47)

C. Nonclaim statutes require creditors to file claims against an estate promptly. This lets personal representatives know the total claims against the estate so they can pay them and distribute the balance promptly. (#11.49)

1. Nonclaim statutes, unlike statutes of limitation, apply to claims not yet due, but not to claims to property in an estate. (#11.50-.53)

2. Claims covered by liability insurance are usually exempt since they do not deplete the estate. (#11.55)

D. Claims Arising during Administration

1. At common law, personal representatives and trustees are personally liable on contracts which they make on behalf of the estate, but they are reimbursed from the estate if they were acting properly. Claimants can reach the assets of the estate only via this right of reimbursement. (#11.62)

2. Many statutes treat personal representatives and trustees like agents, who do not incur personal liability, and they allow claims to be asserted directly against the trust or estate. (#11.63)

CHAPTER 12: PROBATE AND ADMINISTRATION

I. PROBATE

A. Most states do not provide for declaratory judgments as to the validity of a will while the testator is alive. (#12.1)

B. A will can be probated in the state where the testator was domiciled or had property. A probate decree binds persons who reside in other states, but at common law, probate in one state has no effect on land in another states. Many states have changed this rule by statute. (#12.4-.6)

C. Historically a will could be probated without notice to the interested parties, but many states no longer allow this. (#12.7)

D. In most states, a will can be contested even after it has been admitted to probate. (#12.8)

1. Will contests must be brought within a short period after a will is probated. (#12.9)

2. A will can only be contested by someone who has a financial interest in setting it aside. A fiduciary's desire to earn a fee does not confer standing. (#12.10)

3. There is no constitutional right to jury trial in will contests, but many statutes allow it. (#12.11)

E. Many wills provide that any devisee who challenges the will forfeits the devise. These clauses are generally enforceable if the will is upheld unless the contestant had probable cause for contesting the will. (#12.12)

II. NECESSITY FOR ADMINISTRATION

A. Administration is designed to assure the orderly collection of claims against a decedent. (#12.16)

1. In insolvent estates, the personal representative acts like a trustee in bankruptcy. (#12.17)

2. Even in solvent estates, administration is usually necessary to collect and sell assets. (#12.18)

B. Avoiding Administration

1. Assets in a small estate can be collected without administration. (#12.19)

2. Property not in the probate estate is not subject to administration. (#12.20)

III. ANCILLARY ADMINISTRATION

A. Ancillary administration may be necessary because a personal

representative appointed in one state has no power to act outside its boundaries. Many states have modified this rule by statute. Putting property in a living trust can avoid ancillary administration. (#12.21-.23)

CO

B. The ancillary administrator may be ordered to distribute the assets collected either directly to the devisees or heirs of the decedent or to the domiciliary personal representative. (#12.24)

IV. CHOICE OF FIDUCIARY

A. There are various types of fiduciary. The rules governing them are similar but not identical. (#12.25)

1. Normally the court appoints the executor named in the will. (#12.26)

2. If a person dies without a will, a will fails to name an executor, or the one named is unwilling or unable to serve, the court appoints an administrator. Priorities for the choice of an administrator are established by statute. (#12.27)

3. The term "personal representative" covers both executors and administrators. (#12.28)

4. Most trust instruments designate a trustee. If they do not, or if the designated trustee refuses or is unable to act, a court will appoint one. Testamentary trustees are appointed by the probate court, but the trustee of a living trust usually acts without any court appointment. (#12.29)

5. There are two types of guardian, often called guardians of the person and guardians of the estate. The UPC uses the term "conservator" for the latter. (#12.30)

6. Agents are also fiduciaries. Custodians under the Uniform Transfers to Minors Act are much like trustees. (#12.31-.32)

B. Courts sometimes refuse to appoint or remove a fiduciary. (#12.33)

1. A conflict of interest may be disqualifying, especially if it was not apparent to the testator or settlor. (#12.34)

2. Extreme hostility between the fiduciary and the beneficiaries may be disqualifying. (#12.35)

3. Fiduciaries are sometimes removed for a serious breach of duty. (#12.36)

4. Some states prohibit a nonresident from acting as a personal representative. (#12.37)

C. No one can be appointed as trustee or personal representative involuntarily. Once accepted, however, the office cannot be resigned without court approval or the consent of all the beneficiaries unless the trust allows this. (#12.38)

D. Successors

1. Many wills and trust instruments designate successor fiduciaries or provide a way to select one. In the absence of such provision, courts have discretion in choosing a successor. (#12.41)

2. A successor fiduciary has the same powers as the original one unless a power is deemed "personal." (#12.42)

E. Wills and trusts often designate two or more persons to act as fiduciaries. At common law, all the trustees had to agree (except for charitable trusts), but many trust instruments and statutes provide for majority rule. (#12.43-.45)

V. FEES AND OTHER COSTS

A. Under the UPC, a personal representative is entitled to "reasonable compensation." (#12.46)

1. In many states, the fee is a percentage of the estate. (#12.47)

2. The time spent is considered also relevant in determining a reasonable fee. (#12.48)

3. A fee may be denied or reduced because of improper conduct by the fiduciary. (#12.49)

4. When there is more than one personal representative, the compensation is sometimes apportioned among them. In some states, the fee is multiplied. (#12.50)

B. Trustees get "reasonable compensation" in some states. In others, compensation is based on the size of the trust and its income. (#12.51)

C. Contract

1. If the will or trust specifies a fee, the fiduciary may be limited to that fee, but some courts allow higher compensation if the work was more onerous than anticipated. (#12.53)

2. Family members often serve without compensation. This may actually be advantageous to them, since a fee is taxable income whereas a bequest is not. (#12.54)

D. Fiduciaries can be reimbursed for hiring an agent, but not if the agent does acts which the fiduciary ought personally to perform. (#12.55-.56)

E. In some states, attorneys for the personal representative get a percentage of the estate. In others, they get a "reasonable" fee. (#12.57)

1. When the executor is an attorney, some courts allow compensation in both

capacities. In some states, she must elect between an attorney fee or an executor's fee. (#12.59)

2. A fiduciary is not allowed attorney fees as to matters in which he was acting in his own interest and not for the estate. (#12.60)

F. Bond

1. In some states, representatives must file a bond to protect the beneficiaries if the personal representative causes a loss to the estate and is unable to pay damages. The premium on the bond is charged against the estate. (#12.61)

2. Many wills waive bond in order to save the expense. Bonds are usually not required for corporate fiduciaries. (#12.62)

3. In some states, testamentary trustees must have a bond unless the will excuses it, but bonds are not required for living trusts. Guardians/ conservators must give a bond. (#12.63)

G. Many states require the appointment of an appraiser for estates who also gets a fee, but under the UPC this is optional. (#12.64-.65)

VI. SALES BY FIDUCIARIES

A. In many states, trustees have broad powers of sale, but often personal representatives can sell only with court approval. (#12.66-.67)

B. Many wills confer broad powers on executors or trustees to sell; conversely, some direct that assets be retained. (#12.68)

1. Even with a power of sale, it may be necessary to show a proper purpose for the sale. A sale may be necessary because property does not produce income or is speculative or because cash is needed to pay claims or to avoid subdividing property in making distribution. (#12.69)

2. A prohibition on sale can be overridden if drastic change of circumstances makes a sale necessary. (#12.70)

C. Terms of Sale

1. A power to sell does not necessarily include a power to sell on credit. (#12.71)

2. A fiduciary can be surcharged for selling at too low a price. (#12.72)

D. Even if a sale is improper, the buyer can keep the property if she had no notice and paid value. (#12.73)

1. At common law, trustees had to earmark property as property of the trust so purchasers would know they were dealing with a trustee. Many trust instruments and statutes have abolished this rule in order to facilitate sales. (#12.75)

VII. INVESTMENTS

A. Trustees must "make such investments [of trust funds] as a prudent man would make of his own property." In many states a similar standard applies to other fiduciaries. (#12.76-.77)

1. Many states used to have legal lists of proper investments for trustees. Many retain such a legal list of investments for guardians and personal representatives. (#12.78)

2. A higher standard is imposed on professional trustees. (#12.79)

3. Fiduciaries may not make "speculative" investments. Continuing to operate a business owned by the testator may be imprudent, particularly if the business is unincorporated. (#12.80)

4. Prudence requires that investments be diversified. Under the modern "portfolio theory," adopted by the third Restatement of Trusts, a broadly diversified portfolio is proper even if it contains some speculative securities. (#12.81)

5. Fiduciaries may be allowed to retain investments even if they would not have been suitable for purchase, but in some circumstances, even retention may be imprudent. (#12.82)

6. An investment which fails to produce income is ordinarily improper. (#12.83)

B. A will or trust may either restrict or expand the investments allowed. However, broad authority to invest does not necessarily allow investments which are imprudent. Courts sometimes allow trustees to ignore a restriction because of a change in circumstances. (#12.84-.86)

VIII. SELF-DEALING

A. Fiduciaries are not allowed to engage in transactions which involve a conflict of interest, such as buying property of a trust or estate for themselves, even if the price is fair. (#12.87)

1. When a transaction involves a relative of the fiduciary, the rule is less clear. (#12.88)

2. A conflict of interest may also exist if a fiduciary is a director or officer of a company in which a trust or estate holds stock. (#12.89)

B. The prohibition against self-dealing often creates practical difficulties, so exceptions have been made. (#12.91)

1. A will may expressly or implicitly allow self-dealing. (#12.92)

2. Self-dealing may be authorized by a court order. (#12.93)

3. Many statutes allow commercial banks who act as trustees to deposit funds in their own accounts. (#12.94)

4. A conflict of interest also arises when a corporate trustee holds its own stock in a trust, but the Uniform Trustee Powers Act allows them to retain it. (#12.95)

5. Some statutes allow a trustee who administers two trusts to sell property from one to the other if the sale is fair and reasonable. (#12.96)

C. Transactions between a fiduciary and a beneficiary are not ipso facto voidable, but courts scrutinize them for unfairness. (#12.97)

IX. REMEDIES AGAINST FIDUCIARIES

A. Relief against fiduciaries may include specific relief, such as an injunction, or monetary relief, such as a surcharge for loss to the estate or a profit improperly made by the fiduciary. (#12.98-.101).

1. Such relief is generally regarded as equitable, so there is no trial by jury. Traditionally courts refused to award punitive damages, but some more recent cases have done so. (#12.102)

B. Defenses

1. A provision in a will or trust relieving an executor or trustee from liability is effective unless the fiduciary acts in "bad faith" or profits from the breach. (#12.103)

2. A beneficiary who consents to a breach of trust may not thereafter attack it unless the beneficiary lacked capacity or did not know his rights or material facts. Normally consent by one beneficiary does not bar suit by the others. (#12.104)

3. A beneficiary who delays acting may be barred by laches or a statute of limitations. (#12.105)

4. A fiduciary may be protected if the transaction was covered by a court-approved accounting unless the fiduciary was guilty of misrepresentation or concealment in presenting it, or the beneficiary did not get notice of the proceeding and was not represented by others. (#12.106)

5. In some cases a fiduciary may raise as a defense that he relied on advice by others. (#12.107)

C. Each fiduciary must use reasonable care to prevent or redress breaches by the others. (#12.108)

1. A cofiduciary who is held liable may get contribution or indemnification from the others if they were equally or more at fault. (#12.109)

2. Persons who are not fiduciaries may be liable for participating in a breach of trust, but the modern tendency is to protect third parties in order to facilitate administration. (#12.110)

X. ALLOCATIONS BETWEEN PRINCIPAL AND INCOME

A. Most trusts call for the distribution of income to certain beneficiaries. Therefore, the trustee must allocate receipts and expenses between principal and income. (#12.111)

1. Most states have adopted one of two Uniform Principal and Income Acts. (#12.112)

2. The rules of allocation are superseded if the will or trust manifests a different intent. (#12.113)

B. When property is sold, the proceeds are principal, but if the property has not been producing sufficient income, some of the proceeds go to the income beneficiary. (#12.114-.115)

C. Cash dividends on stock are usually income, but in most states, stock dividends go to principal. (#12.116-.117)

D. Certain assets, like oil wells, lose value over time. If all the revenue is allocated to income, there may be nothing left for the remaindermen. (#12.119)

1. The 1962 Uniform Act apportions revenues from natural resources between income and principal. (#12.121)

2. The common law did not require trustees to create a reserve for depreciation, but the 1962 Uniform Act does. (#12.122)

E. When an income item is received after an income beneficiary dies, the part of it earned during his lifetime may be allocated to the beneficiary's estate. (#12.123)

F. Income received by an estate during administration is allocated pro-rata among the devisees except that specific devisees get the income attributable to the devised property, and pecuniary devisees get only interest starting a year after administration begins. (#12.124-26).

XI. DISTRIBUTION

A. Liability for Improper Distribution

1. Fiduciaries are liable for making distribution to the wrong person, even when they act in good faith. (#12.127)

2. Anyone to whom property is improperly distributed is liable to return it, unless he is protected by a statute of limitations or estoppel. (#12.128)

B. If the distributee lacks capacity, it may be necessary to appoint a guardian to receive distribution, but many wills and trusts allow distribution to someone else in this situation. The Uniform Transfers to Minors Act allows distribution to a custodian. (#12.129-.130)

C. Often even pecuniary legacies are satisfied by distributing property rather than cash. The property must be valued at the date of distribution. (#12.131)

INTESTATE SUCCESSION

CHAPTER SUMMARY

I.	Choice of Law	1-2
II.	Surviving Spouse	1-3
III.	Relatives	1-4
IV.	Wrongful Death	1-9
V.	Disadvantages of Intestacy	1-9

INTESTATE SUCCESSION

INTRODUCTION: If you die without a will (and most people do), the rules of intestate succession govern the disposition of your property. Even if you have a will, your heirs may contest it. If the will is found to be invalid, your property will pass by intestate succession. Also many wills leave property to the "heirs" of the testator or someone else. This gives the property to the persons who would take upon intestancy.

This chapter outlines the rules of intestate succession, including who takes, in what shares, and how to determine the governing law. It also discusses the distribution of proceeds from claims for wrongful death. It concludes with a discussion of why it is usually a bad idea to die without a will. For more in-depth coverage of the material in this chapter, see McGovern, Kurtz, and Rein, *Wills, Trusts and Estates,* 1-24 (1988).

CHOICE OF LAW

I. CHOICE OF LAW

A. **State (#1.1):** Each state has its own statute governing intestate succession. About a fourth of the states have adopted the Uniform Probate Code (UPC), but even in those states there are variants, partly because the UPC has been revised often, and some adopting states have not kept pace with the changes. When statutes differ, courts must decide which one applies.

1. ***Land* (#1.2):** Land is governed by the law of the state where it is situated.

2. ***Personal property* (#1.3):** Personal property is governed by the law of the state in which the decedent was domiciled at death.

   Example: An Ohio court followed Vermont law in distributing the personal property of a decedent who died domiciled in Vermont, even though most of his heirs lived in Ohio. *Howard v. Reynolds,* 283 N.E.2d 629 (Ohio 1972).

3. ***Equitable conversion* (#1.4):** When a will directs that land be sold and the proceeds distributed to the "heirs," the court will treat the proceeds as personal property. This is known as "equitable conversion."

   Example: A will directed that land be sold and the proceeds distributed to the testator's heirs. The court applied Illinois law to determine the heirs, even though the land was located in Indiana, because the testator died domiciled in Illinois. *Moore v. Livingston,* 265 N.E.2d 251 (Ind. App. 1970).

   Equitable conversion does not apply if the will simply *allows* the executor to sell the land. Thus when a resident of Virginia owned land in Nebraska that was sold during the administration of the estate, since the will did not require the sale, the proceeds were distributed under the law of Nebraska. *In re Estate of Hannan,* 523 N.W.2d 672 (Neb. 1994).

4. ***Designation in will* (#1.5):** A will can choose the governing law. If a will said the proceeds shall be distributed "to my heirs as determined under the law of New York," the court would apply New York law, even if the testator

had no connection with New York. A well-drafted will should specify the governing law so the court will not have to guess what the testator intended.

B. Time

1. ***Intestate succession* (#1.6):** The intestate succession statute which was in effect when the decedent died controls.

   Example: A court applied the law in effect when a decedent died to give a share to his son even though the law had been changed before the date of the decision. *Estate of Jones v. Jones*, 759 P.2d 345 (Utah App. 1988).

1

2. ***Will* (#1.7):** When a will creates an interest in the "heirs" of someone other than the testator, the law in effect at the testator's death may not control.

   Example: A will of a testator who died in 1912 created a trust. When the trust ended, the property was to be distributed to his "heirs." The court used the law in effect in 1990 when the trust terminated to determine the testator's "heirs" on the theory that the testator knew that the law might change and wanted the current rules to apply. *Boatmen's Trust Co. v. Conklin,* 888 S.W.2d 347 (Mo. App. 1994).

   a. Not all courts would agree with this result. The UPC by its terms applies only to estates of decedents who die after its effective date. Section 8-101(b)(1). A well-drafted will should specify the time that the relevant law is to be determined, *e.g.,* "to my heirs as determined under the laws of the state of New York as of the date of my death."

II. SURVIVING SPOUSE

SURVIVING SPOUSE

A. History

1. ***Land* (#1.8):** Historically a widow got one-third of her husband's land for life as dower. A widower got courtesy, all of his wife's land for life (if children were born of the marriage).

2. ***Personal property* (#1.9):** A widow got one-third of her husband's personal property if he had surviving issue (children, grandchildren, etc), and one-half when he had none. No provision was necessary for a surviving *husband* as to personal property, since he acquired all of his wife's personal property when he married her. This rule was eliminated by Married Women's Property Acts in the nineteenth century.

3. ***Present law* (#1.10):**

   a. Virtually all states have eliminated any distinction between widows and widowers. Those which still existed a few years ago were held to constitute a denial of equal protection. *Stokes v. Stokes,* 613 S.W.2d 372 (Ark. 1981).

b. Nearly all states have increased the surviving spouse's share. Most give the spouse a fee interest, not just a life estate, in land as well as personal property. UPC § 2-102. The feminist movement has played a role in increasing the spouse's share since in a majority of situations the wife is the surviving spouse.

B. Spouse and Issue (#1.11): When the intestate is survived by a spouse and by issue, most statutes give the spouse a fraction of the estate, depending on several factors. In some states, the surviving spouse gets everything.

1. ***Issue of another marriage* (#1.12):** Many states reduce the spouse's share if the intestate has children by another marriage. Under UPC § 2-102(4), the spouse's share is reduced to one-half (plus $100,000) when the intestate has issue who are not issue of the spouse. In this situation, the spouse is less likely to leave the share he/she receives to the decedent's children when the spouse dies. Recall how Cinderella's stepmother treated her.

   a. If the *spouse* has issue who are not issue of the decedent, the spouse's share is $150,000 plus one half the estate under UPC § 1-102(3).

2. ***Number of children* (#1.13):** In some states, the spouse's share depends upon the number of children. *E.g.,* Cal. Prob. Code § 6401(c) (as to separate property, spouse gets one-half if one child, one-third if more than one child). The UPC does not make this distinction.

3. ***Community property* (#1.14):** Eight states have special rules for community property. This is defined as property acquired during the marriage by the labor of either spouse. Property which either spouse owns at the time of marriage, or which is acquired during marriage by gift or inheritance, is separate rather than community. See #3.49, *infra.* In most community property states, when a spouse dies intestate the other spouse inherits all the community property, even if there are children. *E.g.,* UPC § 2-102A.

4. ***Length of marriage* (#1.15):** The longer a marriage lasts, the more community property is likely to exist. In separate property states, on the other hand, the length of the marriage is irrelevant; a wife of thirty years gets the same share as one who married the decedent three days before he died.

C. *Spouse and Other Relatives* (#1.16): The spouse typically gets a larger share if the intestate has no surviving issue or other close relatives. UPC § 2-102(1), for example, gives everything to the spouse if the decedent is not survived by issue or parents.

RELATIVES

III. RELATIVES

A. Preference for Issue (#1.17): Whatever does not go to the surviving spouse goes to the issue of the decedent. UPC § 2-103. Issue (or descendants — the two words are synonymous) includes grandchildren, great-grandchildren, etc.

B. Remoter Issue

1. ***Parents living* (#1.18):** More remote issue do not get a share if their parents are living.

   Example: A will left property to the heirs of Virginia. She was survived by three children and four grandchildren. The grandchildren took nothing because their parents (Virginia's children) were alive. *Central Trust Bank v. Stout,* 579 S.W.2d 825 (Mo. App. 1979).

   This rule helps to prevent property going to minors and reduces the subdivision of property into many small shares.

2. ***Representation* (#1.19):** If one of the decedent's children predeceases her, the dead child's children take his share "by representation", *i.e.,* they divide the share which their parent would have received. Thus if the dead child would have received one-third of the estate and he had five children, they would each get 1/15.

   a. These grandchildren take directly from the decedent; their share is not subject to claims of the parent's creditors or the terms of the parent's will. UPC § 2-110.

   b. Representation is not limited to one generation. If a *grandchild* of the decedent also predeceases her, the grandchild's children would take the grandchild's share by representation.

C. Shares

1. ***Division among grandchildren* (#1.20):** Suppose that a decedent has three children who all predecease her. She has four grandchildren. Three are the children of her son, James, and one is the child of her daughter, Lynn. One child died without issue. All states agree that the four grandchildren would inherit, and that no share would be allotted to the child who died without issue, but there are two views as to how to divide the estate. Under UPC § 2-106, the grandchildren would take an equal (one-quarter) share. (This is sometimes called *per capita,* but the UPC does not use this term). In some states, the grandchildren would take by representation or *per stirpes.* Lynn's child would get one-half of the estate as the representative of Lynn, while James's children would divide his share, getting one-sixth each. *E.g.,* Ky. Rev. Stat. § 391.040.

2. ***Division among children and grandchildren* (#1.21):** Now suppose that one of the decedent's three children survived her. All states agree that the surviving child would take one-third of the estate, but they disagree on how to divide the other two-thirds. In some states, Lynn's child would take one-third representing Lynn, and James's children would divide his one-third. Cal. Prob. Code § 240. This gives James's children a smaller share even though they are in the same relationship to their grandmother as the child of Lynn. UPC § 2-106 would divide the two-

thirds equally among the four grandchildren (who would thus get one-sixth each). This is called the "per-capita-at-each-generation" system.

3. ***Division among grandchildren and great-grandchildren* (#1.22):** Assume that all the decedent's children predeceased her and so did one grandchild, a son of James, who had two children who survived the decedent. All states agree that the three surviving grandchildren (Lynn's child and the two surviving children of James) and the two great-grandchildren (the children of James's deceased son) would inherit. There are two views as to how to divide the estate.

   a. Under one view, all the heirs would take by representation. The initial division occurs at the level of the children even if they are all dead. This "pure *per stirpes*" approach gives Lynn's child one-half, James's two surviving children one-sixth each, and the two great-grandchildren 1/12 each.

   b. Under UPC § 2-106, only the more remote heirs (the great-grandchildren) take by representation. The estate is divided at the nearest degree of kinship in which there are surviving heirs — here the grandchildren. Under this method, sometimes called "*per capita* with representation," each grandchild of the decedent would take one-quarter, and the two great-grandchildren would take one-eighth each.

D. **Parents (#1.23):** If a decedent has no surviving issue, parents are next in line. In most states, the decedent's parents or surviving parent take everything if there are no issue. UPC § 2-103(2). In some states, the parents share with siblings of the decedent on some basis. *E.g.,* Tex. Prob. Code § 38(a) (if one parent dead, half to siblings).

E. **Issue of Parents (#1.24):** If there are no issue or surviving parents, the property goes to the issue of the parents or either of them by representation. UPC § 2-103(3).

1. ***Half blood* (#1.25):** If one of the decedent's parents had children by another marriage, they would be the decedent's half brothers and sisters. They would take the same share as whole brothers and sisters under the UPC, but a few states give half-blood relatives a smaller share.

   Example: A father had two children by his first marriage and three by his second. When one of the former died without a spouse or issue, 40% of her estate went to her whole brother and 20% to each of her father's children by the second marriage. *Curry v. Williman,* 834 S.W.2d 443 (Tex. App. 1992). Under the UPC § 2-107, each sibling would have received 25%.

   a. Historically half-blood relatives were not allowed to inherit land at all, but no state follows this rule today.

2. ***Representation* (#1.26):** Many states limit representation among collateral relatives, distinguished from issue of the decedent.

Example: Decedent was survived by first cousins and first cousins once removed (children of deceased first cousins, sometimes called second cousins). The latter could not inherit, since the statute limited representation to children of siblings of the decedent. *In re Estate of Task*, 543 A.2d 416 (N.H. 1988). UPC § 2-103(4), however, would allow representation in this case.

3. **Shares (#1.27):** Questions like those discussed above regarding division among issue also arise when collateral heirs inherit.

   Example: Decedent had four siblings who all predeceased him. *P* had two children, both dead but one survived by three children and the other by four. *H* had four children, all living. *L* had five children, four of them living and one dead, survived by a child. *E* had one child who survived. Thus the decedent was survived by eight nephews and nieces and by the issue of three who died before him. Each living niece and nephew took 1/11, and the share of each deceased niece or nephew was divided among his or her children. *Matter of Estate of Mebust*, 843 P.2d 310 (Mont. 1992).

   a. Under the "pure *per stirpes*" division which prevails in some states (*see* #1.22, *supra*), the estate would originally have been divided into at the level of the decedent's siblings into fourths, and *E*'s child would have taken one-fourth instead of one-eighth.

   b. In some states the children of the dead nieces and nephews would not be allowed any share. *See* #1.21, *supra*.

   c. Under UPC § 2-106, the 3/11 which went to the eight children of deceased nieces and nephews would have been equally divided among them. *See* #1.21, *supra*.

F. **Grandparents and Their Issue (#1.28):** If a decedent is not survived by issue, parents or issue of parents, the grandparents, or their issue (uncles, aunts, first cousins) take.

1. ***Maternal/paternal* (#1.29):** Everyone has two sets of grandparents, maternal and paternal. Under UPC § 2-103(4), half the estate goes to the paternal grandparents (or their issue if they are not living), and half to the maternal grandparents or their issue. In this situation persons in the same degree of kinship with the decedent may take unequal shares.

   Example: Suppose a decedent has six maternal cousins (grandchildren of his maternal grandparents) and four paternal cousins (grandchildren of his paternal grandparents). Under the UPC, the maternal cousins would each take 1/12 of the estate and the paternal cousins would each receive one-eighth. In some states, each cousin would receive 1/10. Cal. Prob. Code § 6402(d).

G. **"Laughing Heirs" (#1.30):** Remote relatives are sometimes called "laughing heirs" because their connection with the decedent is so tenuous that they are not aggrieved by her death. Many states allow any relative, however remote, to inherit. The UPC, however, does not allow relatives more remote than issue of

1

grandparents to inherit (though the decedent can leave her estate to them by will if she wants to).

1. ***Other states* (#1.31):** Many states that otherwise follow the UPC have rejected this innovation on the theory that the typical decedent would prefer a remote relative to inherit rather than have an escheat to the state.

   Example: A decedent was survived only by second cousins (issue of great-grandparents). They inherited. Although the intestacy statute generally followed the UPC, it did not limit inheritance in the same way. *In re Estate of Brunel,* 600 A.2d 123 (N.H. 1991).

2. ***Heir-hunting* (#1.32):** Remote relatives of a decedent are often hard to locate, and an industry has arisen to search for them.

   Example: A firm located relatives of the decedent who agreed to give the firm 40% of their inheritance if it revealed the location of the estate. The court held this contract was enforceable. *Matter of Estate of Katze-Miller*, 463 N.W.2d 853 (Wis. App. 1990).

H. **Spouse's Relatives (#1.33):** Under the UPC, relatives of the decedent's spouse (sometimes called relatives by affinity) do not inherit from the decedent. But in some states they do in some cases.

1. ***No other heirs* (#1.34):** Under Cal. Prob. Code § 6402(e), if the decedent has no surviving close relatives, the issue of a predeceased spouse take. As to stepchildren, *see also* #2.66, *infra*.

I. **Source of Property (#1.35):** Under the UPC, the source from which the decedent acquired the property is irrelevant, but in a few states it makes a difference.

Examples: In Kentucky if a person dies without issue, land which was given to him by one parent is inherited by that parent. Ky. Rev. Stat. § 391.020. Under Cal. Prob. Code § 6402.5, if a decedent dies without a spouse or issue, property derived from a predeceased spouse returns to relatives of the spouse.

The common law had a similar "ancestral property" rule, but most states have abandoned it because of the administrative problems of determining where property in an estate came from.

J. **Escheat (#1.36):** If there are no heirs, the property of a person who dies intestate escheats to the state. There may be a controversy as to which state gets escheated property.

Example: A resident of Illinois died without heirs. He had a bank account in Seattle. The state of Washington got the money on the theory that it was located there, even though in choosing the governing law, Illinois, as the state of the decedent's domicile, would be preferred. *See* #1.3, *supra*. *O'Keefe v. State Department of Revenue,* 488 P.2d 754 (Wash. 1971). Some states in this situation would give the property to the state of the decedent's domicile, if it would do the same in the converse case. Cal. Prob. Code § 6805(b).

IV. WRONGFUL DEATH

WRONGFUL DEATH

A. **Importance (#1.37):** For many persons the most important "asset" at death is a claim for wrongful death. Unlike ordinary property, this claim is not subject to disposition by the will of the decedent.

B. **Relationship to Intestacy Statutes (#1.38):** The intestacy statutes are often the basis for dividing the recovery.

Example: Decedent's father and mother got an equal share of the proceeds even though the father had failed to support his child; the wrongful death statute tracked the intestacy law, which took no account of this. *Pogue v. Pogue,* 434 So.2d 262 (Ala. App. 1983).

1. ***Flexibility* (#1.39):** In many states, however, the wrongful death statute departs from the intestacy rules, often giving the court discretion on how to divide the recovery.

   Example: Decedent was survived by a child who was his only heir, but his mother and siblings could share in recovery for wrongful death. Under the statute, the court or jury had discretion as to how to divide the proceeds. *Butler v. Halstead,* 770 P.2d 698 (Wyo. 1989).

V. DISADVANTAGES OF INTESTACY

DISADVANTAGES OF INTESTACY

A. **General Rules (#1.40):** The intestacy statutes are based on what the legislators think decedents want done with their property. Scholars have attempted to throw light on this question (1) by studying wills of decedents who died testate and (2) interviewing people to find out how they would like to have their property distributed when they die. These studies have helped to shape the law. Nevertheless, the statutes are imperfect because general rules may not be appropriate in a particular case.

Example: All states give an equal share to each child of the decedent, but some parents prefer to favor a child who is especially needy, or to disinherit a child who has been unkind to them.

B. **Distribution to Incapacitated Persons (#1.41):** Intestacy statutes often give a share to persons who are legally incompetent, such as minor children. Lawyers usually recommend that property passing to minors be put into a trust.

C. **Trusts (#1.42):** Many wills create trusts, not only to manage property for minors but also provide for a spouse while assuring that at the spouse's death the property will pass to the testator's children. This is particularly useful (1) if the spouse is not the other parent of the children, or (2) to reduce estate taxes in large estates by using the exemptions of both spouses.

D. **Division of Property (#1.43):** Often intestacy statutes divide property among several persons, such as the decedent's spouse and children. This division of ownership may make it hard to manage or to sell the property. Therefore, many wills leave all the estate to the testator's spouse.

E. **Nonrelatives (#1.44):** Most statutes provide only for the decedent's spouse and blood relatives. The decedent may prefer to have the property go to a friend or a charity, particularly if her only heirs are distant relatives.

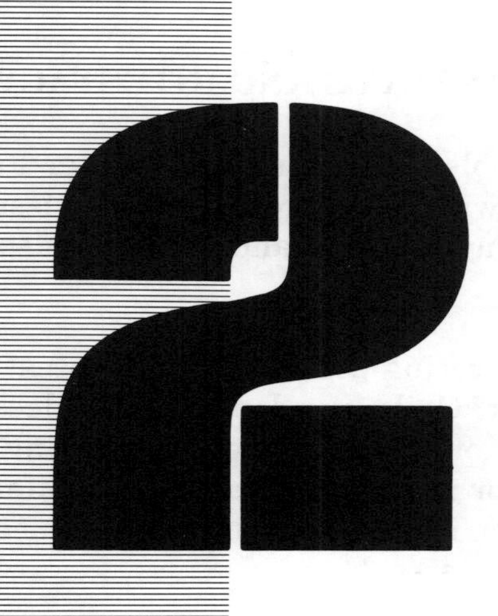

COMMON PROBLEMS IN WILLS AND INTESTACY

CHAPTER SUMMARY

I.	Claims by Remoter Issue	2-2
II.	Lapse	2-3
III.	Shares	2-8
IV.	Children Born Out of Wedlock	2-9
V.	Adoption	2-13
VI.	Spouses	2-16
VII.	Misconduct	2-18
VIII.	Advancements	2-20
IX.	Disclaimer	2-22

COMMON PROBLEMS IN WILLS AND INTESTACY

INTRODUCTION: Some of the problems discussed in Chapter 1 also arise when interpreting a will. For example, when a will leaves property "to my issue," how should it be divided? If a will leaves property "to my children" and a child predeceases the testator, what happens to the child's share?

Other problems arise both in interpreting wills and under intestacy. Does "children" include children born out of wedlock? Children adopted by the decedent? Children adopted by someone else? When is an heir or devisee barred from taking because of misconduct, such as deserting the decedent or murdering him? Should lifetime gifts made by a decedent to an heir or devisee be taken into account in distributing an estate? What if an heir or devisee disclaims his or her interest?

These problems also arise as to property which passes neither by will or intestacy, such as life insurance, and property held in joint tenancy or in a living trust. Such assets are not included in the "probate" estate and are commonly referred to as "nonprobate" property. The rules applied to nonprobate property are often the same as those governing the probate estate, but not always. For a more in-depth discussion of the subjects covered in this chapter, see McGovern, Kurtz, and Rein, *Wills, Trusts and Estates*, 25–184, 420–35 (1988).

CLAIMS BY REMOTER ISSUE

I. CLAIMS BY REMOTER ISSUE

A. Devise to Issue (#2.1): In intestate succession more remote relatives do not inherit if their parents are living. *See* #1.18, *supra*. Similarly a devise to "issue" is usually construed to exclude the descendants of any living child. *Restatement (Second) of Property (Donative Transfers)* § 28.2(2) (1987).

1. ***Per stirpes* (#2.2):** The exclusion of remoter issue is even more likely if the devise includes the words *"per stirpes"* or its English equivalent, "by representation."

   Example: Property was given *"per stirpes"* to my living children and grandchildren." The grandchildren got nothing because their parents were living. *Estate of Stowers v. Northwest Bank Indiana, N.A.*, 624 N.E. 2d 485 (Ind. App. 1993).

2. ***Per capita* (#2.3):** A devise "to my issue *per capita,"* on the other hand, may include all descendants. *Restatement (Second) of Property (Donative Transfers)* § 28.2, comm. d (1987).

B. "Children" (#2.4): A devise to "children" does not usually include grandchildren. Nor does a devise to "nephews and nieces" include grandnephews and grandnieces. Id. §§ 25.1, comm. a, 25.8.

II. LAPSE

LAPSE

A. Condition of Survival (#2.5): An heir must survive an intestate decedent in order to inherit. So also devisees must survive the testator in order to take under a will.

B. Antilapse Statutes

2

1. ***Effect* (#2.6):** Nearly all states have antilapse statutes which operate like representation in intestacy. *See* #1.19, *supra*.

   Example: A will leaves property "to my son James," and James dies before the testator leaving two children who survive the testator. James's children would take his share under a typical antilapse provision like UPC § 2-603.

   a. The devisee's issue take directly from the testator, so the property is not subject to claims by the devisee's creditors or taxable in the devisee's estate.

2. **Relationship of devisee to testator (#2.7):** Most antilapse statutes apply only if the devisee is a relative of the testator, but some are broader.

   Example: A will left property to nephews of the testator's wife. The antilapse statute did not apply to the nephews who predeceased the testator since they were not related to him. *Matter of Estate of Burcham*, 811 P.2d 1208 (Kan. 1991). Under UPC § 2-603 the result in this case would be the same, but devises to stepchildren are included.

   a. Some statutes apply only if the devisee is a descendant of the testator. *Matter of Estate of Ross*, 604 N.E.2d 982 (Ill. App. 1992) (devise to siblings of testator not covered). UPC § 2-603, however, applies if the devisee is a grandparent or a descendant of a grandparent of the testator.

3. ***Contrary Intent* (#2.8):** The antilapse statutes do not apply if the will otherwise provides. A devise "to John if he survives me" is usually held to show an intent that the statute should not apply. *Restatement (Second) of Property (Donative Transfers)* § 18.6, comm. a (1984). However, this is not true under UPC § 2-603(b)(3) (1990).

   Example: A will which left property to the testator's sisters said that if they did not survive, the property should go to their brother. The sisters and the brother all predeceased the testator. The court held that the antilapse statute did not apply. *Matter of Estate of Simpson*, 423 N.W.2d 28 (Iowa App. 1988). However, under UPC § 2-603(b)(4) the substitute gift to the brother would trump the antilapse statute only if he had survived; since he did not, the sisters' children would take.

4. ***"For John or his issue"* (#2.9):** A will can produce the same result as an antilapse statute by appropriate language. A devise "to my friend, John, or

if he dies before me, to his issue" would go to John's issue if John predeceased the testator, even though this was not covered by the statute. A devise which simply says "to John or his issue" is usually construed to mean the same thing.

5. ***Class gifts* (#2.10):** A devise to a group such as "my brothers and sisters" is a "class gift." Some courts do not apply the antilapse statute to class gifts. *Estate of Kalouse,* 282 N.W.2d 98 (Iowa 1979) (devise "to my cousins"; issue of cousins who predeceased the testator do not take). UPC § 2-603, however, like many statutes, applies to class gifts.

   a. The UPC even covers class members who were dead when the will was executed. Many states disagree, reasoning that a testator who wanted the children of a relative who was already dead to take would have said so explicitly.

      Example: A will left property "to my brothers and sisters." The children of a sister who had been dead for many years when the will was signed did not take under the statute, *Haynes v. Williams,* 686 S.W.2d 870 (Mo. App. 1985), but they would take under the UPC.

C. **If the Statute Does Not Apply (#2.11):** The antilapse statute may not apply because the devisee is not covered by the statute (*e.g.*, a nonrelative), or because the devisee had no issue who survived the testator. In such cases, several dispositions are possible.

1. ***Intestacy* (#2.12):** The property may go intestate.

   Example: A will left property "to my sisters, Ruth and Mary." Mary died before the testator without issue. Her share passed by intestacy to the testator's heirs. *McGill v. Johnson,* 775 S.W.2d 826 (Tex. App. 1989).

2. ***Class gifts* (#2.13):** Class gifts are divided among the members of the class who qualify (if the antilapse statute does not apply). Sometimes there is dispute as to whether a devise is a class gift.

   a. Many courts hold that if the devisees are named, as in *McGill v. Johnson, supra* #2.12, it is not a class gift. But not always.

      Example: A will left property "to my nephews Marshall and David and my niece Martha." The court held that this was a class gift. The court wished to avoid an intestacy because the testator was estranged from his heirs. *Sullivan v. Sullivan,* 529 N.E.2d 890 (Mass. App. 1988).

   b. A devise to a named individual and a group, such as "to Frank and the children of Mary," is usually construed as a class gift, with Frank being a member of the class. *Estate of Kalouse,* 282 N.W.2d 98 (Iowa 1979).

c. Designating the share of each member of the group, *e.g.*, "1/3 to each of my children," indicates an intent not to create a class gift. *Dawson v. Yucus,* 239 N.E.2d 305 (Ill. App. 1968).

d. Even a class gift lapses if all the members of the class die before the testator.

3. ***"To John or Mary"* (#2.14):** Even without a class designation, a will can produce the same result by appropriate language, such as "to John and Mary or the survivor" or "to John and Mary as joint tenants." In joint tenancy, the right of survivorship continues; if John and Mary both survive the testator, when one later dies, the other will take the property.

4. ***Residue* (#2.15):** Most wills make a series of devises, followed by a "residuary" clause, *e.g.,* "I leave the residue of my estate to *X*." If one of the earlier devises lapses, the property passes to *X* under the residuary clause (assuming it does not pass to the issue of the devisee under the antilapse statute or to the other members of the class in a class gift).

a. If a will says, "I leave the residue of my estate to *X* and *Y*," and *X* predeceases the testator, UPC § 2-604 gives *X*'s share to *Y*, just as if it were a class gift.

b. In some states, *X*'s share passes intestate to the heirs of the testator.

Example: A will said, "I leave everything I own to Chester and Roxy." Roxy was a dog who could not take. (Some courts would have upheld this as a trust for Roxy.) Roxy's share went to the testator's heir. *Estate of Russell,* 444 P.2d 353 (Cal. 1968). Present California law, however, is like the UPC; the failed devise would go to Chester. Cal. Prob. Code § 21111. Many courts reach the same result even without a statute on the basis of a preference for avoiding an intestacy. *Matter of Estate of Kirkendall*, 642 N.E.2d 548 (Ind. App. 1994).

c. If the will does not use the word "residue," a lapse may lead to an intestacy.

Example: A will left one-third of the estate to the testator's wife and the remaining two-thirds to designated relatives. When the wife predeceased, her share passed intestate because this was not a residuary devise. *Estate of Allen,* 388 N.W.2d 705 (Mich. App. 1986). But a comment to UPC § 2-604 (1990) says that a devise of "all my estate" should be treated as a residuary devise.

D. Nonprobate Property

1. ***Condition of survival* (#2.16):** Most insurance policies expressly require the beneficiary to survive the insured in order to take. Under UPC § 6-212,

the beneficiary of a multiperson bank account takes only if she survives. However, a condition of survival is not always implied in a living trust.

Example: A trust provided that when the settlor and his wife died, the assets were to go to designated children. The share of a child who predeceased the settlor was held to pass to his estate because this was a living trust, not a will. *First Nat. Bank v. Anthony*, 557 A.2d 957 (Me. 1989).

2. ***Antilapse statutes*** **(#2.17):** By their terms, most antilapse statutes apply only to wills, but some courts have applied them by analogy to living trusts. *Dollar Savings v. Turner,* 529 N.E.2d 1261 (Ohio 1988). UPC § 2-706 (1990) applies the antilapse statute, like other rules of construction, to all "instruments."

3. ***Payment to probate estate*** **(#2.18):** If an insurance policy does not designate an alternate beneficiary (or if the alternate beneficiary also fails to survive the insured), and no antilapse statute applies, the proceeds are paid to the insured's probate estate.

   a. If *A* and *B* hold property as joint tenants and *B* dies, the property will become *A*'s by right of survivorship and be part of *A*'s probate estate when he dies.

E. **Future Interests (#2.19)** Many wills and other instruments create future interests, for example, property is left "to my wife for life, remainder to my children." The children have a future interest (a remainder).

1. ***Presumption of vesting*** **(#2.20):** Courts often say the law favors early vesting of remainders.

   Example: A will left property in trust to the testator's son for life, remainder to his other children. Three of these children survived the testator but died before the son. Their interest passed to their estates because the law favors vesting and no condition of survival was expressed. *Dauer v. Butera*, 642 N.E.2d 848 (Ill. App. 1994). (If these children had predeceased *the testator* the antilapse statute would have given their interests to their issue.)

2. **UPC (#2.21):** UPC § 2-707 (1990) extends the antilapse idea to future interests. This applies only to trusts so as not to impede the alienability of land. (In a trust the trustee can sell the trust property regardless of who the beneficiaries are. *See* #12.66, *infra*) In *Dauer v. Butera*, *supra*, under the UPC, the children's interest would have been contingent on their survival until distribution, with a substitute gift to their descendants if they did not survive. Thus the shares of the children who died before the life tenant would have passed directly to their issue. If they had no issue their interest would have failed.

3. ***"Heirs"* (#2.22):** When a future interest is given to "heirs" of the testator or another, it often makes a difference when the heirs are determined, since anyone who dies before the time of determination is excluded from sharing.

   Example: A will left land to the testator's nephew for life, remainder to the testator's heirs. This was held to include a brother of the testator who survived him but died before the nephew, because the testator's heirs were determined as of his death. *Tate v. Kennedy*, 578 So.2d 1079 (Ala. 1991). But in *Warren-Boynton State Bank v. Wallbaum*, 528 N.E.2d 640 (Ill. 1988), when land was deeded to a daughter for life, remainder "to my heirs," the heirs were determined as of the daughter's death. Otherwise the daughter would have received the remainder since she was an heir of the donor when he died, but she was intended to have only a life estate.

   a. Under UPC § 2-711 (1990), "heirs" are determined as "if the designated individual died when the disposition is to take effect in possession," *i.e.*, the same result as in *Wallbaum*. Since this rule (unlike § 2-707) is not limited to trusts, it may impede alienability. In *Wallbaum*, for example, since the remaindermen were not determined until the daughter died, the land could not have been sold while she was alive because the owners could not be identified.

2

F. **Simultaneous Death (#2.23):** Since a condition of survival is imposed in inheritance, wills, insurance policies, etc., it is necessary to determine the order of deaths when two persons die at about the same time. Nearly all states have adopted a Uniform Simultaneous Death Act (USDA) to deal with this situation.

   1. ***Wills and intestacy* (#2.24):** Under the USDA, a devisee is treated as if he predeceased the testator if the order of deaths cannot be proved. The same rule applies to heirs. If a person survives the decedent, even if only by a fraction of a second, the statute does not apply.

      Example: *H* and *W* were critically injured in a collision. *H* died in the ambulance on the way to the hospital. *W* died a few minutes later. USDA was inapplicable, so *H*'s will leaving his estate to *W* took effect and the property then passed under *W*'s will to members of her family. *Matter of Estate of Villwock*, 418 N.W.2d 1 (Wis. 1987).

      a. UPC § 2-702 would change the result in *Villwock*; it requires a devisee to survive by 120 hours unless the will provides otherwise. UPC § 2-104 requires heirs to survive by the same period.

         Rationale: When a couple dies at about the same time, it is usually desirable to avoid multiple administration of the same property, *e.g.*, in both the husband's and the wife's estates. For this reason, many wills require devisees to survive by an even longer period, such as thirty days or six months.

b. Some wills provide that a devise lapses if the devisee dies "before the property is distributed to him." This language may lead to claims that the devise did not lapse because the estate *should have been* distributed more promptly. *Matter of Estate of Johnson*, 871 P.2d 360 (Ariz. App. 1991).

2. ***Nonprobate property* (#2.25):** If the insured and the beneficiary die simultaneously, the insured is presumed to have survived under USDA § 5. A new version of USDA, promulgated in 1991, parallels the UPC in requiring survival by 120 hours in all "donative dispositions." USDA § 3 (= UPC § 2-702 (1990).

a. If two persons holding property in joint tenancy die simultaneously, the property is equally divided between the two estates. USDA § 3. Under the latest version, this also applies if they die within 120 hours of each other. USDA § 4 (1991) (= UPC § 2-702(c)).

b. Provisions in a will dealing with simultaneous death do not control nonprobate assets.

Example: *H* and *W* died simultaneously. His will provided that in case of simultaneous death, she would be deemed to have survived. (Such provisions are often used in wills to get the federal estate tax marital deduction). Nevertheless, property which they held in joint tenancy was divided equally between the two estates. *Keegan v. Estate of Keegan*, 384 A.2d 913 (N.J. Super. 1978).

3. ***Determination of Death* (#2.26)**: UPC § 1-107 contains other rules relating to the determination of death.

a. Death occurs when there is an irreversible cessation of circulatory, respiratory, or all brain functions. (Based on a Uniform Determination of Death Act). A death certificate is prima facie evidence of the time of death.

b. A person who is absent without explanation for five years and not heard from after diligent search is presumed to have died at the end of that period unless evidence indicates an earlier death.

SHARES

III. SHARES

A. **"Equally" (#2.27):** Many wills say that property should be "equally divided," or "share and share alike." These terms have been variously interpreted.

Example: A decree of distribution said that property was to pass to heirs "share and share alike." The heirs were a daughter and two children by a deceased son. Under the intestacy statute, the daughter would have taken one-half and the two grandchildren one-quarter each. *See* #1.25, *supra*. But the court gave each heir one-third because of the words "share and share alike." *Black v. Unknown Creditors,* 155 N.W.2d 784 (S.D. 1968). Other courts, however, interpret such words to mean that *each branch of the family* receives an equal share. *Dewire v. Haveles,* 534 N.E.2d 782 (Mass. 1989).

B. *"Per stirpes"* (#2.28): The words *"per stirpes"* or "by representation" are also subject to conflicting interpretations.

Example: A trust called for property to pass "to my issue, share and share alike per stirpes." The settlor had six grandchildren. The court held that each grandchild took an equal share; the words *"per stirpes"* simply meant that if any great-grandchildren took by representation, the grandchildren were to be the basis of division. *Bonney v. Granger,* 356 S.E.2d 138 (S.C. App. 1987). But other courts construe *"per stirpes"* to mean that the testator's children, even though they are all dead, should be the basis for the division. *First Nat. Bank v. Singer,* 549 N.E.2d 940 (Ill. App. 1990). UPC § 2-709(c) agrees with this result when the words "per stirpes" are used, but "by representation" requires division per capita at each generation. *See* #1.21, *supra*.

C. "Grandchildren" (#2.29): An undefined devise to persons who are all in the same generation, like "to my grandchildren," is normally construed to give each person an equal share.

1. **"Issue" (#2.30):** Under UPC § 2-708, a devise "to issue" without qualifying language calls for a division under the rules of intestate succession. Under *Restatement (Second) of Property (Donative Transfers)* § 28.2 (1987), on the other hand, it calls for a *per stirpes* distribution as in *Singer, supra*.

2. ***"Heirs"* (#2.31):** Under UPC § 2-711, a gift to "heirs" calls for a division under the applicable rules of intestate succession. *Accord, Restatement (Second) of Property (Donative Transfers)* § 29.6 (1987).

IV. CHILDREN BORN OUT OF WEDLOCK

CHILDREN BORN OUT OF WEDLOCK

A. History (#2.32): Historically, a child born out of wedlock was *"filius nullius"* (the child of no one) for purposes of intestate succession. The child did not inherit from his parents nor did they inherit from the child. In construing devises "to children," courts presumed that children born out of wedlock were not included.

B. Constitution (#2.33): The United States Supreme Court has held that bars against inheritance by children born out of wedlock are an unconstitutional denial of equal protection. *Trimble v. Gordon,* 430 U.S. 762 (1977). However, the problems in proving paternity have been held to justify some limitations on inheritance from or by the *father* of the child.

1. ***"Clear" proof* (#2.34):** Some states require "clear and convincing" proof of paternity before a child born out of wedlock can inherit from the father. Ky. Rev. Stat. § 391.105 (b).

2. ***Writing or adjudication*** **(#2.35):** Some require that there be an adjudication of paternity while the father is alive. Cf. Wis. Stat. § 852.05(1) (adjudication or written acknowledgement of paternity). Such a requirement was held constitutional in *Lalli v. Lalli,* 439 U.S. 259 (1978), on the ground that proof of paternity is difficult after the father is dead.

C. **Terminology (#2.36):** Children born out of wedlock were traditionally called illegitimates (or bastards). Today these terms have been generally eliminated from statutes.

2

1. ***"Lawful"*** **(#2.37):** Nevertheless, a gift to "lawful" descendants is usually construed to exclude children born out of wedlock. *Continental Bank, N.A. v. Herguth*, 617 N.E.2d 852 (Ill. App. 1993).

D. **Parentage (#2.38):** The question whether a parent-child relationship exists is important for other purposes than inheritance. Many states have adopted a Uniform Parentage Act (UPA). Under UPC § 2-114, this act also controls succession in most cases.

1. ***Invalid marriage*** **(#2.39):** Most states treat a child as legitimate if the parents were married even if the marriage was invalid. The Constitution may require this. *Reed v. Campbell,* 476 U.S. 852 (1986) (unconstitutional to deny inheritance when parents participated in a marriage ceremony which was invalid because the father was already married). Under UPA § 4, a man is presumed to be the father of a child if he was married to the mother "by a marriage solemnized in apparent compliance with the law, although the marriage is or could be declared invalid."

2. **Later marriage (#2.40):** At common law, a child was legitimate if the parents were married when the child was born, even if the child was conceived out of wedlock. Under UPA § 4, a man is presumed to be the father of a child if he married the mother after the child was born if he indicated his paternity, *e.g.*, by consenting to being named the father on the child's birth certificate.

3. ***No marriage*** **(#2.41):** Even if the parents never married, a man who "receives the child into his home and openly holds out the child as his natural child" is presumed to be the father under UPA § 4. Even if there is no basis for any presumption of paternity, it may be established by proof under § 6(c).

4. **Rebutting presumptions (#2.42):** At common law a husband was irrebuttably presumed to be the father of his wife's children. This presumption has been considerably weakened. Under UPA § 4(b), the presumptions of paternity can be rebutted by "clear and convincing" evidence.

   Example: When a child was born, his mother was married to Jones, but the court admitted DNA evidence showing that Boyd was actually the father. *Batcheldor v. Boyd*, 423 S.E.2d 810 (N.C. App. 1992).

a. Under UPA § 6, a presumption of paternity created by a marriage can only be rebutted by the child, the mother, or a presumed father. Other statutes have similar limitations.

Example: A husband's sister was not allowed to prove that a child born during her brother's marriage was not his. *Matter of Estate of Raulston,* 805 P.2d 113 (Okl. 1990).

5. ***Time limits* (#2.43):** A claim of paternity may be barred by lapse of time.

Examples: A child's claim of paternity was denied under a statute requiring that such claims be asserted within five months of the father's death, even though the child was not born until eight months after the father died. The court distinguished *Clark v. Jeter*, 486 U.S. 456 (1988) which held that a six-year limitation on paternity actions was unconstitutional. The present statute was justified by the need for prompt disposition of decedents' estates. *S.V. v. Estate of Bellamy*, 579 N.E.2d 144 (Ind. App. 1991). But in *Woods v. Harris*, 600 N.E.2d 163 (Ind. App. 1992), a forty-eight-year-old man was allowed to claim that a decedent was his father in order to inherit; the statute of limitations on actions for child support was inapplicable.

a. When a marriage creates a presumption of paternity under UPA, an action to rebut the presumption must be brought "within a reasonable time after obtaining knowledge of relevant facts, but in no event later than five years after the child's birth." UPA § 6(a)(2).

Example: A husband was listed as the father of a child on the birth certificate. When the parents later divorced, the mother claimed the husband was not the father, but the court held it was too late to do so. *Mak-M v. SM,* 854 P.2d 64 (Wyo. 1993).

6. **Artificial insemination (#2.44):** Under UPA § 5, when a wife is inseminated artificially with her husband's consent, the husband is deemed the father and not the donor of the semen. *Accord, Restatement (Second) of Property (Donative Transfers)* § 25.3 (1988) (construing gifts to "children").

E. Inheritance

1. ***From mother* (#2.45):** All states today allow a child to inherit from the mother regardless of the marital status of the parents because proof of maternity is not a problem.

2. **Inheritance by parents (#2.46):**

a. The Supreme Court has been less receptive to claims by fathers, since, unlike a child born out of wedlock who had no choice, an unmarried father is responsible for his status. *Parham v. Hughes,* 441 U.S. 347 (1979). *But see Adoption of Kelsey*, 823 P.2d 1216 (Cal. 1992) (unconstitutional to deny claim of unwed father who tried to maintain contact with child).

b. Under UPC § 2-114, inheritance from a child by or through a parent is barred "unless the parent has openly treated the child as his [or hers], and has not refused to support the child." Apparently this includes children born in wedlock.

F. Construction of Gifts to "Children," etc.

2

1. ***Following intestacy rules* (# 2.47):** When construing words like "children" or "issue" in instruments, courts often use the intestacy statutes as a guide to the maker's intent with respect to children born out of wedlock. UPC § 2-705 (1990) follows this view. (The earlier UPC had the same rule but was limited to wills.) When "child" or "issue" is used in the UPC itself, *e.g.*, the antilapse provision, the intestacy rules control. UPC § 1-201(5)(9).

2. ***Intent to exclude* (#2.48):** Children born out of wedlock, even if they would inherit in intestacy, may be excluded by the terms of a particular will. *Herguth*, #2.37, *supra*. Enforcement of such a restriction does not violate the Constitution since no state action is involved. However, a statute which presumed that gifts to issue did not include children born out of wedlock was held unconstitutional. *Estate of Dulles,* 431 A.2d 208 (Pa. 1981).

G. Choice of Law

1. ***Wills* (#2.49):** Instruments which create future interests often come before courts many years after the testator died. Some courts apply the law in effect when the testator died to determine intent. This may bar children born out of wedlock. *Powers v. Wilkinson,* 506 N.E.2d 842 (Mass. 1987) (presumption that children born out of wedlock are included in class gifts applied only prospectively). *But see Wilmington Trust Co. v. Amian,* 531 A.2d 1209 (Del. Ch. 1987) (applying law at the date of distribution, even though trust was created in 1933).

2. ***Intestate succession* (#2.50):** In intestate succession, normally the statute in effect when the intestate died controls (*see* #1.6, *supra*), but not if that statute was unconstitutional. *Reed v. Campbell,* 476 U.S. 852 (1986). On the other hand, a distribution which has taken place under an unconstitutional statute will not be disturbed. *Stallworth v. Hicks*, 434 So.2d 229 (Ala. 1983).

3. ***Status* (#2.51)**: Personal property is ordinarily governed by the law of the decedent's domicile, and land is governed by the law of the situs. *See* ##1.2, 1.3, *supra*. But another law may determine a child's status.

   Example: A trust gave property to issue. Even though it was governed by Massachusetts law which construed "issue" to include only children born in wedlock, a son born out of wedlock was allowed to take because he had been legitimated by his father under the law of New Hampshire, where they were domiciled. *Powers v. Steele,* 475 N.E.2d 395 (Mass. 1985).

V. ADOPTION

ADOPTION

2

A. History (#2.52): Adoption was recognized in Roman law. Julius Caesar adopted Augustus, for example. The common law, however, did not recognize adoption. American statutes began to authorize it in the nineteenth century and now over 100,000 adoptions occur annually in the United States.

B. Strangers to the Adoption (#2.53): Originally, adoptees could not inherit or take under a will of a "stranger-to-the-adoption."

Examples: If Mary adopted a child, the child would inherit from Mary, but not from Mary's relatives because they were not parties to the adoption. If John left property "to the children of Mary," courts presumed that he did not intend to include her adopted children, but this presumption could be rebutted.

1. ***Intestate succession* (#2.54):** Most states reject the stranger-to-the-adoption idea today. For example, UPC § 2-114 says that "an adopted individual is the child of his [or her] adopting parents" for purposes of succession "by, through, or from a person." Under this provision, Mary's adopted child would inherit not only from her but also from her relatives.

2. ***Class gifts* (#2.55):** In construing gifts to "children" and the like, UPC § 2-705 (1990) generally includes adopted persons in accordance with the rules governing intestate succession. (The earlier UPC applied the same rule only to wills.) Even without such a statute, courts often refer to the intestacy statutes in construing wills and other instruments.

   a. The UPC rules of construction apply "in the absence of a finding of a contrary intention" UPC § 2-701 (1990). Courts usually require clear language to overcome the presumption that adoptees are included.

      Example: A gift to the "bodily issue" of the testator's son was held to include an adoptee. *Hagaman v. Morgan,* 886 S.W.2d 398 (Tex. App. 1994). *But see Hyman v. Glover,* 348 S.E.2d 269 (Va. 1986) (devise to "issue" does not include adopted children).

3. ***Change in the law* (#2.56):** In construing wills which were probated when the stranger-to-the-adoption idea prevailed, some courts exclude adoptees on the ground that the law in effect at the testator's death controls. *Foley v. Evans,* 570 N.E.2d 179 (Mass. App. 1991). Some pro-adoptee statutes, on the other hand, expressly apply to instruments previously drafted. This is constitutional, *First Nat. Bank v. King,* 635 N.E.2d 755 (Ill. App. 1994), but if property has already been distributed under the old rule, the adopted child has no remedy. *Estate of Sewell,* 409 A.2d 401 (Pa. 1979); *cf.* #2.50, *supra.*

2

C. Adults

1. ***Is adoption possible?* (#2.57):** Most states permit the adoption of an adult, but some do not. *Matter of Adoption of Chaney*, 887 P.2d 1061 (Idaho 1995). In *Matter of Paul,* 471 N.E.2d 424 (N.Y. 1984), the court refused to allow a homosexual to adopt his lover on the ground that this was inconsistent with the parent-child relationship. *See also In re Jones,* 411 A.2d 910 (R.I. 1980) (married man not allowed to adopt his mistress); Cal. Family Code § 9320 (adult may adopt "another adult who is younger, except the spouse of the prospective" adopter).

2. ***Effect* (#2.58):**

   a. Even where an adoption of an adult has taken place, some courts refuse to recognize it in construing a gift to "children" of the adopter, but others treat adult adoptions no differently than others.

      Example: A gift to a son's "issue" was held not to include his wife, whom he had adopted. *Matter of Trust Created by Belgard*, 829 P.2d 457 (Colo. App. 1991). *But see Boatmen's Trust Co. v. Conklin*, 888 S.W.2d 347 (Mo. App. 1994) (adult adoptees were not "issue" but they were "heirs" under the same will); *Hagaman v. Morgan*, 886 S.W.2d 398 (Tex. App. 1994) (adult adoptee included in a gift to "bodily issue").

   b. Under UPC § 2-705(b) (1990), in construing a disposition by a stranger to the adoption, "an adopted individual is not considered the child of the adopting parent unless the adopted individual lived while a minor...as a regular member of the houshold of the adopting parent."

      Example: *H* marries a woman with young children by a prior marriage. He would like to adopt them but cannot while they are minors because the father, *W*'s former husband, will not consent. When they become adults, and their father's consent is no longer needed, the adoption takes place. These children would qualify as *H*'s "children" under a will of *H*'s father.

      The limitations in § 2-705(b) do not apply to intestate succession or to a will of the adopting parent. Thus if a person adopts a fifty-year-old friend, the friend would take under the adopter's will as a "child" and would inherit from the adopter's mother by representation if the adopter predeceased his mother. Of course, if the mother did not like that, she could disinherit the adoptee.

D. Biological Relatives

1. ***Inheritance from* (#2.59):**

   a. Under UPC § 2-114, the tie between the adoptee and blood relatives is severed unless the adoption is by a stepparent.

Example: If a mother remarries after a divorce or the death of the father and her new husband adopts the child, the child continues to inherit from his biological father and his relatives (as well as from his adoptive father and his relatives). But a child adopted by his maternal grandparents could no longer inherit from his father. *Aldridge v. Mims*, 884 P.2d 817 (N.M. App. 1994).

b. In some states, the adoptee inherits from biological kindred only if they have "maintained a family relationship" with the adoptee. 20 Pa. Stat. § 2108. Maryland severs the tie between an adoptee and the biological parents in all cases. *Hall v. Vallandingham*, 540 A.2d 1162 (Md. App. 1988).

2. ***Class gifts* (#2.60):** When a will leaves property to "children of *X*," does this include a child of *X* who has been adopted by someone else? UPC § 2-705 follows the rules of intestate succession on this issue also, but evidence of a contrary intent may control.

   Example: If *X* had no other children, a court may construe the word to include an adopted-away child even if the child would not inherit under the intestacy rules. *Restatement (Second) of Property (Donative Transfers)* § 25.5, comm. c (1987).

3. ***Double share* (#2.61):** A child adopted by a relative may have two bases for inheriting from the same decedent, *e.g.*, as an adopted child and as a biological grandchild. UPC § 2-113 prohibits the child from getting a double share in this situation.

4. ***Inheritance by biological relatives* (#2.62):** UPC § 2-114 limits the rights of the biological parent(s) and their relatives to inherit from a child who has been adopted by others, even when the child continues to be able to inherit from them. This can be justified by the fact that a minor child's consent is not required for the adoption, but the consent of the parents is.

E. Equitable Adoption

1. ***Inheritance by child* (#2.63):** Many courts treat a child who has been raised by foster parents as "equitably adopted" and thus entitled to inherit. The theory is usually that the foster parents expressly or impliedly promised to adopt the child, and the child can enforce the promise as a third party beneficiary.

2. ***Inheritance by parents* (#2.64):** The foster parents are not usually permitted to rely on an equitable adoption. *Reynolds v. City of Los Angeles,* 222 Cal. Rptr. 517 (Cal. App. 1986) (foster parents of equitably adopted child can't sue for wrongful death). *Contra, Lawson v. Atwood,* 536 N.E.2d 1167 (Ohio 1989).

F. Stepchildren

1. ***Inheritance* (#2.65):** Stepchildren (the children of an intestate's spouse) normally do not inherit. *See* UPC § 1-201(5). But in some states they inherit in the absence of other heirs. *Cf.* #1.34, *supra*. They may also be allowed to claim damages for wrongful death if they were dependent on their stepparent. Cal. Code Civ. Proc. § 377(b)(2).

2. ***Class gifts* (#2.66):** A devise to "children" does not usually include stepchildren. *National Home Life Ins. Co. v. Patterson,* 746 P.2d 696 (Okl. App. 1987) (insurance policy). However, the circumstance may show otherwise.

   Example: A trust for "my nieces and nephews" was held to include the nieces and nephews of the settlor's husband because the settlor had none of her own. *Clymer v. Mayo,* 473 N.E.2d 1084 (Mass. 1985).

G. Choice of Law (#2.67): Courts usually recognize an adoption which took place in another state, unless it offends the public policy of the forum. *Tsilidis v. Pedakis,* 132 So.2d 9 (Fla. App. 1961) (adoption in Greece which would not have been allowed in Florida disregarded).

1. ***Effect of adoption* (#2.68):** The law of the state where an adoption occurred does not necessarily govern its effect. Thus an adoption in Rhode Island barred the adoptee from inheriting from his biological relatives under New York law, even though the law of Rhode Island was otherwise. *Matter of Estate of Chase*, 515 N.Y.S.2d 348 (App. Div. 1987).

SPOUSES

VI. SPOUSES

A. Importance (#2.69): All intestacy statutes give a share to the decedent's surviving spouse. Spouses may also have rights to an elective share, family allowance, etc. This may raise a question as to whether persons were legally married.

1. ***Construction* (#2.70):** If a will leaves property "to my wife, Mary," Mary will get it whether or not she was validly married to the testator. But if an instrument simply says "spouse" without naming her, only a legal spouse qualifies. *Seradell v. Hartford Acc. and Indem. Co.,* 843 P.2d 639 (Alaska 1992).

B. Bigamy (#2.71): If John marries Mary when he is already married to Sally, the marriage is invalid, but in many states Mary may acquire rights as a "putative spouse" if she married John in good faith. Uniform Marriage and Divorce Act § 209.

1. ***No marriage ceremony* (#2.72):** A person can claim to be a putative spouse only if there was a marriage ceremony between the "spouses." *Thomas v. Sullivan*, 922 F.2d 132 (2d Cir. 1990) (Social Security claim).

2. ***Cohabitation after divorce of other spouse* (#2.73):** In some states Mary would also be John's spouse if he later divorced Sally and he and Mary continued to cohabit, even though their original marriage was invalid. *Estate of Whyte v. Whyte*, 614 N.E.2d 372 (Ill. App. 1993).

C. No Ceremony

1. ***History* (#2.74):** If a couple live together without a marriage ceremony, some states treat them as married on the theory that a marriage only requires consent. Such marriages are called "common law" marriages because English law did not require a ceremonial for marriage until a statute of 1753. Most states have abolished common law marriage, but a statute abolishing common law marriage does not invalidate those which were previously contracted.

2. ***Choice of law* (#2.75):** A common law marriage contracted in a state where it is valid will be recognized in other states. *Allen v. Storer*, 600 N.E.2d 1263 (Ill. App. 1992) (Illinois recognizes common law marriage of a couple domiciled in Ohio.)

3. ***Enforceability of contract* (#2.76):** Even in states which do not recognize common law marriage, parties who cohabit may acquire rights on the basis of an express or implied contract. *Connell v. Francisco,* 872 P.2d 1150 (Wash. App. 1994) (marriage rules govern division of property of unmarried cohabitants who separate). *Cf. Whorton v. Dillingham*, 248 Cal. Rptr. 405 (Cal. App. 1988) (similar claim by homosexual lover). But this theory does not give them the right to inherit. *Peffley-Warner v. Bowen*, 778 P.2d 1022 (Wash. 1989).

   a. Cases are split on whether an unmarried cohabitant can sue for wrongful death; the result depends on the terms of the relevant statute. *See Lealaimatafoa v. Woodward-Clyde Consl.*, 867 P.2d 220 (Haw. 1994) (cohabitant can claim as a "dependent"); *Sykes v. Propane Power Co.*, 541 A.2d 271 (N.J. Super. 1988) (no recovery as "spouse").

D. Capacity (#2.77): A marriage may be voidable for lack of capacity but some states do not allow a marriage to be challenged on this basis after one spouse has died.

Example: A son was not allowed to annul the marriage of his dead father for lack of capacity, though he could have done so while the father was alive. *Hall v. Nelson*, 534 N.E.2d 929 (Ohio App. 1987). *Contra, Matter of Estate of Hendrickson,* 805 P.2d 20 (Kan. 1991).

E. Divorce (#2.78): Divorce terminates the spousal relationship only if it has become final.

Example: Although a couple was separated and divorce proceedings were pending when the husband died, his wife could claim an elective share of his estate. *Hamilton v. Hamilton*, 879 S.W.2d 416 (Ark. 1994). *But see Carr v. Carr,* 576 A.2d 872 (N.J. 1990) (husband denied elective share when spouses were separated at death).

1. ***Invalid divorce* (#2.79):** A divorce issued by a court which has no jurisdiction does not dissolve a marriage. *In re Estate of Newton*, 583 N.E.2d 1026 (Ohio App. 1989) (Mexican divorce invalid because parties did not reside there). However, a person who obtains or "consents to" a divorce, or remarries after a divorce, is estopped to claim the divorce was invalid. UPC § 2-802(b). *Cf. In re Estate of Dalton*, 647 N.E.2d 78 (Ohio Comm. Pl. 1995) (even without any divorce, a wife who remarried after *H* left her could not claim to be *H*'s spouse).

MISCONDUCT

VII. MISCONDUCT

A. Desertion (#2.80): Some states bar spouses who abandon a decedent or commit adultery from sharing in the decedent's estate.

Example: A husband was barred from a family allowance because he was living with another woman when his wife died. Adultery could be inferred from the circumstances despite his denial. *Oliver v. Estate of Oliver,* 554 N.E.2d 8 (Ind. App. 1990).

1. ***Narrow construction* (#2.81):** Courts tend to construe such statutes narrowly on the ground that they impose a "forfeiture."

   Example: In *Estate of Harris*, 391 N.W.2d 487 (Mich. App. 1986), a husband who lived with his wife only periodically was held not to be barred by such a statute.

2. ***No statute* (#2.82):** Without a statute, misconduct does not bar a spouse from inheriting, *Estate of Miller,* 768 P.2d 373 (Okl. App. 1988).

B. Homicide

1. ***History* (#2.83):** Historically, the property of a convicted felon escheated. This rule was later abandoned as unfair to the heirs of the felon since they had done no wrong. Many state constitutions prohibit forfeiture for crime.

2. ***Statutes* (#2.84):** Most states today have statutes which bar a killer from inheriting or otherwise taking property from the person killed. Many of them are similar to UPC § 2-803.

3. ***Degree of crime* (#2.85):** UPC § 2-803 bars anyone who "feloniously and intentionally kills the decedent."

   a. Some statutes bar only those who are guilty of murder. Louisiana, on the other hand, bars anyone who is "criminally responsible" for the death, even if the crime was unintentional. *In re Hamilton,* 446 So.2d 463 (La. App. 1984).

b. Killing in self-defense or while insane does not disqualify the killer from taking. *Estate of Artz v. Artz,* 487 A.2d 1294 (N.J. Super. 1985). *But see* Ohio Rev. Code § 2105.19(A) (person found not guilty by reason of insanity is barred).

c. Although the statute literally only covers the killer, some courts have applied it to an accessory. *Matter of Estate of Gibbs*, 490 N.W.2d 504 (S.D. 1992) (devisee who conspired to kill testator disqualified even though actual killing was accomplished by another).

4. ***Proof of crime* (#2.86):** Under some statutes the bar operates only if the killer is convicted. Thus a killer who is incompetent to stand trial or who was erroneously acquitted can take. *Button v. Elmhurst Nat. Bank*, 522 N.E.2d 1368 (Ill. App. 1988).

   a. UPC § 2-803, on the other hand, allows a court to determine guilt by a preponderance of the evidence in the absence of a conviction. If a killer has been convicted, the conviction is conclusive. UPC § 2-803(g).

5. ***Effect of disqualification* (#2.87):** In most states, if the killer is disqualified, the property passes as if the killer had predeceased the decedent. UPC § 2-803. The effect of this depends on the terms of the relevant instrument.

   Examples: When a beneficiary who killed the insured was disqualified, the proceeds went to her children, who were named as alternate beneficiaries. *Seidlitz v. Eames,* 753 P.2d 775 (Colo. App. 1987). But when a policy named no alternate beneficiary, the proceeds went into the insured's estate when the beneficiary murdered him. *Estate of Chiesi v. First Citizens Bank*, 613 N.E.2d 14 (Ind. 1993).

   a. If the killer took out the policy intending to kill the insured, the policy is voidable for fraud and so no proceeds are paid. *Federal Kemper Life Assur. v. Eichwedel*, 639 N.E.2d 246 (Ill. App. 1994).

6. ***Joint tenancy* (# 2.88):** Under UPC § 2-803(c), if the killer and victim owned property in joint tenancy, one-half of it goes to the estate of each. Most courts adopt this solution, regardless of who paid for the asset.

   Example: A husband killed his wife. They owned a home in joint tenancy. Half of it was awarded to the wife's estate even though she had not contributed to its purchase. *Sundin v. Klein,* 269 S.E.2d 787 (Va. 1980).

7. ***Killer's own property* (#2.89):** Disposition of the killer's own property is not affected by the crime.

   Example: A son killed his mother. This barred him from inheriting her property, but she (*i.e.*, her estate) did not succeed to *his* property on the basis of the fiction that he died first. *Mothershed v. Schrimsher*, 412 S.E.2d 123 (N.C. App. 1992).

a. A spouse who kills the other spouse does not lose his or her share of the community property. *Armstrong v. Bray*, 826 P.2d 706 (Wash. App. 1992).

8. ***Protection of third parties* (#2.90):** An insurance company which pays the proceeds to a beneficiary without notice that he is disqualified is protected.

Example: A company paid the proceeds of insurance to the wife as beneficiary. She later pleaded guilty to killing the insured. The company was not liable to his children who claimed that it was negligent in making payment. UPC § 2-803(h) protects an insurer unless it has "written notice" of a claim prior to payment. *Lundsford v. Western States Life Ins.*, 872 P.2d 1308 (Colo. App. 1993).

a. Similar protection is given to bona fide purchasers of property by UPC § 2-803(i).

ADVANCE-MENTS

VIII. ADVANCEMENTS

A. Effect of Advancement (#2.91): Most parents wish their children to receive equal shares of their property. If a parent has previously given property to one child as an "advance," the law takes this into account in dividing an intestate estate.

Example: Suppose *F* has three children (*A, B,* and *C*) and dies with an estate of $100,000. During his life he had made advancements to *A* of $50,000 and to *B* of $30,000. These amounts are brought into "hotchpot," *i.e.*, figuratively added to *F*'s estate. With a $180,000 estate, each child would be entitled to $60,000. *A* has already received $50,000, so she would get $10,000 more. *B* would get $30,000 more. This would leave $60,000 for *C*. See UPC § 2-109, comment.

1. ***Excess advancement* (#2.92):** If *F* had advanced $100,000 to *A, A* would already have received more than her share. She would not have to return this excess (assuming that the $100,000 was an advancement and not a loan), but she would get no part of *F*'s probate estate. Now the estate after hotchpot would amount to $130,000, taking into account the advancement to *B* but ignoring the one to *A*. *B* would get $35,000 and *C* would get the remaining $65,000.

2. ***Valuation* (#2.93):** If advancements were in property rather than cash, the property would be valued as of the date of the gift, rather than at *F*'s death. UPC § 2-109(b).

3. ***Heirs covered* (#2.94):** Under UPC § 2-109, advancements are taken into account as to all heirs. In some states, they affect only issue of the intestate. In Massachusetts, for example, if *F* was survived by a wife, her share of her estate would be computed without reference to his advancements to the children. Mass. Gen. Laws c. 196 § 3.

4. ***Death before donor* (#2.95):** If *A* or *B* predeceased *F* but had children who survived him, the children would take by representation, and their share would not be affected by the advancements under UPC § 2-109, unless *F* manifested this intent in writing.

5. ***Transfers covered* (#2.96):**

   a. A sale is not an advancement, but courts look behind a recital of consideration in a deed to see if the transfer was actually a gift. *Thomas v. Thomas,* 398 S.W.2d 231 (Ky. 1965).

   b. Small gifts, like birthday presents and payments for a child's support, are not treated as advancements.

2

B. Proof of Advancement (#2.97): In many states gifts to a child are presumed to be advancements. But under UPC § 2-109, a gift is an advancement "only if declared in a contemporaneous writing by the decedent or acknowledged in writing by the heir to be an advancement." This seriously diminishes the importance of the doctrine since few donors who make advancements are sophisticated enough to satisfy the requirement.

C. Relationship to Wills

1. ***Gifts prior to execution of will* (#2.98):** If a person dies with a valid will, any prior advancements are irrelevant; the law assumes that the testator already took them into account.

2. ***Satisfaction of devises* (#2.99):** Gifts made *after* a will is executed may be treated as satisfaction of devises in the will.

   Example: A will left $5,000 to a charity. The testator later gave the charity $5,000. This was held to satisfy the devise so the charity got nothing from the estate. *In re Kreitman's Estate,* 386 N.E.2d 650 (Ill. App. 1979). The result may differ if the "match" between the devise and the gift is less clear. *Maestas v. Martinez,* 752 P.2d 1107 (N.M. App. 1988) (deed of specific land does not satisfy devise of a share of *T*'s real estate to the donee).

   a. Under UPC § 2-609, a gift satisfies a devise only if this intention is stated in the will or a contemporaneous writing.

      Example: A will made a devise of $75,000. The testator later made gifts to the devisee, and then signed a statement that the gifts were to reduce the devise. The devisee got the full $75,000 because the statement was not contemporaneous with the gift. *In re Estate of McFayden*, 454 N.W.2d 676 (Neb. 1990).

   b. When a devise is satisfied, the issue of the devisee who take under the antilapse statute if the devisee predeceases the testator are also barred. UPC § 2-609(c). *Contrast* #2.95, *supra.*

D. Loans (#2.100): When a transfer is a loan rather than an advancement, no writing is needed, and the loan is set off against the share of the heir or devisee. *Matter of Estate of Button*, 830 P.2d 1216 (Kan. App. 1992); UPC § 3-903.

DISCLAIMER

IX. DISCLAIMER

A. Reasons for Disclaimer

2

1. ***Tax avoidance* (#2.101):** Usually an heir or devisee disclaims property in order to save taxes. Someone who does not want property can give it away, but this may require paying a gift tax. A qualified disclaimer, however, is not a taxable gift. Int. Rev. Code § 2518.

   a. A disclaimer may also reduce state inheritance taxes, or allow an estate to get a larger marital deduction if it causes more property to go to the decedent's spouse.

   b. Historically, state law governed disclaimers, but to avoid treating citizens in different states differently, Int. Rev. Code § 2518 now allows disclaimers regardless of their effectiveness under state law.

2. ***Avoiding creditors' claims* (#2.102):** An heir or devisee who is insolvent may disclaim so that members of his family get the property rather than his creditors. In most states, a disclaimer is not subject to challenge by creditors.

   Example: A devisee disclaimed a devise before he filed for bankruptcy. This was not a fraudulent transfer because a disclaimer "relates back," so there is no transfer to the disclaimant at all. *Matter of Simpson*, 36 F.3d 450 (5th Cir. 1994). If the devisee had waited until he was actually in bankruptcy the disclaimer would have been ineffective.

B. Requirements for Disclaimer

1. ***Formalities* (#2.103):** A disclaimer must be in writing and filed in the probate court. UPC § 2-801; *Matter of Estate of Griffin*, 812 P.2d 1256 (Mont. 1991) (disclaimer revocable until it is filed).

   a. A disclaimer requires no consideration, unlike the release or assignment of an expectancy by a prospective heir while the ancestor is still alive. These are unenforceable without a "fair consideration." *Restatement of Property* § 316. This requirement prevents an improvident disposition of an expected inheritance. After the ancestor or testator is dead, there is less risk of an improvident disposition because the right is no longer speculative.

2. ***Time limits* (#2.104):** At common law a donee had a "reasonable time" after learning of a gift to disclaim it. Many statutes impose more specific limits.

a. Under Int. Rev. Code § 2518(b)(2), the disclaimer must be made within nine months of the transfer. *See also* UPC § 2-801(b). This means nine months from the death of the testator or the intestate.

b. Federal law differs from that of many states as to when holders of a future interest must disclaim.

Example: A trust was created in 1917 which gave a remainder to the settlor's issue. When the remainder took effect in 1979, one of the issue disclaimed her interest. This was effective under state law because her interest had not yet vested, but for tax purposes the time started to run when she learned (or should have learned) of her interest, so her disclaimer was treated as a gift. *U.S. v. Irvine,* 114 S.Ct. 1473 (1994).

C. Disclaimers by Fiduciaries

1. ***UPC* (#2.105):** UPC § 2-801(a) allows disclaimers by a personal representative, guardian, conservator, or agent of the person who has an interest.

2. ***Fiduciary obligations* (#2.106):** The fiduciary's duties to act in the interests of those whom they represent may nevertheless preclude a disclaimer.

Example: An administrator of a deceased heir could not disclaim when a creditor of the heir objected. *Estate of Heater v. Illinois Dept. of Public Aid,* 640 N.E.2d 654 (Ill. App. 1994). But in *McClintock v. Scahill,* 530 N.E.2d 164 (Mass. 1988), trustees for the settlor's grandchildren were allowed to disclaim since this would have favorable tax consequences for the settlor's estate and thus be in the beneficiaries' "best interests." Under UPC § 5-407 a conservator can disclaim only if this is in the best interests of the conservatee.

D. Effect of Disclaimer (#2.107): Disclaimed property ordinarily passes as if the disclaimant had predeceased the testator. UPC § 2-801(d). This may not be what the disclaimant wants.

Example: A will devised land to three children. One son disclaimed so his sisters could take it, but in fact his share passed to his children under the antilapse statute instead. *Ernst v. Shaw,* 783 S.W.2d 400 (Ky. App. 1990).

A will may expressly provide what happens when a devisee disclaims; if it does, this provision controls.

1. ***Future interests* (#2.108):** A disclaimer by a life tenant accelerates subsequent future interests.

Example: A will created a trust for the testator's son for life, remainder to the testator's grandchildren. When the son disclaimed, the property passed to the grandchildren immediately, even though the will said the trust was not to terminate until the son died. *Pate v. Ford*, 376 S.E.2d 775 (S.C. 1989).

E. **Agreements among Successors (#2.109):** Successors may agree to alter the distribution of an estate. Such an agreement is not subject to the rules governing disclaimers.

Example: A will left the estate to one daughter but she agreed to divide it with her siblings. This was valid, but the inheritance tax was based on the will and not on the distribution under the agreement. *Estate of McNicholas v. State*, 580 N.E.2d 978 (Ind. App. 1991).

LIMITATIONS ON THE RIGHT OF DISPOSITION

CHAPTER SUMMARY

I.	Protection of Children	3-2
II.	Protection of the Spouse	3-7
III.	Elective Share	3-7
IV.	Community Property	3-10
V.	Choice of Law	3-13
VI.	Omitted Spouse	3-14
VII.	Waiver	3-16
VIII.	Other Limitations	3-17

LIMITATIONS ON THE RIGHT OF DISPOSITION

INTRODUCTION: This chapter discusses the rights of children who are disinherited by a parent's will. Unlike the civil law which gives children a forced share, most American states provide only a family allowance for support while the estate is administered.

Spouses receive more protection than children in American law. Most states provide an elective share to a surviving spouse as an alternative to taking under the will. In eight states that recognize community property, each spouse owns half of the assets accumulated by gainful activity of either spouse during the marriage. The rights of the spouse can be waived by an agreement made before or during the marriage, but courts view such agreements with suspicion because of the confidential relationship which exists between persons who are or about to be married.

Both spouses and children not mentioned in a will may be able to get an intestate share of the testator's estate on the theory that their omission was an oversight. This usually applies only if they were born or married to the testator after the will was executed. For a more detailed treatment of the topics in this chapter, *see* McGovern, Kurtz, and Rein, *Wills, Trusts and Estates* 86-154 (1988).

PROTECTION OF CHILDREN

I. PROTECTION OF CHILDREN

A. General Rule (#3.1): Children receive very little protection in American law from being disinherited by a parent. Like other heirs, they can contest a will, and juries are sometimes sympathetic to will contests by disinherited children, but unless the testator lacked capacity or was unduly influenced or the will fails to satisfy formal requirements (*see* chapters 4 and 7, *infra*), the contest will fail.

B. History

1. ***Land* (#3.2):** English law did not allow wills of land before the Statute of Wills of 1540. Feudalism was partly responsible for this; a tenant who could devise land could escape the feudal incidents like wardship. In the later Middle Ages, landowners evaded the prohibition on devises by putting land in "use." Uses came to an end with the Statute of Uses of 1536. This caused a public outcry, and a few years later the king had to agree to the Statute of Wills.

2. ***Personal property* (#3.3):** The law always allowed wills of personal property where feudal considerations did not apply. In the early Middle Ages, parts of a man's estate were reserved for his wife and children, and he could only dispose of a fraction by will. (Married *women* could not make wills at all until the Married Women's Property Acts). Later the fixed portions reserved for wives and children disappeared in England.

C. Policy

1. ***Arguments* (#3.4):** Since parents are obligated to support their children, they arguably should not be permitted to disinherit them. However, the duty to support normally applies only to minor children. Since minor children cannot handle property, any share they receive must be managed by a guardian, so many parents prefer to leave their property to the other parent who can provide for the children. This argument is less persuasive when the parent is no longer married to the other parent of the children.

2. ***Discretionary vs. fixed share* (#3.5):**

   a. The law might protect children from disinheritance by giving them a fraction of the estate, as in the early Middle Ages. This is the rule in many civil law countries. *See* #3.6, *infra*. But such fixed shares fail to take account of the needs of the children or their conduct toward the parent.

   b. An alternative is to give courts discretion to award property to deserving members of the family. This system prevails in the British Commonwealth. American law has rejected it because it gives judges so much discretion, although the family allowance in most American states follows this path. *See* #3.10, *infra*.

D. *Legitime* (#3.6): Louisiana's system of forced heirship or *"legitime"* is derived from the French Civil Code. A person with two or more children must leave them half the estate, one-quarter if there is only one child. This share is protected against *inter vivos* gifts as well as wills. La. Civ. Code Art. 1493.

1. ***Limitations* (#3.7):** In 1989 the Louisiana legislature limited *legitime* to children who were under age 23 or incapacitated. This was held to violate the state constitution which protects forced heirship. *Succession of Lauga*, 624 So.2d 1156 (La. 1993). Nevertheless, children can be disinherited for twelve "just causes."

   Example: A will disinheriting daughters who had cursed their father and refused to visit him when sick was upheld; this was "cruelty" under La. Civil Code Art. 1621. *Ambrose Succession v. Ambrose*, 548 So.2d 37 (La. App. 1989).

2. ***Choice of law* (#3.8):** American courts outside Louisiana look unfavorably on forced heirship and often avoid applying it.

   Example: A child's claim to a forced share of his father's estate was denied, even though the father was domiciled in Switzerland and had property there, because his will said that it should be governed by the law of Maine. *Matter of Estate of Wright*, 637 A.2d 106 (Me. 1994).

   a. Even the courts of Louisiana do not apply their law to the personal property of persons who die domiciled in other states. *Cohn v.*

Heymann, 544 So.2d 1242 (La. App. 1989) (*legitime* applies to land in Louisiana but not stock owned by Pennsylvania domiciliary).

E. **Survival of Support Decrees (#3.9):** When parents divorce, the father is usually ordered to make payments for the support of any minor children. Courts often hold that the support obligation ends when the obligor dies. Under the Uniform Marriage and Divorce Act (adopted in only a few states), the duty to make support payments does not terminate when the father dies, but the amount may be modified.

3

Example: A divorce decree provided that the father's support obligation would be a lien on his estate. After he died, his executor claimed that the obligation should be reduced by the amount of Social Security payments received by his children as a result of his death. The court rejected this claim but said that the claim for support would not have survived except for the special provision in the decree. *Pessein v. Pessein*, 846 P.2d 1385 (Wash. App. 1993).

F. **Family Allowance and Homestead (#3.10):** When a person dies, the estate is held in administration while the assets are collected and claims are paid. In order to support the decedent's family during administration, a "family allowance" is paid. UPC § 2-404. Most states have similar provisions.

1. ***Precedence over will and creditors* (#3.11):** The family allowance is payable regardless of the provisions of the will. It also takes precedence over claims of creditors.

   Example: A creditor with a judgment against a decedent was unable to enforce it because her entire estate was needed to satisfy the family allowance. *Estate of Wilhelm,* 760 P.2d 718 (Mont. 1988).

   a. Under UPC § 2-404, if an estate is insolvent, the family allowance cannot continue for more than one year.

2. ***Discretion* (#3.12):** Trial courts have discretion in fixing the amount of the allowance. They take into account the family's station in life and other resources.

   Example: A family allowance award of $1,000 a month for 24 months was upheld for an estate with $1.6 million. The court took into account the family's standard of living and the widow's own property. *Matter of Estate of Hamilton*, 869 P.2d 971 (Utah App. 1994).

   a. Under UPC § 2-405 the personal representative can fix the family allowance up to a certain amount without court approval, subject to court review if anyone complains.

3. ***Spouse vs. children* (#3.13):** If a decedent was survived by both children and a spouse, the allowance is paid to the latter "for the use of" the children. However, if children are not living with the spouse, their allowance

goes to the "child or his guardian or other person having his custody." The UPC limits payments to minor children and children whom the decedent was supporting.

4. ***Compared with family maintenance* (#3.14):** The family allowance resembles family maintenance in the British Commonwealth, #3.5, *supra,* but it only provides support while the estate is being administered.

5. ***Homestead and Exempt Property* (#3.15):** Many states have a homestead exemption. Like the family allowance, it protects the spouse and minor children from disinheritance and from claims of the decedent's creditors.

   a. Under UPC § 2-402 (1990), homestead is $15,000 for the spouse, or for each minor or dependent child if there is no surviving spouse. Section 2-403 (1990) allows $10,000 in "exempt property."

   b. In some states, homestead and the statutory exemptions are larger but may be limited in other ways.

   Example: A decedent's farm was awarded to his widow as homestead even though he had devised it to others. Homestead only gave her the right to occupy it for life. *Matter of Estate of Heimbach*, 847 P.2d 824 (Okl. App. 1993).

   c. In some states homestead property cannot be alienated *inter vivos*. *Sims v. Cox*, 611 So.2d 339 (Ala. 1992) (husband's deed of residence to his daughters without his wife's signature was voidable).

G. **Pretermitted Heirs (#3.16):** Nearly all states have "pretermitted heir" statutes designed to protect children from being disinherited unintentionally.

Example: A bachelor executes a will leaving all his property to his brothers and sisters. He later marries and has children. He never gets around to changing his will. UPC § 2-302 would give his children their intestate share.

1. ***Existing vs. after-borns* (# 3.17):** Some statutes cover all children, even though it seems unlikely that a testator would forget about existing children when executing a will. UPC § 2-302 applies only to children who are born (or adopted) after the execution of the parent's will.

   Example: A will provided for the testator's three children. After a fourth child was born, the testator executed a codicil to his will which did not mention the child. The child's claim under the statute was rejected since the codicil republished the will after the child's birth. *Azunce v. Estate of Azunce*, 586 So. 2d 1216 (Fla. App. 1991).

   a. The UPC provides for any child living when the will was executed whom the testator mistakenly thought was dead.

2. ***Children vs. grandchildren* (#3.18):** UPC § 2-302 only covers children, but some statutes provide for all issue.

   Example: A testator was survived by three grandchildren, his only child having predeceased him. His will failed to mention one of them. She was given her intestate share under the Oklahoma statute but would have lost under the UPC. *Crump's Estate v. Freeman,* 614 P.2d 1096 (Okl. 1980).

3. ***Adoption, etc.* (#3.19):** The rules governing intestate succession govern who is a "child" under the pretermitted heir statute.

   Example: The testator had a child out of wedlock after executing his will. A statute provided that the subsequent birth of a legitimate child revoked a will. The will was revoked since the restriction to legitimate children was unconstitutional. *Talley v. Succession of Stuckey*, 614 So.2d 55 (La. 1993). Under the definition of "child" in the UPC, the result would be the same except that the whole will would not be revoked.

4. ***Contrary intent* (#3.20):**

   a. An intention to disinherit a child expressed in the will bars any claim under the statute. Questions of construction arise as to whether particular language is sufficient to show such an intent.

      Example: A will left the testator's estate to his wife and provided that if she did not survive, the estate would go to his heirs. His wife survived. The substitutional gift to "heirs" in the will barred a claim by the testator's daughter under the statute. *Leatherwood v. Meisch,* 759 S.W.2d 559 (Ark. 1988). But in *Matter of Estate of Woodward*, 807 P.2d 262 (Okl. 1991) a statement in a will that "all other persons are excluded" did not bar a claim by pretermitted heirs).

   b. Evidence outside the will showing an intent to disinherit may not be enough to bar the claim.

      Example: A will left the testator's estate to his daughter. Statements by the testator that he intended to exclude his son were not admissible because this intent had to appear "in the will." *Estate of Jones v. Jones,* 759 P.2d 345 (Utah App. 1988). The UPC agrees but makes two exceptions:

      (1) If the testator gave property to the child in lieu of a bequest in the will, the child cannot claim. The intent that the gift was in lieu of a devise can be inferred from the size of the gift or from statements made by the testator.

      (2) If a will leaves the estate to the other parent of the testator's children, *e.g.,* the testator's wife, the children have no claim.

5. ***Share*** **(#3.21):** Most statutes give pretermitted children their intestate share. In some cases this can amount to the whole estate. But under UPC § 2-302, if the will provided for the testator's existing children, the share of any after-born is limited to that amount.

6. ***Nonprobate property*** **(#3.22):** The pretermitted heir statutes are usually limited to the probate estate. Thus if a person names children as beneficiaries of insurance, an after-born child does not get a share of the proceeds. *Penn Mutual Life Ins. Co. v. Abramson*, 530 A.2d 1202 (D.C. App. 1987).

II. PROTECTION OF THE SPOUSE

PROTECTION OF THE SPOUSE

A. **Policy (#3.23):** Almost all states protect the spouse against disinheritance.

Rationale: Spouses get more protection than children. Since they are adults, property awarded to a spouse usually requires no guardianship. Also, even a spouse who needs no support has a moral basis for claiming a share of an estate, since both spouses contribute to the accumulation of property during marriage to a much greater extent than children do.

B. **Dower and Curtesy (#3.24):** Traditionally, widows got dower, and widowers got curtesy. *See* #1.8, *supra*. This was their intestate share, and it could not be taken away from them by will.

1. ***Deficiencies*** **(#3.25):** Dower and curtesy only covered land. The most important assets in many estates today are personal property, such as stocks and bonds.

   a. Dower makes alienation of property difficult. *Sterling v. Wilson*, 621 N.E.2d 767 (Ohio App. 1993) (sale voidable because *W* had not released dower).

   b. Modern statutes give the same share to the surviving spouse regardless of sex.

2. ***Present status*** **(#3.26):** UPC § 2-112 abolishes dower and curtesy. Some statutes preserve the name "dower" but give it a different meaning. Ky. Rev. Stat. § 392.020 ("dower" includes personal property).

III. ELECTIVE SHARE

ELECTIVE SHARE

A. **Size of Share (#3.27):** In most states today, a surviving spouse can elect to take a share of the decedent's property regardless of the decedent's will. State laws vary as to the size of the share.

1. ***Size of the estate*** **(#3.28):** The fraction allowed to the spouse by the UPC elective share does not depend on the size of the estate, but the spouse can get at least $50,000. This is designed to implement the "support" rationale for the elective share. UPC § 2-202(b) (1990).

2. ***Length of the marriage* (#3.29):** The UPC elective share now depends upon the length of the marriage; a spouse of less than two years gets 3% as compared with a spouse of fifteen years or more, who gets 50%. This is not typical in separate property states, but it roughly reproduces the result in community property systems. *See* #3.46 et.seq, *infra.*

3. ***Other resources* (#3.30):** In most states the elective share does not depend upon need; a spouse with ample resources can claim it. However, the UPC gives the spouse a percentage of the "augmented estate" which includes the property of *both* spouses, and the spouse's own property reduces the claim. §§ 2-203, 2-209 (1990). Thus a wealthy spouse may get nothing under the elective share rules. The pre-1990 UPC only took into account any property of the spouse which came from the decedent.

   Example: A husband had received property as surviving joint tenant with his wife. Under the pre-1990 UPC, his property was presumed to have come from his wife, but he could and did rebut this presumption by showing that he had contributed his own funds to the joint tenancy. As a result he was only charged with one-half of it. *Matter of Estate of Lettengraver*, 813 P.2d 468 (Mont. 1991). Under the present UPC § 2-207, even if he had been the sole contributor to the joint tenant property, it would have reduced his elective share.

B. **Subject to claims (#3.31):** The spouse's elective share is based on the estate after the payment of claims. UPC §§ 2-203-4. In this respect, it differs from dower, the family allowance, and homestead, which have priority over claims. *See* #3.11, *supra.*

C. **Nonprobate Assets (#3.32):** Dower and curtesy attached to all land owned by either spouse at any time during the marriage. Many modern elective share statutes, in contrast, only cover the decedent's probate estate, so a spouse can defeat the elective share by gifts or will substitutes.

   Example: A husband gave a house to his children by a prior marriage but continued to live in it. The house was not part of his estate for computing his widow's share. *Dalia v. Lawrence*, 627 A.2d 392 (Conn. 1993).

   1. ***Augmented estate* (#3.33):** UPC § 2-203 includes nonprobate transfers in the augmented estate subject to the spouse's claim. This would include the house in *Dalia* because the husband retained possession of the house until his death. UPC § 2-205(2).

   2. ***Illusory transfers* (#3.34):** Even without such legislation, some courts allow a surviving spouse to attack nonprobate transfers as "illusory."

      Example: A husband created a revocable trust worth $1.3 million, as compared with his probate estate of $158,000. His widow was allowed a share of the trust assets on the theory that the husband retained so much control over the trust that it was "illusory." *Johnson v. Farmers & Merchants*

Bank, 379 S.E.2d 752 (W. Va. 1989). The result would be the same under UPC § 2-205.

3. ***Fraud* (#3.35):** A few statutes allow the surviving spouse to attack "fraudulent" transfers made by the decedent. It is not clear what this means.

   Example: A widow recovered money which her husband had transferred shortly before he died because this was a "fraud" on her rights. *Matter of Estate of Froman*, 803 S.W.2d 176 (Mo. App. 1991). But a widow could not reach joint bank accounts which her husband had created for his children; this was not fraudulent. *In re Estate of Mocny*, 630 N.E.2d 87 (Ill. App. 1993). Under UPC § 2-205, the joint bank account would have been included in the augmented estate and so would the eve-of-death transfer in *Froman* to the extent that it exceeded $10,000.

4. ***Insurance and pensions* (#3.36):** UPC § 2-205, unlike the pre-1990 version, includes life insurance in the augmented estate. Most pension plans are subject to ERISA, a federal statute which prevents a spouse from being cut out of pension benefits. 29 U.S.C. § 1055(a).

5. ***Transfers for consideration* (#3.37):** UPC § 2-208 exempts transfers for which the decedent received full consideration. Such transfers do not deplete the resources available for the spouse's support, since the consideration received is substituted for the item sold.

6. ***Transfers prior to marriage* (#3.38):** Some states allow spouses to upset transfers made on the eve of marriage as "fraudulent." *Efird v. Efird*, 791 S.W.2d 713 (Ark. App. 1990) (land deeded to children the day before the marriage). UPC § 2-205(2), however, in the case of irrevocable transfers, only covers those made "during marriage."

D. Other Benefits Given to Spouse

1. ***By will* (#3.39):** The common law allowed a spouse to claim dower or curtesy *and* take any benefits given to the spouse by the decedent's will unless the will otherwise provided. The same rule applies today to the family allowance and homestead. UPC §§ 2-402-404. But in most states the spouse must elect between the elective share and the decedent's will.

   Example: A widow could not reach a joint account the decedent had created with his brother because she had not renounced the decedent's will. *Hannah v. Hannah*, 824 S.W.2d 866 (Ky. 1992).

   a. Under UPC § 2-209, the benefits received by the widow under the will would have reduced her share but not eliminated it unless they were worth more than the elective share.

b. Formerly spouses were charged with any devise to them in the will even if they disclaimed it, but this provision was eliminated in 1993. UPC § 2-209, comment.

2. ***Benefits outside the will* (#3.40):** UPC § 2-209 also charges the spouse with benefits received from the decedent by gift or a will substitute.

E. Time for Election (#3.41): A spouse has a limited period in which to elect. UPC § 2-211 allows nine months from the date of the decedent's death or six months from the probate of the decedent's will.

1. ***Extensions* (#3.42):** A court may extend the time, for example, if the will is ambiguous, and the spouse needs to know how it will be construed in order to decide what to do.

F. Election by Guardian (#3.43): Sometimes the surviving spouse is incompetent when the decedent dies. Under the pre-1990 UPC, a spouse's guardian could claim the elective share only if it was "necessary to provide adequate support" for the spouse. Many courts adopt the same approach.

Example: When *H* died, his widow was under guardianship. Since she had $1 million of her own, the court refused to allow her guardian to elect against *H*'s will. *Estate of Lynch*, 421 N.E.2d 953 (Ill. App. 1981).

1. ***UPC* (#3.44):** Under UPC § 2-212(b) (1990), the right of a guardian to elect is not limited, but the assets taken under the elective share go into a trust for the spouse's life and return to the decedent's estate after the spouse dies.

G. Death of Spouse (#3.45): If the spouse dies before making an election, the spouse's executor or administrator cannot claim the elective share. UPC § 2-212. *Contra, Estate of Bozell*, 768 P.2d 380 (Okl. App. 1989).

COMMUNITY PROPERTY

IV. COMMUNITY PROPERTY

A. Significance (#3.46): In the eight community property states, one-half of the community property belongs to each spouse. This recognizes the fact that both spouses contribute to the acquisition of property during marriage. This concept affects the way property is divided when a couple divorces, or when one spouse dies intestate. *See* #1.14, *supra*.

1. ***Elective share* (#3.47):** A spouse who is disinherited can claim one-half of the community property but has no rights in the testator's separate property if the decedent leaves it to another person. This right replaces the elective share in community property states.

2. ***Differences* (#3.48):** Although there are many common rules in community property states, there are important differences in the details. The ultimate source of American community property is Spanish law, but the concept exists in many other European countries in various forms.

B. **Classification (#3.49):** All property acquired during the marriage by gainful activity is community property. Property which a spouse owned prior to the marriage or which was inherited or acquired by gift or will during the marriage is separate.

1. ***Presumption* (#3.50):** A spouse who claims that an asset is separate property must prove it, since all property acquired during marriage is presumed to be community. The fact that title to an asset is held in the name of only one spouse does not rebut the presumption that it is community property.

   Example: *H* was seventy-eight when he married, and the marriage only lasted eight years. This was not enough to rebut the presumption that an asset which he had purported to give away was community property. *Estate of Hull v. Williams,* 885 P.2d 1153 (Idaho App. 1994).

2. ***Tracing* (#3.51):** Property which was acquired during a marriage can be proved to be separate by tracing.

   Example: When he married, *H* owned 200 shares of Texaco stock. He later sold them and bought 200 shares of Trans World with the proceeds. The Trans World stock was held to be *H*'s separate property. *Estate of Hanau v. Hanau,* 730 S.W.2d 663 (Tex. 1987).

3. ***Income* (#3.52):** In some states, income from separate property is separate, but in others it is community if it accrues during the marriage. Separate property continues to be separate even though it appreciates during the marriage.

4. ***Commingling* (#3.53):** Often both community and separate property go into the acquisition of an asset. There are various solutions to this problem.

   Example: A husband bought a house prior to the marriage. During the marriage, community property was used to make payments on the mortgage and to improve the house. The house was apportioned between separate and community property based on the number of mortgage payments made from each. But the community was simply reimbursed for its expenditures on the improvements. *Malmquist v. Malmquist,* 792 P.2d 372 (Nev. 1990).

   a. Sometimes the community contribution is in the form of services provided by either spouse during the marriage. *Smith v. Smith*, 837 P.2d 869 (N.M. App. 1992) (*H* and *W* both worked for a company owned by *H* before the marriage; since they were undercompensated for their work, the community was entitled to a lien on the company).

5. ***Agreement* (#3.54):** Parties can "transmute" separate property into community by agreement. Such an agreement may be inferred when, for example, *W* uses her separate property to buy land and has title taken in the

names "*H* and *W*." *In re Estate of Hansen*, 892 P.2d 764 (Wash. App. 1995). *But see In re Marriage of Shannon,* 777 P.2d 8 (Wash. App. 1989) (alleged transmutation of house to community property rejected because no written agreement).

6. ***Separation* (#3.55):** Property acquired while a couple is separated may be deemed separate. However, some states apply this rule only when there is a separation decree. *Lynch v. Lynch*, 791 P.2d 653 (Ariz. App. 1990) ($2.2 million won by *H* in lottery while couple separated and divorce proceedings were pending was community property).

A. **Differences between Community Property and Elective Share (#3.56):** Although the elective share and community property perform similar functions, they differ in important ways. Each spouse *owns* a share of the community property, whereas the elective share is only an expectancy until one spouse dies.

1. ***Nonprobate property* (#3.57):** Since both spouses have a present interest in community property, they can usually set aside transfers made by the other spouse during life.

   Example: *H* deeded land to his children by a prior marriage. *W* had the deed set aside because both spouses must consent to a gift of land which is community property. *Bosone v. Bosone,* 768 P.2d 1022 (Wash. App. 1989). Under the UPC, the land would not have been subject to *W*'s elective share unless the deed was executed less than two years before *H* died. Even then it would not be included if *H* had received consideration for it, whereas sales of community property by one spouse may be voidable. *Arch Ltd v. Yu*, 766 P.2d 911 (N.M. 1988) (contract by *H* to sell community land is unenforceable).

   a. *Inter vivos* transactions by one spouse involving community property are not always voidable since each spouse has certain "managerial" rights over community property.

      Example: *W* selected an option for her pension which provided larger benefits during her life but no benefits to *H* if he survived her. The court rejected *H*'s claim for benefits; the pension was community property, but *W* could select the option. *O'Hara v. Public Employees Retirement Board,* 764 P.2d 489 (Nev. 1988).

   b. Even gifts by one spouse to a third person may be upheld in some states if they are "reasonable" in amount. *Redfearn v. Ford,* 579 S.W.2d 295 (Tex. App. 1979) ($73,000 gift upheld).

2. ***Spouse who fails to survive* (#3.58):** Community property rights do not depend on which spouse dies first.

Example: *W* died before *H* and left her estate to her children. They received half the community property as *W*'s successors. *Allard v. Frech*, 754 S.W.2d 111 (Tex. 1988). They would have no claim to *H*'s property under the UPC which only gives rights to a surviving spouse.

3. ***Other benefits given to spouse* (#3.59):** Normally a spouse does not have to elect between community property and property given or devised to the spouse by the decedent.

   Example: *W* used community property to create joint accounts for her sister and for *H*. *H* was allowed to keep the latter while claiming half of the account for the sister. *Chesnin v. Fischler,* 717 P.2d 298 (Wash. App. 1986). Under the UPC, his joint account would have reduced his elective share.

   a. On the other hand, if a will purports to dispose of both halves of the community property, the other spouse is put to an election. Usually a devise of "all my property" is construed to mean only the testator's half of the community so the spouse does not have to elect.

V. CHOICE OF LAW

CHOICE OF LAW

A. Land (#3.60): The law of the situs usually controls land.

Example: *H*'s will made no provision for *W*. Her claim to a half-interest in land in Louisiana under its community property law was allowed even though *H* was domiciled in New York, a separate property state. *Estate of Crichton,* 228 N.E.2d 799 (N.Y. 1967).

1. ***Exceptions* (#3.61):** There is a modern tendency to abandon the situs rule. For example. Cal. Family Code § 760 makes all property, wherever situated, community property if it is acquired by a married person domiciled in California. Conversely, Cal.Prob.Code § 120 follows the law of domicile when a married person domiciled elsewhere owns land in California. UPC § 2-202 also makes the spouse's rights depend upon the law of the decedent's domicile.

B. Personal Property

1. ***Domicile at death* (#3.62):** Personal property is normally governed by the law of the decedent's domicile. Thus the court in *Crichton, supra,* rejected *W*'s claim to a half share of *H's* personal property.

2. ***Domicile at time of acquisition* (#3.63):**

   a. If a couple is domiciled in a community property state when property is acquired, it remains community property if they later move to a separate property state. Uniform Disposition of Community Property Rights at Death Act. Not all states have adopted this statute, but courts have recognized the same rule.

b. Conversely, property acquired while a couple is domiciled in a separate property state remains separate when they move to a community property state. This leaves the spouse with no protection from disinheritance, so California treats such property as "quasi-community property" and gives a surviving spouse half of it. Cal. Prob. Code §§ 66, 101.

Example: *H* and *W* spent most of their life in a separate property state but moved to California when they retired. Their property would not be community property because they were not domiciled in a community property state when they acquired it. But if *H* devised his property to someone else, *W* could claim one-half of it (assuming it was acquired during the marriage). But if *W* died before *H*, she would have no rights in *H*'s separate property, comparable to the rights she would have in true community property.

3

C. Designation of Governing Law

1. ***In will* (#3.64):** A will sometimes designates the governing law, but a testator cannot reduce the elective share by designating the law of a state where the elective share is smaller. UPC § 2-703.

2. ***Nonprobate assets* (#3.65):** Courts of the state where a person dies may not have power over nonprobate assets in another state.

   Example: A person created a living trust in Nevada and later moved to Montana, where he died. The Montana court had no power over the Nevada trust since it had no jurisdiction over the trustee. *Matter of Estate of Ducey*, 787 P.2d 749 (Mont. 1990).

D. Federal Law (#3.66): Federal law may supersede community property claims.

Example: A wife's attempt to devise her community property share in her husband's pension failed because ERISA, a federal statute governing pensions, prevailed over state community property rights. *Ablamis v. Roper*, 937 F.2d 1450 (9th Cir. 1991).

OMITTED SPOUSE

VI. OMITTED SPOUSE

A. Intestate Share (#3.67): UPC § 2-301 gives a spouse not mentioned in a will an intestate share of the testator's estate if the marriage occurred after the will was executed. The provision, like the one for pretermitted children, #3.16, *supra,* assumes that the testator never got around to changing the will. Such provisions are common but not universal, since some states regard the elective share as sufficient protection for spouses.

1. ***Comparison with elective share* (#3.68):** The intestate share granted by § 2-301 is usually larger than the elective share, but it only includes property in the probate estate, unlike the elective share. See #3.33, *supra*.

Example: A man executed a will and at the same time put assets into a revocable trust. He later married. His wife got her intestate share of his probate estate under a statute like UPC § 2-301, but received none of the assets in the trust. *Estate of Heggstead*, 20 Cal. Rptr.2d 433 (Cal. App. 1993).

2. ***Will revoked by marriage*** **(#3.69)**: Some states retain the rule of the English Wills Act of 1837 that marriage revokes a will, but under UPC § 2-301, after the spouse's intestate share is distributed, the rest of the estate is governed by the will. *Matter of Estate of Groves*,788 P.2d 127 (Ariz. App. 1990) (spouse gets all the estate under the statute but appointment of executor in the will still takes effect).

3. ***Devise to child*** **(#3.70):** The 1990 version of UPC § 2-301 applies only to the portion of the estate not devised to prior children of the testator or their descendants.

   Example: A widower's will leaves his estate to his children. He then marries and fails to change his will. Even though his widow would get a substantial share of the estate in intestacy, she would have no rights under § 2-301. She would, however, have rights to an elective share. See *Mongold v. Mayle*, 452 S.E.2d 444 (W. Va. 1994).

4. ***Remarriage*** **(#3.71):** Such statutes have been held to apply to a person whom the testator remarried after executing a will. *Estate of Katleman*, 16 Cal. Rptr.2d 468 (Cal. App. 1993). According to the comment, UPC § 2-301 does not apply if the will was executed during a prior marriage to the same spouse.

B. Proof of Contrary Intent

1. ***Provision in will*** **(#3.72):** UPC § 2-301 is subject to a contrary provision in the will, unlike the elective share. A devise to a person whom the testator later marries is not enough to show such contrary intent.

   Example: A will left property to the testator's friend, with the residue devised to the testator's siblings. He later married the friend and died without changing his will. She took his estate as an omitted spouse. *In re Estate of Gaspelin*, 542 So.2d 1023 (Fla. App. 1989). Under UPC § 2-301 (1990) the result would be the same, but the devise would reduce the spouse's share, assuming that she was entitled to only a share of the estate.

2. ***Extrinsic evidence*** **(#3.73):** UPC § 2-301 does not generally allow evidence outside the will to prove an intent to bar the spouse. *Noble v. McNerny*, 419 N.W.2d 424 (Mich. App. 1988) (oral statements insufficient).

   a. However, if the testator transferred property to the spouse outside the will, this may bar the spouse's claim if the testator so intended. *Compare Estate of Shannon*, 274 Cal. Rptr. 338 (Cal. App. 1990) (small payment from *H*'s pension not enough to bar spouse) *with Matter of Estate of Bartell*, 776 P.2d 885 (Utah 1989) (transfer of $230,000 to wife showed intent to bar her). Unlike an ordinary advancement, *see* #2.10, *supra*, the decedent's intent can be inferred from oral statements or the size of the transfer; no writing is required.

b. The spouse is also barred under UPC § 2-301 if "it appears from the will or from other evidence that the will was made in contemplation of" the marriage. Presumably, this would include evidence that the will was executed shortly before the marriage.

VII. WAIVER

WAIVER

A. Joinder in Conveyance (#3.74): The UPC excludes from the augmented estate any property transferred with the written consent or joinder of the surviving spouse. UPC § 2-208(a).

B. Transmutation of Community Property (#3.75): Just as parties may agree to turn separate property into community, #3.54, *supra,* they may do the reverse. Many states require that such an agreement be in writing. Cal. Fam. Code § 852.

Example: A wife signed a consent to the husband's designation of a beneficiary of pension benefits which were community property. Nevertheless, the wife's estate took half the benefits when she died, since the writing she signed did not contain an "express declaration" of an intent to transmute the property. *In re Estate of MacDonald*, 794 P.2d 911 (Cal. 1990).

C. General Waivers (#3.76): UPC § 2-213 provides that a spouse's right to an elective share, homestead, or family allowance may be waived by a written contract signed by the spouse. Such agreements often raise questions as to what they cover.

Example: A premarital agreement provided that "all our property shall remain separate." This was construed not to bar *H* from claiming an elective share and family allowance after *W* died. *Estate of Calcutt v. Calcutt*, 576 N.E.2d 1288 (Ind. App. 1991). But in *Matter of Estate of Beesley*, 883 P.2d 1343 (Utah 1994), an agreement stating that *W* would get one half of *H*'s estate was held to bar her from getting a larger share when he died intestate.

1. ***UPC* (#3.77):** UPC § 2-213(d) says that a "waiver of 'all rights' or equivalent language" bars the elective share, family allowance, homestead, exempt property, and an intestate share.

D. Defenses (#3.78): Historically, all contracts between married persons were voidable. This is no longer true, but since the relationship between spouses (or prospective spouses) differs from the relationship between parties to commercial contracts, courts avoid waivers if there is an abuse of the confidence which spouses typically repose in each other. UPC § 2-213 (1990) follows a Uniform Premarital Agreement Act on this subject.

1. ***Voluntary* (#3.79):** UPC § 2-213(b)(1) says the waiver is unenforceable if the spouse "did not execute the waiver voluntarily." Some courts invalidate waivers if the spouse had no opportunity to examine it before signing. *Matter of Marriage of Foran*, 834 P.2d 1081 (Wash. App. 1992) (*W* only saw the contract the day the honeymoon began).

2. ***Unconscionability* (#3.80):** UPC § 2-213(b)(2) also makes the waiver unenforceable if it was "unconscionable when it was executed" and there was inadequate disclosure. An agreement which gives the spouse substantially less than the spouse's statutory rights may be deemed unconscionable. *In re Estate of Geyer*, 533 A.2d 423 (Pa. 1987) (waiver invalid because it gave spouse property worth $70,000 when her elective share would have been $300,000). But not all courts take this view.

   Example: A premarital agreement which barred *H* from any share of *W*'s estate was binding. The marriage itself was sufficient consideration. *Beatty v. Beatty*, 555 N.E.2d 184 (Ind. App. 1990).

3. ***Disclosure* (#3.81):** Even an "unconscionable" agreement is enforceable under UPC § 2-213 if there was "reasonable disclosure" of the decedent's property, or the spouse had adequate knowledge thereof or waived disclosure.

   Example: Even though *W* got nothing under *H*'s will, her claim to an elective share was barred by a premarital agreement. She had some business experience, had visited his farm, and so knew something about his assets. *Matter of Estate of Ascherl*, 445 N.W.2d 391 (Iowa App. 1989).

   a. Arguably, even a full disclosure of the other spouse's property is meaningless unless the waiving spouse is also informed about the rights being waived. Some cases hold that a waiver by a spouse who does not have independent counsel is unenforceable. *Rowland v. Rowland,* 599 N.E.2d 315 (Ohio 1991) (agreement drafted by *H*'s lawyer who failed to advise *W*, age 18, to get her own counsel). *But see In re Estate of Gagnier,* 26 Cal. Rptr.2d 128 (Cal. App. 1993) (agreement valid even though *W* had no counsel).

4. ***ERISA* (#3.82):** ERISA 29 U.S.C. § 1055(c) imposes special requirements for waivers of rights in the other spouse's pension. The waiver must be witnessed by a plan representative or a notary and designate a beneficiary who cannot be changed without the spouse's consent. Arguably, it cannot be executed prior to the marriage.

OTHER LIMITATIONS

VIII. OTHER LIMITATIONS (#3.83): Some limitations on testamentary freedom can be asserted by any heir, not just a spouse or child of the testator. These are relatively unimportant.

A. **Mortmain (#3.84):** Several states once limited devises to charity, usually by requiring that the will be executed a certain period prior to the testator's death. Most states have now repealed such statutes, and a few courts have held them to be unconstitutional. *Shriners Hospital v. Zrillic,* 563 So.2d 64 (Fla. 1990).

1. ***Rationale* (#3.85):** The statutes were designed to guard against undue influence over a dying testator, but they were arbitrary. A testator in good health might happen to die a few weeks after making a will and the statute would apply, whereas it did not apply to devises to noncharities who might also exercise undue influence. As to undue influence, *see* #7.11, *infra.*

B. **Public Policy (#3.86):** A direction in a will that property be destroyed may be unenforceable as contrary to a public policy against waste. *Eyerman v. Mercantile Trust Co.*, 524 S.W.2d 210 (Mo. App. 1975).

1. ***Divorce* (#3.87):** Devises which encourage divorce have been held to violate public policy, but this rule is narrowly applied, particularly in more recent cases.

   Example: A will provided that the property for the testator's daughter should go into a trust so long as she was married. The daughter claimed this violated public policy, but the court held that encouraging divorce was acceptable if the parent reasonably believed it would promote the child's welfare. *Hall v. Eaton*, 631 N.E.2d 805 (Ill. App. 1994).

C. **Disinheritance Clauses (#3.88):** Many cases refuse to give effect to a clause which disinherits particular heirs without devising the property to another.

Example: A will expressly disinherited the testator's heirs, but they took most of her estate because the will contained no residuary clause. *Matter of Estate of Krokowsky*, 896 P.2d 247 (Ariz. 1995).

1. ***UPC* (#3.89):** UPC § 2-101 rejects this rule "which defeats a testator's intent for no sufficient reason." It treats the disinherited heirs as if they had executed a disclaimer.

FORMAL REQUIREMENTS

CHAPTER SUMMARY

I.	Wills	4-2
II.	Gifts	4-9
III.	Trusts	4-13
IV.	Joint Tenancy	4-17
V.	Payable-on-death Contracts	4-18

FORMAL REQUIREMENTS

INTRODUCTION: Wills must be in writing, signed, and (usually) witnessed. Some states allow "holographic" wills which are not witnessed, but these must be entirely in the testator's handwriting. These requirements are designed to guard against false claims as to what a decedent intended. They also perform a cautionary function since rash statements are less likely to be reduced to writing.

Gifts *inter vivos* are subject to less stringent requirements. A signed writing is necessary to transfer land, but not personal property. Delivery is required for both land and personal property, but courts interpret this laxly. No consideration is necessary for a gift, but statements that a gift will be made in the future, and gifts of "expectancies," are treated as promises for which consideration is necessary.

For trusts, no delivery is necessary if the settlor declares herself trustee, but a writing is required to create a trust of land. Joint tenancy is not subject to the requirements for wills even though it operates to pass property at death to the surviving tenant. Insurance and pension contracts that provide for payment on death to a designated beneficiary are also free from the formalities prescribed for wills.

The distinction between the formalities required for wills and for other transfers is questionable. Sometimes a gift or trust is held to be "testamentary" because it takes effect only at death, but this rarely happens today. If is no claim of fraud, courts are reluctant to deny effect to a clear manifestation of intent, particularly since the use of these will substitutes has become so common. A more in-depth discussion of the material covered in this chapter appears in McGovern, Kurtz, and Rein, *Wills, Trusts and Estates,* 156–206 (1988).

WILLS

I. WILLS

A. History

1. ***English statutes* (#4.1):** The Statute of Wills of 1540, which first allowed wills of land, required that they be in writing. Later statutes imposed additional requirements.

   a. The Statute of Frauds added that wills must be signed and attested by three witnesses.

   b. The Wills Act of 1837 reduced the number of necessary witnesses to two, but it added other requirements, *e.g.*, that the will be signed at the end, and that the witnesses be present at the same time.

2. ***American statutes* (#4.2):** Most American statutes are based either on the Wills Act or the Statute of Frauds.

   a. Some American statutes impose additional requirements, *e.g.*, that the will be "published," *i.e.*, that the testator declare to the witnesses that this is his will.

b. The UPC reduces the formal requirements for wills.

B. Policy

1. ***Reasons for formalities* (#4.3):**

   a. Evidentiary function. If wills did not have to be in writing, witnesses might falsely claim that the decedent wanted her property to pass in a particular way. Even honest witnesses might not remember correctly what the decedent said.

   b. Cautionary function. Persons often make rash oral statements. The writing requirement guards against this.

   c. Channeling function. It is sometimes hard to know whether a person meant an oral remark to be taken seriously, or whether it was just a tentative idea. If the testator's wishes are expressed in a signed and attested writing, there is less reason to doubt that it was meant to be dispositive.

2. ***Substantial compliance* (#4.4):** Some have argued that "substantial compliance" with the statutes should suffice. Under UPC § 2-503 (1990), a will can be probated if there is "clear and convincing evidence that the decedent intended" it to be a will even if it does not comply with the statutory requirements. There are two reasons for this change.

   a. In the past, many wills were made when the testator was near death and thus subject to undue influence. Today, most wills are executed long before the testator dies.

   b. The formal requirements for will substitutes like joint tenancy are less stringent than those for wills. It seems illogical to differentiate between the two since they perform similar functions.

   c. Nevertheless, the substantial compliance idea has had a mixed reception in the courts. *Compare Matter of Will of Ranney*, 589 A.2d 1339 (N.J. 1991) (accepting it) with *Burns v. Adamson*, 854 S.W.2d 723 (Ark. 1993) (rejecting a will because not signed by a witness).

3. ***Distinction between wills and contracts* (#4.5):** The trend to relax formal requirements has not been carried as far for wills as it has for contracts. The Statute of Frauds does not require witnesses for contracts, but most states still require them for wills. Courts often enforce oral contracts, but oral wills are almost never valid. *See* #4.28, *infra*. There are two reasons for this distinction.

   a. The testator is always dead when a will is probated and thus cannot rebut false claims as to her intent. Both parties can usually testify when a suit is brought to enforce an alleged contract.

b. Refusal to allow a will which is formally insufficient only means that the testator's property passes by intestate succession (or a prior valid will). This is not as troubling as the refusal to enforce a contract since the parties have often acted in reliance on it.

C. **Signature (#4.6):** All states require that wills be signed. The signature is a symbol that the testator has finished the will.

1. ***Mark*** **(#4.7):** The testator's full name is not required; initials or an "X" is sufficient. *Trim v. Daniels*, 862 S.W.2d 8 (Tex. App. 1993) (initials). Typewritten signatures have also been upheld.

2. ***Proxy*** **(#4.8):** Someone else may sign for the testator if he does it "in the testator's conscious presence and by the testator's direction." UPC § 2-502. *Cf. Matter of Estate of Dethorne,* 471 N.W.2d 780 (Wis. 1991) (will signed by testator's wife denied probate because no proof she signed at his request).

3. ***Place of signature*** **(#4.9):** Some statutes, following the 1837 Wills Act, require that the will be signed "at the end." Others, like the UPC, do not. However, if the name is not at the end, it may not count as a signature because it was not intended as such. The many cases on this issue are hard to reconcile. *Compare Matter of Estate of Erickson,* 806 P.2d 1186 (Utah 1991) (will denied probate because testator's name was at the beginning) *with Clark v. Studenwalt,* 419 S.E.2d 308 (W.Va. 1992) (testator's name at the beginning was a sufficient signature).

   a. A court may uphold a will on the theory that the signature was at the "logical" end.

      Example: The testator filled a sheet of paper with writing, then signed it on the top margin, the only space available. The court held that the will was signed "at the end." *Estate of Stasis,* 307 A.2d 241 (Pa. 1973).

   b. Sometimes failure to sign at the end renders the whole will invalid; sometimes only the parts which follow the signature will be rendered invalid.

      Example: The testator signed the first of four pages of a will. The whole will was denied probate. *Keener v. Archibald,* 533 N.E.2d 1268 (Ind. App. 1989). But in New York, only the parts which follow the signature are invalid, unless this would subvert the testator's intent. N.Y. E.P.T.L. § 3-2. l(a)(1)(A).

   c. If a testator signs a will and later adds words, the additional words cannot be probated but the original will remains valid.

   d. The testator's signature on the last page of a multipage will is valid, but many lawyers, out of an abundance of caution, have the testator sign or initial every page.

e. Some courts have denied probate to wills when the testator signed only an affidavit attached to the will, but UPC § 2-504(c) expressly allows this.

D. Witnesses

1. ***Number*** **(#4.10):** Nearly all states now only require two witnesses.

2. ***Competency*** **(#4.11):** In most states, general competency to testify is enough. Texas requires the witnesses to be over age 14. Tex. Prob. Code § 59.

   a. A drafter who anticipates a will contest should select the witnesses carefully, *e.g.*, they should be familiar enough with the testator to be able to give credible testimony as to her capacity.

   b. The civil law gives special status to wills executed in the presence of a notary, but this is not generally true in America. However, many states give special status to "international wills" which are executed pursuant to a 1973 convention signed by many countries. International wills must be signed before two ordinary witnesses and an "authorized person." Active lawyers admitted to practice are "authorized persons" for this purpose. See UPC § 2-1009.

3. ***Interested witnesses*** **(#4.12):** The Statute of Frauds required "credible" witnesses. The then prevailing rules of evidence did not allow interested witnesses to testify. Therefore, if a devisee witnessed a will, the will was invalid. A statute was then passed whereby only the devise to the witness was void. Most U.S. states have such a statute. *E.g.*, Tenn. Code § 32-1-103(b).

   a. In some situations, a devise to a witness is valid.

      (1) A devise to an extra or "supernumerary" witness is allowed.

      Example: There are three witnesses but only one of them is interested, and the statute only requires two witnesses. The interested witness can take. *Brickhouse v. Brickhouse,* 407 S.E.2d 607 (N.C. App. 1991).

      (2) The devise is valid if the witness would take just as much if the will were not probated because he is the testator's heir, or a devisee under an earlier will. Tex. Prob. Code § 62.

      (3) A witness can act as executor or trustee. They are not regarded as interested because they must work to earn the fees they get. Ky. Rev. Stat. § 394.200(2).

      (4) Some states allow the *spouse* of a witness to receive a devise, *Estate of Harrison,* 738 P.2d 964 (Okl. App. 1987), but others do not, *Matter of Estate of Webster,* 574 N.E.2d 245 (Ill. App. 1991) (devise to wife of witness void).

(5) The devise is valid if the witness benefits only indirectly – *e.g.,* a devise to the church of which the witness is the minister.

b. Many commentators have criticized the bar against interested witnesses. UPC § 2-505 provides that "the signing of a will by an interested witness does not invalidate the will or any provision of it." *Compare* Cal. Prob. Code § 6112 (devise to witness creates a presumption of undue influence).

E. What Witnesses See

1. ***Signature or acknowledgment* (#4.13):** Normally the witnesses watch the testator sign the will, but it suffices if they see the testator acknowledge a signature previously made. Some courts allow this only if the witnesses see the signature at the time of the acknowledgment. But under UPC § 2-502, the witnesses may see either the signing or the testator's acknowledgment of the signature or of the will. Thus it is enough if the testator tells the witnesses "this is my will" even if they cannot see the signature.

2. ***Publication and request* (#4.14):** Some statutes (not including the UPC) require the testator to tell the witnesses that this is a will and request them to sign it. Courts tend not to be very strict about this.

   Example: A will was upheld even though the witnesses did not recall hearing the testator declare that it was his will, since the purpose of the requirement was simply to make sure that the testator knew he was signing a will. *Matter of Estate of Bearbower*, 426 N.W.2d 392 (Iowa 1988).

   a. No state requires that the witnesses know *the contents* of the will (which many testators want to keep secret until they are dead).

3. ***Present at the same time* (#4.15):** In most states a testator may sign the will before one witness and later acknowledge her signature before another, but some require that the witnesses be present at the same time. Cal. Prob. Code § 6110(c).

F. Signature by Witnesses

1. ***Presence of the testator* (#4.16):** Traditionally, witnesses had to sign the will in the presence of the testator. Wills have been held invalid because the witnesses took the will into another room to sign it. UPC § 2-502 merely requires that witnesses sign "within a reasonable time after" witnessing the will. But a signature by a witness after the testator dies has been held insufficient. *Matter of Estate of Royal*, 826 P.2d 1236 (Colo. 1992).

2. ***Signature as witness* (#4.17):** Unless a person signs *as a witness,* some courts hold that the requirement is not satisfied. Thus a signature by a notary acting as such has been held insufficient. *Estate of Overt,* 768 P.2d 378 (Okl. App. 1989). *Contra, In re Estate of Price,* 871 P.2d 1079 (Wash. App. 1994).

G. **Attestation Clause and Affidavit (#4.18):** Most lawyers have the witnesses sign an "attestation clause," which recites that the proper formalities were observed. Such a clause is not required, but it has several advantages.

1. ***Advantages*** **(#4.19):** Sometimes the witnesses deny that the requirements for proper execution were satisfied or do not remember.

   Example: A court probated a will on the basis of the attestation clause even though the witnesses did not remember whether it had been properly executed. *In re Estate of Carrol*, 548 N.E.2d 650 (Ill. App. 1989).

2. ***Self-proved wills*** **(#4.20):** UPC § 2-504 (like many other statutes) allows a will to be "self-proved" by having the witnesses sign an affidavit. This allows the will to be probated without having the witnesses appear in court.

3. ***Signing the clause alone*** **(#4.21):** Some courts hold that if the witnesses sign only the affidavit, they have not signed *the will* as required by the statute, *Wich v. Fleming,* 652 S.W.2d 353 (Tex. 1983), but others treat the clause as part of the will. *Matter of Petty's Estate,* 608 P.2d 987 (Kan. 1980). Accord, UPC § 2-504(c).

4. ***Unavailability of witnesses*** **(#4.22):** Even if a will is not self-proved, it can be probated without the witnesses' testimony if they are not available, *e.g.*, because they have died or have moved out of state. UPC § 3-406.

H. **Holographic Wills (#4.23):** UPC § 2-503 allows unwitnessed wills if they are in the testator's handwriting. Such wills are called "holographic." Not all the states allow them. They are usually drafted without the benefit of a lawyer, since lawyers understand that the benefits of having witnesses to a will outweigh any costs involved.

1. ***Rationale*** **(#4.24):** A handwritten will provides a more extensive specimen of the testator's handwriting than one in which the signature is the only mark made by the testator. Therefore, witnesses are not needed to prove its authenticity. (Pennsylvania allows unwitnessed wills which are not in the testator's handwriting; this is unique. 20 Pa. Stat. § 2502.)

2. ***Testamentary intent*** **(#4.25):** In holographic wills, the absence of witnesses may cause doubt as to whether the writing was intended to be a will.

   Example: A court refused to probate a letter which said, "I want my daughters to share 1/3, 1/3, 1/3," saying that the author had no testamentary intent. *Wolfe v. Wolfe,* 448 S.E.2d 408 (Va. 1994). But in *Matter of Estate of Ramirez,* 869 P.2d 263 (Mont. 1994) the court probated a letter saying "mom should have everything if anything happens to me."

   a. Courts refuse to probate writings which are only a preliminary draft for a future will. *Matter of Will of Smith*, 528 A.2d 918 (N.J. 1987) (letter of instructions to lawyer).

b. Some courts allow extrinsic evidence to show that a writing was made with testamentary intent, but others say that the intent must appear on the face of the will. In North Carolina, a holograph must be found among the testator's "valuable papers" or "deposited... for safekeeping" in order to be effective. N.C. Gen. Stat. § 31-3.4(a).

3. ***Date*** **(#4.26):** Since witnesses are not available to establish the date of a holograph, some states require that they be dated. Louisiana. Civ. Code Art. 1588. California requires this only if the date is relevant, *e.g.*, because the testator lacked capacity at some time before she died. Cal. Prob. Code § 6111(b). UPC § 2-502 does not require a date.

4. ***Printed matter*** **(#4.27):** Many wills have been denied probate as holographs because the writing contained matter not in the testator's handwriting. UPC § 2-502 only requires that "material portions" be in the testator's handwriting, and the parts showing testamentary intent need not be in the testator's handwriting.

   Example: A testator used a printed form for his will, filling in the blanks by hand. The court held that this qualified as a holograph. *Estate of Muder,* 765 P.2d 997 (Ariz. 1988).

I. **Oral Wills (#4.28):** The Statute of Frauds allowed oral wills when they were made in the testator's last illness. The Wills Act abolished them, but a proviso allowed wills by soldiers in service and seamen at sea based on the liberal rules of Roman law for soldiers' wills. Some American states have similar provisions, but they are rarely used. The UPC does not allow oral wills.

J. **Choice of Law**

1. ***Traditional rule*** **(#4.29):** Traditionally the law of the situs governed land, and the law of the testator's domicile governed personal property.

2. ***Liberal rule*** **(#4.30):** Under UPC § 2-506 (and many similar statutes) a will is valid if its execution complies either with the law of the place of execution, or of the place of the testator's domicile at death or at the time of execution.

3. ***Change in law*** **(#4.31):** A similar liberal choice of law rule covers cases where the law changes after a will is executed.

   Example: A testator executed a holographic will at a time when they were not allowed. Before he died, the state enacted the UPC. The will was held to be valid. *Estate of Fitzgerald,* 738 P.2d 236 (Utah App. 1987). If the change had been in the other direction, the will would also have been upheld. UPC § 2-506 validates wills which are valid at the time of execution, despite changes which occur thereafter.

K. **Malpractice (#4.32):** Lawyers who draft wills which are invalid for failure to comply with formal requirements may be held liable to the intended beneficiaries.

1. ***Privity* (#4.33):** Some states still adhere to the view that a lawyer who drafts a will for a testator is not liable to the intended beneficiary because there is no "privity" between the lawyer and the beneficiary. *Spivey v. Pulley,* 526 N.Y.S.2d 145 (App. Div. 1988). However, most courts have rejected this view in recent years. *Simpson v. Calvert,* 650 A.2d 318 (N.H. 1994).

   a. Plaintiffs in a malpractice action must show that the testator intended to benefit them. Some courts require that proof of the testator's intent be as strong as the proof needed to establish a will. This requirement may defeat the malpractice action. *Ryan v. Ryan,* 642 N.E.2d 1028 (Mass. 1994).

2. ***Ways to guard against invalidation* (#4.34):** Use of an attestation clause or affidavit is desirable. *See* #4.18, *supra.* A lawyer should personally supervise the execution in order to assure it is properly carried out. The will should recite the place of execution, as this may make the will valid in other states. *See* #4.30, *supra.* But most lawyers follow the most stringent formal requirements in order to assure that the will can qualify in every state, *e.g.*, by using three witnesses even though most states require only two.

GIFTS

II. GIFTS

A. Policy

1. ***Comparison with wills* (#4.35):** The formalities required for *inter vivos* gifts are less stringent than those for wills. No writing is required for gifts of personal property. As to land, a signed writing is necessary, but usually witnesses are not required. Two reasons are often suggested for the difference:

   a. Delivery is necessary for a gift, and it performs the same protective function as a writing or attestation. However, courts have so watered down the delivery requirement that it has become almost meaningless.

   b. A testator is dead and so cannot rebut false claims, but this is a weak distinction since litigation concerning gifts also often arises after the donor dies.

2. ***Testamentary gifts* (#4.36):** Courts sometimes hold that a gift was testamentary and invalid for failure to comply with the formalities prescribed for wills.

   Example: A father executed a deed of land to his sons but kept the income until he died. The court held that the deed was ineffective as testamentary. *Matter of Estate of Dittus,* 497 N.W.2d 415 (N.D. 1993).

   However, such holdings are becoming relatively rare. *See* #4.66, *infra.*

3. ***Clear and convincing evidence* (#4.37):** Courts sometimes say that a donee must produce clear and convincing evidence to prove a gift, especially after the donor has died. *Hocks v. Jeremiah,* 759 P.2d 312 (Or. App. 1988).

B. Writing

1. ***Land* (#4.38):** Virtually all states have provisions based on the Statute of Frauds which require a signed writing to convey an interest in land. However, an oral gift of land may be effective on an estoppel theory.

   Example: A mother orally gave land to her children. The gift was held valid because the donees had acted in reliance on the gift in making improvements on the land. *Montoya v. New Mexico Human Services Dept.,* 771 P.2d 196 (N.M. App. 1989).

4

   a. Even if a deed is lost, the transfer can be proved by clear evidence of the execution and delivery of the deed. *Cole v. Guy*, 539 N.E.2d 436 (Ill. App. 1989).

2. ***Personal property* (#4.39)**

   a. A writing is not necessary to transfer personal property.

      Example: A husband, intending to give securities to his wife, delivered the certificates without indorsing them. This was effective under Uniform Commercial Code § 8-307, which says that the transfer of a security is complete upon delivery. *Andrews v. Troy Bank and Trust Co.,* 529 So.2d 987 (Ala. 1988).

   b. Most personal property of substantial value is in the form of "intangibles" which represent claims against an institution, *e.g.*, a bank account, stock, or corporate bond. Usually the institution has rules governing the transfer of such claims. Failure to comply with these rules may make a gift ineffective.

      Example: A woman delivered United States Savings Bonds to her granddaughters, intending to make a gift. The gift was held invalid because United States Treasury Regulations required a re-registration in order to transfer bonds. *United States v. Chandler,* 410 U.S. 257 (1973).

   c. But many courts hold that such rules are only designed to protect the institution from liability if it pays without notice of a transfer.

      Example: A father delivered a boat to his daughter. Although he failed to have a new certificate of title issued in her name, the daughter was held to own the boat. A statute requiring title certificates was only to protect bona fide purchasers and did not affect the validity of the gift between donor and donee. *Abney v. Western Res. Mut. Cas. Co.*, 602 N.E.2d 348 (Ohio App. 1991).

   d. Checks are subject to special rules; even if signed and delivered, they are not effective as gifts if the drawer dies before the check is cashed. *DeLuca v. Bancohio Natl. Bank, Inc.*, 598 N.E.2d 781 (Ohio App. 1991).

C. Delivery

1. ***Necessity of delivery* (#4.40):** Occasionally a gift fails for lack of delivery.

   Example: Even though a father intended to forgive debts of his children, there was no effective gift because he did not give them back their notes. *Matter of Estate of Hoyle*, 866 P.2d 451 (Okl. App. 1993).

2. ***Symbolic delivery* (#4.41):** Delivery can be symbolic or "constructive" only.

   Example: A man handed bonds to his sister as a gift. She refused them so he could put them in his safe deposit box. The gift was valid even though the donor was in possession of the bonds when he died. *Hocks v. Jeremiah,* 759 P.2d 312 (Or. App. 1988).

3. ***Donee already in possession* (#4.42):** If the intended donee is already in possession of property, delivery is unnecessary, *e.g.*, where the donee has been holding property for safekeeping and the donor says she can keep it as a gift. *Restatement (Second) of Property (Donative Transfers)* § 31.1, illus. 4.

4. ***Delivery of instrument of gift* (#4.43):** The donor can keep the property but deliver a writing to the donee indicating donative intent.

   Example: A father sent a letter to his son saying, "I wish to give you the painting by Klimt which hangs in my living room." The gift was upheld even though the son never got possession of the painting during his father's life. *Gruen v. Gruen,* 496 N.E.2d 869 (N.Y. 1986).

5. ***Delivery to a third person* (#4.44):** Delivery can be made to someone other than the donee.

   Example: A man executed a deed conveying land to his children. He handed the deed to his sister, telling her to give it to the children after he died. This was heldto be an effective delivery. *Herron v. Underwood,* 503 N.E.2d 111 (Ill. App. 1987).

   However, if delivery is made to someone characterized as an agent of the donor rather than the agent of the donee, the gift fails on the ground that the agent's powers expire when the donor dies. *See Kesterson v. Cronan*, 806 P.2d 134 (Or. App. 1991).

6. ***Registration* (#4.45):** Registration of a bank account or a security may be a valid substitute for delivery.

   Example: A father wished to give stock to his son. He turned in his certificate and had the company issue one in the son's name. The father kept the new certificate in his possession, but the gift was held effective. *Estate of Ross v. Ross,* 626 P.2d 489 (Utah 1981). *See also* Uniform Transfers to Minors Act (UTMA) § 9(a).

7. ***Authorization to take* (#4.46):** Sometimes the donor's authorizing the donee to take possession is treated as delivery.

   Example: A terminally ill man in the hospital told his brother to go to the donor's safe deposit box and take some bonds which were in the box. This was held an effective gift. *Brown v. Metz*, 393 A.2d 402 (Va. 1990).

D. Consideration

1. ***History* (#4.47):** In the early Middle Ages, a transfer of land required delivery of the land itself ("livery of seisin"). When courts first began to allow land to be transferred by deed, they required "consideration" for the deed, but this was defined broadly to include affection for a spouse or relative. Today deeds usually recite a consideration, but this is not necessary for validity.

2. ***Promises* (#4.48):** Promises require consideration (or some substitute therefor like promissory estoppel).

   a. The distinction between a gift and a promise often turns on whether the donor used words indicative of a present transfer.

      Example: A man signed and delivered to his secretary a paper which said, "I give you 5% of my profits from the musical version of *Pygmalion*." (This later became the enormously successful "My Fair Lady.") The court held that this was a gift which required no consideration. *Speelman v. Pascal,* 178 N.E.2d 723 (N.Y. 1961). But a document saying a woman would convey land "at the expiration of the life estate" held by her mother was held to be a promise, ineffective for lack of consideration. *Larabee v. Booth,* 463 N.E.2d 487 (Ind. App. 1982).

   b. Even with words of the present tense, a person cannot make an effective gift of an "expectancy" which he does not yet own. However, an assignment of an expectancy, such as an heir's hope of inheriting from a parent who is still living, is effective if the assignment is supported by adequate consideration. *Johnson by and through Lackey v. Schick*, 882 P.2d 1059 (Okl. 1994).

E. Recording

1. ***Effect of failure to record* (#4.49):** An unrecorded deed may be invalid as to some third persons but valid as to others.

   Example: A creditor with a judgment against a husband sought to reach land which he had conveyed to his wife by an unrecorded deed. The creditor failed because unrecorded deeds are valid except against bona fide purchasers or mortgagees; the statute did not protect judgment creditors of the transferor. *Siegel Mobile Home Group v. Bowen,* 757 P.2d 1250 (Idaho App. 1988).

In some states the result would be different. Therefore it is usually desirable to record a deed of gift of land to prevent creditors of the donor from later reaching it.

2. ***Recording as a substitute for delivery* (#4.50):** Recording of a deed creates a presumption of delivery.

   Example: A man recorded a deed putting property into joint tenancy with his son. He later claimed he did not intend to make a gift, but the court held that the presumption of delivery was not rebutted, even though the father still possessed the deed. *Gross v. Gross*, 781 P.2d 284 (Mont. 1989).

III. TRUSTS

A. "Equity Follows the Law" (#4.51): Most of the rules governing gifts also apply to trusts. Trusts are either created by will (testamentary trusts) or *inter vivos* (often called living trusts). A will which creates a testamentary trust must comply with the formalities prescribed for wills. But there is a difference between living trusts and other gifts in that a trust can be created without delivery when the settlor declares himself trustee.

B. Writing (#4.52): Most American states have adopted § 7 of the Statute of Frauds. It requires that trusts of land be "proved by some writing signed by the party who is by law enabled to declare such trust."

1. ***Nature of the writing* (#4.53):** The terms of the trust can be pieced together from several writings.

   Example: A woman conveyed land to her nephews "to hold in trust." She later executed a will which set forth the terms of the trust. The court held that the will and the deed together were sufficient. *Ramage v. Ramage,* 322 S.E.2d 22 (S.C. App. 1984).

   a. If the deed had not mentioned the trust, the will would have been insufficient. The will is a signed writing, but after a person conveys land, she is no longer "enabled to declare such trust" since she no longer has title.

   b. The writing need not have created the trust. If the trustees in *Ramage* had later acknowledged in writing that the land was given to them in trust, that would satisfy the statute. *Restatement (Second) of Trusts* § 47 (1959).

2. ***Waiver of the statute* (#4.54):** The trustee may waive the defense of the statute by failing to raise it when sued or by admitting the existence of the trust. If he does so, his creditors may not object.

   Example: Frank conveyed a house to his brother on an oral trust for himself. The brother later ran into financial difficulties and conveyed the house back to Frank. This was valid because the oral trust was not void. However, if the brother had taken possession of the house and his creditors had relied on his apparent ownership, they would be protected on an estoppel theory. *In re Gustie,* 36 B.R. 473 (D. Mass. 1984). *See* #6.64, *infra.*

3. ***Constructive trusts* (#4.55):** Section 8 of the Statute of Frauds makes an exception for constructive and resulting trusts. In *Gustie, supra,* if the brother had refused to give the house back to Frank, he might have been compelled to do so on the theory of a constructive trust. *See* #6.46, *infra.*

4. ***Personal property* (#4.56):** A writing is not required to create a trust of personal property.

   Example: A man had stock registered in his name "as trustee for Audrey," saying she should get the stock when he died. This was effective. *In re Estate of Zuckerman*, 578 N.E.2d 248 (Ill. App. 1991).

C. **Delivery**

1. ***Declaration of trust* (#4.57):** A settlor can declare himself trustee of property without delivering anything to the beneficiary. To require a settlor to deliver trust property would be impractical, since the settlor as trustee continues to manage the property for the beneficiary.

   Example: A man signed a declaration of trust with an attached schedule of assets. Land included in the schedule was held to be part of the trust, even though the man never executed a deed to himself as trustee. *Estate of Heggstead*, 20 Cal. Rptr. 2d 433 (Cal. App. 1993).

2. ***Conveyance to trustee* (#4.58):** Delivery is necessary if someone other than the settlor is going to be the trustee.

   Example: The owner of stock indorsed the certificate to a trust but failed to deliver it to the trustee. The stock did not become part of the trust, because delivery is required when the settlor is not the trustee. *Papale-Keefe v. Altomare*, 647 N.E.2d 722 (Mass. App. 1995).

D. **Custodianships (#4.59):** Because of the tax advantages of gifts to minors, most states have adopted the Uniform Transfers to Minors Act. This Act facilitates the creation of custodianships for minors which operate much like a trust, except they terminate when the minor reaches age twenty-two, whereas many trusts go on for a longer period.

1. ***Language* (#4.60):** Under the Act, a person can create a custodianship by registering property in the name of the donor or another "as custodian for [name of minor] under the [state] Uniform Transfers to Minors Act." UTMA § 3. This incorporates the terms of the Act by reference, and it is not necessary to draft a trust instrument.

2. ***Delivery* (#4.61):** When property is registered in this form, or if title to land is recorded in this form, no delivery is necessary. UTMA § 9.

E. Consideration (#4.62): No consideration is necessary to create a trust. However, language indicating an intent to create a trust in the future is enforceable only if supported by consideration. Also without a *"res,"* a property interest, a trust fails, just as an attempt to give an expectancy is ineffective without consideration. *See* #4.48, *supra.*

Examples: A man signed a document which said that if he sold certain land, "I will hold the sale proceeds in trust." The trust failed because the sale proceeds were not in existence when he signed the document, and the language used was only a promise to create a trust in the future. *Kavanaugh v. Estate of Dobrowolski,* 407 N.E.2d 856 (Ill. App. 1980). But when a grandfather agreed to create a trust for his grandchildren if their father gave their mother custody, this was enforceable because there was consideration for the promise. *Estate of Chaitlen,* 534 N.E.2d 482 (Ill. App. 1989).

F. Language (#4.63): Attempts to enforce a trust sometimes fail because the settlor did not use appropriate language for a trust.

Example: A letter authorizing a stepchild to remove bonds from a safe-deposit box was held "insufficient to prove any intent to establish a trust." *Duggan v. Keto*, 554 A.2d 1126 (D.C. App. 1989).

However, a trust can be created without using the word "trust" expressly. Thus when a woman signed a paper stating that certain stock "belongs to Miss Peck in the event of my death," this was held to be an effective trust. *Mahoney v. Leddy,* 223 A.2d 456 (Vt. 1966).

1. ***Precatory language* (#4.64):** When *A* transfers property to *B* with a statement indicating how *B* is to use the property, no trust is created if the suggestion was merely precatory.

   Example: A will left land to the testator's children and said, "it is my desire" that it not be sold during their lifetime. The court held this was only precatory. *Dwyer v. Allyn*, 596 N.E.2d 904 (Ind. App. 1992) However, the word "desire" is sometimes construed as imposing an obligation. *Gillespie v. Davis,* 410 S.E.2d 613 (Va. 1991).

2. ***Charge and condition* (#4.65):** Language may impose an enforceable obligation other than a trust. In a trust, the trustee must return the property to the settlor after the purposes of the trust have been accomplished, whereas one who gets property subject to a charge can keep it after he fulfills the charge.

   Example: A will left stock to the testator's son "provided that he pay the net income to my other children for two years." The older children argued that this was a trust and so after the first two years, the stock should pass under the residuary clause of the will. But the court held this language only created a charge. *Estate of Krotz,* 522 N.E.2d 790 (Ill. App. 1988).

a. Another possible construction of the language in *Krotz* is to say it created a condition. This would mean that if the son failed to pay two years' income to the other children, the legacy would fail since he would not have satisfied the condition.

b. Another possible construction would be that by accepting the devise, the son promised to pay two years' income to the other children. This construction would give the older children no interest in the stock, but they could sue the son for breach of his promise.

G. Is the Living Trust Testamentary? (#4.66): If the grantor in a deed reserves a life estate and a power to revoke, the deed may be challenged on the theory that it is in effect a will and therefore requires the same formalities. *See* #4.36, *supra*. A similar attack is sometimes made on revocable living trusts, but modern cases nearly always uphold them. *Restatement (Second) of Trusts* § 57 (1959).

1. ***Rationale* (#4.67):**

   a. Courts often say that living trusts do not have to comply with the requirements for wills because they give the beneficiaries a "present interest." *Farkas v. Williams,* 125 N.E.2d 600 (Ill. 1955). However, this interest seems tenuous so long as it can be destroyed by revocation.

   b. A better rationale for upholding revocable living trusts is that usually the settlor signs a formal writing which substantially fulfills the policy behind the formalities prescribed for wills.

2. ***Totten trusts* (#4.68):** Many persons open bank accounts "as trustee" for someone else, without indicating what the terms of the trust are. A leading case, *In re Totten,* 71 N.E. 748 (N.Y. 1904), held that such trusts were valid and the account passed to the designated beneficiary when the "trustee" died. Modern cases have followed this view also.

3. ***Insurance trusts* (#4.69):** Often the owner of an insurance policy designates a trustee as the beneficiary. Even though the trust does not begin to operate until the settlor dies, many cases have upheld such trusts and many statutes expressly authorize them.

4. ***Dacey trusts* (#4.70):** A mutual fund salesman named Dacey published a very popular book called *How to Avoid Probate!*, advocating the use of revocable trusts to avoid probate and providing forms for this purpose. These forms allow assets other than insurance and bank accounts to pass at death. Many sophisticated lawyers also use revocable living trusts to pass property at death without probate.

H. Designation of Trustee (#4.71): Normally the instrument which creates a trust designates the trustee, but failure to do so does not invalidate the trust. Nor does a trust fail if the designated trustee is unwilling or unable to serve unless the settlor would not have wanted the trust without the designated trustee.

Example: A will said that the testator's friends, Harriet Fogg and Mr. and Mrs. Robie, should decide who should get her furniture. When Fogg predeceased the testator, the court held that the Robies could exercise the power, but a dissenting judge thought it should fail since all three did not survive. *Estate of Worthley,* 535 A.2d 433 (Me. 1988). *See* #12.42, *infra.*

I. **Designation of Beneficiaries (#4.72):** Some trusts have been held invalid on the ground that the settlor failed to designate beneficiaries.

Example: A will left the estate "to Kenneth to distribute among my relatives as he sees fit." The court held that the beneficiaries were so indefinite that the trust failed, and the estate passed intestate. *Binns v. Vick,* 538 S.W.2d 283 (Ark. 1976).

1. ***Power* (#4.73):** Under *Restatement (Second) of Trusts* § 122 (1959), however, Kenneth would have a power to convey the property to one of the testator's relatives.

2. ***Outright gift* (#4.74):** If the court had construed the language in *Binns* as only precatory, Kenneth would own the property outright. *See* #4.64, *supra.*

3. ***Class gifts* (#4.75):** The beneficiaries of a trust do not have to be named. Often a trust is created for the settler's "issue," for example. "Relatives" is sometimes construed to mean "heirs." Under this construction the trust is valid. *Restatement (Second) of Trusts* § 415 (1959).

JOINT TENANCY

IV. JOINT TENANCY

A. **Testamentary Nature (#4.76):** Joint tenancy is not subject to the formal requirements for wills even though it operates to transfer property at death to the surviving joint tenant.

Rationale: Sometimes joint tenancy is expressly validated by a statute such as UPC § 6-212, which deals with joint bank accounts. Sometimes it is said that the creation of a joint tenancy creates a present interest. *Compare* #4.67, *supra.* Perhaps courts accept joint tenancy because they sympathize with the desire to avoid the cost of probate. *See* #10.3, *infra.*

B. **Language Needed to Create (#4.77):** Historically, a gift "to *A* and *B*" was presumed to make them joint tenants, but many states change this presumption to tenancy in common.

Example: Land was conveyed to a husband and wife "as joint tenants." When *W* died, *H* did not succeed to all the property because the intent to create a right of survivorship did not "manifestly appear" in the deed. *Hoover v. Smith,* 444 S.E.2d 546 (Va. 1994). Therefore, they held as tenants in common, and *W*'s children succeeded to her half-interest.

1. ***Spouses* (#4.78):** In many states, when the tenants are spouses, it is presumed that they hold in joint tenancy or as tenants by the entirety. *See* #5.41*, infra. Cf. Matter of Estate of Snyder,* 880 S.W.2d 596 (Mo. App. 1994) (presumption inapplicable to a couple who were cohabiting but not legally married).

2. ***UPC* (#4.79):** Under UPC §§ 6-201(5), 6-212, a bank account payable to two or more persons passes to the survivor "whether or not a right of survivorship is mentioned," but the terms of the account may provide otherwise. Section 6-204 provides a model form which banks can use to make the depositor's intent clear.

   a. The presumption of a right of survivorship in bank accounts has been held inapplicable to other forms of property. *Matter of Estate of Ashe*, 787 P.2d 252 (Idaho 1990) (brokerage account).

C. **Writing (#4.80):** In most states a joint account can be created without any writing.

Exceptions: A few states require a writing. In Illinois, no right of survivorship exists as to someone who fails to sign the deposit agreement. *Estate of Wrage*, 550 N.E.2d 1115 (Ill. App. 1990).

D. **Delivery**

1. ***Straw man* (#4.81):** Historically if a person wanted to put land which he owned into joint tenancy with another, he would have to convey it to a straw man who would then convey it back to him and the other as joint tenants because all the joint tenants had to acquire title at the same time. Most states have dispensed with this formality.

2. ***Bank accounts* (#4.82):** If *A* creates a joint bank account for herself and *B*, this is effective even though she never delivers anything to *B*. This is usually explained by saying that *B* is the beneficiary of a contract between *A* and the bank, and delivery is not necessary to make a contract valid.

E. **Safe-Deposit Boxes (#4.83):** Persons sometimes jointly rent a safe-deposit box. Courts usually hold that the contents of the box do not become the property of the surviving tenant. *Wright v. Union Nat. Bank*, 819 S.W.2d 698 (Ark. 1991). *But see Matter of Estate of Langley*, 546 N.E.2d 1287 (Ind. App. 1989).

PAYABLE-ON-DEATH CONTRACTS

V. PAYABLE-ON-DEATH CONTRACTS

A. **Insurance and Pensions (#4.84):** If *A* takes out life insurance and designates *B* as the beneficiary, *B* will get the proceeds when *A* dies, even though the beneficiary designation did not comply with the formal requirements prescribed for wills. UPC § 6-201 so provides, and courts for many years have reached this result without a statute. The same is true of the designation of a beneficiary for death benefits under a pension plan.

B. Other Interests

1. ***Bank accounts* (#4.85):** UPC § 6-212(b) validates bank accounts which provide that at the death of the depositor, the funds shall pass to a designated beneficiary.

2. ***Securities* (#4.86):** UPC § 6-307 now also authorizes securities to be held in "beneficiary form." The rules are similar to those for bank accounts. The drafters wished to provide "an alternative to the frequently troublesome joint tenancy form of title" which creates problems when the co-owners disagree or one becomes insolvent. *See* #10.13, *infra*.

3. ***Sale contracts* (#4.87):** In the case of bank accounts and insurance policies, the bank or insurance company performs a role analogous to witnesses to a will. Where there is no institutional setting for the transaction, validity is more doubtful.

   Example: A contract for the sale of land provided that when the seller died, the payments should go to his sister. The court held this was invalid for failure to comply with the statute on wills. *Martinson v. Holso,* 424 N.W.2d 664 (S.D. 1988). Other cases, however, have upheld such provisions, and it would be valid under UPC § 6-201.

Notes

REVOCATION

CHAPTER SUMMARY

I.	Wills	5-2
II.	Gifts	5-7
III.	Trusts	5-8
IV.	Insurance	5-9
V.	Joint Tenancy	5-9
VI.	Change of Circumstances	5-11

REVOCATION

INTRODUCTION: A will can be revoked. It is not necessary to reserve a power to revoke in the will. However, the law imposes formal requirements for revoking wills. They are similar to the formal requirements for making wills, but they are not the same. All states allow a will to be revoked by physical act. There is no counterpart to this for making wills. In most states, a devise to the testator's spouse is automatically revoked if the two get a divorce.

This chapter also deals with the revocation of other transfers. Gifts, unlike wills, are not revocable, but there are certain exceptions. Trusts are also presumed to be irrevocable in most states, but many trust instruments reserve a power to revoke. An attempted revocation may fail because it does not comply with the terms of the power, which normally require written notice to the trustee. Insurance policies usually give the insured the right to change the beneficiary by notice to the insurer. Courts hold that substantial compliance with this requirement is sufficient. In many states divorce has no effect on the designation of a spouse as beneficiary of a living trust or an insurance policy as distinguished from a will.

Joint tenancy presents special problems with respect to revocation. Joint bank accounts are usually held to belong to the person who deposited the money so long as she is living. It is harder to recover land which you have put into joint tenancy, but usually either joint tenant can "sever" so the land becomes a tenancy in common with no right of survivorship. The topics covered by this chapter are discussed in depth in McGovern, Kurtz, and Rein, *Wills, Trusts and Estates,* 207–233 (1988).

WILLS

I. WILLS

A. Physical Act

1. ***Nature of the act* (#5.1):** UPC § 2-507(2) says a will can be revoked "by performing a revocatory act on the will" which "includes burning, tearing, cancelling, obliterating, or destroying the will or any part of it." Other states have similar provisions which go back ultimately to the Statute of Frauds.

   a. Total destruction of the will is not necessary.

      Example: A will was found with "VOID" written over several parts. The court held the will was revoked. *Matter of Estate of Ausley*, 818 P.2d 1226 (Okl. 1991).

   b. Marks on a will which do not touch any of the words have been held not to be a "cancellation" under the statute, but UPC § 2-507(a)(2) rejects this view.

2. ***Intent to revoke* (#5.2):** Unless the act is done with the intent to revoke, the will is not revoked. The intent to revoke must be simultaneous with the

act. A testator cannot "ratify" a prior accidental destruction. *McKenzie v. Francis,* 197 S.E.2d 221 (Va. 1973).

3. ***Presence of the testator* (#5.3):** The physical act can be performed by the testator or by another person, but it must be done in the testator's presence.

   Example: A testator asked his wife to destroy his will. She went into another room to do it. The revocation was held to be ineffective. *Estate of Bancker,* 232 So.2d 431 (Fla. App. 1970). However, UPC § 2-507 says the testator's "conscious" presence is enough.

4. ***Partial Revocation* (#5.4):**

   a. Most states allow partial revocation by physical act, but some do not.

      Example: A will left the estate to "Michael and Edward." The testator later crossed out Edward's name. This was held to be ineffective. *Estate of Eastman v. Eastman,* 812 P.2d 521 (Wash. App. 1991). The result under UPC § 2-507 would probably be different because it says "a will *or any part thereof*" may be revoked by cancellation. A few statutes expressly prohibit partial revocation by physical act. N.Y.E.P.T.L. § 3-4.1 (a).

   b. Physical act revocation does not allow a testator to add words to a will. For example, if a will says, "I devise Blackacre to John," and the testator crosses out "John" and writes in "Mary," Mary will not get Blackacre unless the will is re-executed.

5. ***Presumptions* (#5.5):** If a will cannot be found after the testator dies, or is found in a mutilated condition, courts presume that the testator intended to revoke it. For example, in *Ausley, supra,* there was no evidence as to who put the writing on the will or why, but on the basis of the presumption the court held that the will was revoked.

   a. The presumption only applies to an executed copy of the will which was in the testator's possession. The fact that an unexecuted carbon copy is missing is irrelevant. *Cf. In re Estate of Tolin,* 622 So.2d 988 (Fla. 1993) (tearing up a xerox copy does not revoke).

   b. If a will is executed in duplicate and one copy is missing, preservation of the duplicate may rebut the presumption of revocation. *Estate of Shaw,* 572 P.2d 229 (Okl. 1977). *But see Succession of Talbot,* 530 So.2d. 1132 (La. 1988) (finding intent to revoke even though only one copy was destroyed).

   c. Courts presume that marks on a will were made after it was executed.

      Example: A will was found with "$500" in a legacy crossed out and "$100" written above. If this change was made before the will was executed, the legatee would have received $100, but since the court presumed it was done later, the change was ineffective. *Ruel v. Hardy,* 6 A.2d 753 (N.H. 1939).

6. ***Rebutting the presumption*** **(#5.6):** The presumption of revocation can be rebutted by any evidence.

   Example: A will could not be found after the testator died. Nevertheless, the court probated a copy on the basis of testimony that the testator was always losing things and disliked his heirs. *Matter of Estate of Kaspar*, 887 P.2d 702 (Kan. App. 1994).

7. ***Proof of lost wills*** **(#5.7):** Even if a missing will was not destroyed with the intent to revoke it, proof of its contents may be impossible.

   Example: A court refused to probate a copy of a lost will because a statute required that the provisions of a lost will be proved "clearly and distinctly" by a witness, and the witness was unable (not surprisingly) to remember the forty-eight bequests contained in the will. *Estate of Kleefeld,* 433 N.E.2d 521 (N.Y. 1982).

   a. Proof of a lost will must be "clear and convincing." *Conkle v. Walker,* 742 S.W.2d 892 (Ark. 1988) (testimony was too vague).

8. ***Avoiding problems*** **(#5.8):** Many lawyers advise the testator to sign only one copy of a will, in order to avoid the presumption that the will was revoked in case a copy is lost. Some lawyers keep the executed will in their possession to guard against its loss. Others consider this practice unethical, since it appears to induce the testator to come back to the same lawyer in order to change the will. Many states allow wills of a living testator to be deposited in court for safekeeping. *E.g.*, UPC § 2-515.

B. Subsequent Instrument (#5.9): A will can also be revoked by a subsequent instrument which is executed with the formalities prescribed for wills.

1. ***Formalities*** **(#5.10):** A holograph can revoke an attested will.

   Example: A written will was found with the names of some devisees crossed out and others substituted. The testator had initialed the bottom of the page. The court held the change was effective; the typewritten words on the same page did not destroy the holographic character of the alteration. *Estate of Nielson,* 165 Cal. Rptr. 319 (Cal. App. 1980). If the testator had not initialed the changes, most courts would hold that the signature requirement was not satisfied. *But see Hancock v. Krause,* 757 S.W.2d 117 (Tex. App. 1988) (in making the changes the testator "adopted" his prior signature).

2. ***Dispositive provisions*** **(#5.11):** The subsequent instrument need not contain dispositive provisions. A paper which just says that the testator wishes to revoke all prior wills is enough.

3. ***Implied revocation* (#5.12):** The later instrument can revoke the earlier will "expressly or by inconsistency." UPC § 2-507. However, without an express revocation, courts often reconcile the provisions of the two instruments so as to avoid an implied revocation.

   Example: A will executed in 1965 left the estate to twenty-two persons. A 1970 will left certain furniture "and the rest of my personal property" to four others. If "personal property" was given its ordinary meaning, the 1965 will would have been revoked by inconsistency, but the court construed it to mean only household goods, so the testator's securities passed under the 1965 will. *Estate of Francoeur,* 290 N.E.2d 396 (Ill. App. 1972).

4. ***Date* (#5.13):** An undated will cannot revoke other wills unless there is proof that it was executed subsequent to them. Cal. Prob. Code § 6111(b)(2).

C. Revival

1. ***Physical act revocation* (#5.14):** Suppose that a testator executes will # 1, then executes will # 2 which revokes will # 1, then destroys will # 2. Most states presume that the testator did not intend to revive will # 1 and so died intestate. UPC § 2-509; *May v. Estate of McCormick,* 769 P.2d 395 (Wyo. 1989).

   a. UPC § 2-509 allows evidence to show that the testator did intend to revive will # 1, but some states would not allow will # 1 to be revived unless it was re-executed or "republished." Md. Estates and Trusts Code § 4-106. *See* #5.15, *infra*.

   b. UPC § 2-509 creates a presumption *in favor of* revival in this situation if will # 2 only partially revoked will # 1.

2. ***Republication by codicil* (#5.15):** Testators often make minor revisions in a will by executing a "codicil." A codicil must be executed with the formalities prescribed for wills. It usually refers to the will which it modifies, and is said to "republish" the will. This may revive a will which has been revoked.

   Example: A testator executed a codicil "to my will of July 16, 1948," which he had previously revoked. This was held to revive the will. *Barrett's Estate,* 260 N.E.2d 107 (Ill. App. 1970).

D. Dependent Relative Revocation

1. ***Physical act revocation* (#5.16):** Sometimes a testator cancels a will under the mistaken assumption that a new will, made at the same time, is valid. In such cases, courts may find there was no revocation because the testator's intent to revoke was "dependent" on the validity of the new will. This is called dependent relative revocation.

Example: A will executed in 1963 was found with pencil marks through it and an unsigned will dated in 1978. The court probated the 1963 will despite the markings on it because "the revocation of the old will was so related to the making of the new as to be dependent upon it." *Carter v. United Methodist Church,* 271 S.E.2d 493 (Ga. 1980).

a. But a court may find that the revocation of the old will was not dependent on the validity of the new one.

Example: A testator revoked a will by physical act, intending to make a new one, but died before it was completed. The court refused to apply dependent relative revocation because of differences between the revoked will and the contemplated new one. However, a dissenting judge noted that this allowed property go to the testator's heirs who were disinherited by both wills. *Matter of Estate of Ausley*, 818 P.2d 1226 (Okl. 1991).

5

2. ***Subsequent instrument* (#5.17):** Dependent relative revocation may also apply when a later will revokes an earlier one but was invalid, for example, because it violated the Rule against Perpetuities.

3. ***Contrast with revival* (#5.18):** Dependent relative revocation is sometimes confused with revival, but the two ideas may produce different results.

Example: A testator destroyed a will she had made in 1959, intending to revive a will she had executed in 1955. Her intent could not be given effect because a statute barred revival without a re-execution of the will. *See* #5.14, *supra.* However, the court probated the 1959 will (which was similar to the 1955 will) on the theory that her intent to revoke it was dependent on reviving the 1955 will. *Alburn's Estate,* 118 N.W.2d 919 (Wis. 1963).

E. Change of Circumstances

1. ***Divorce* (#5.19):** Under UPC § 2-804, if a testator gets a divorce after executing a will, any devise to the former spouse is revoked. Most states have similar statutes. The entire will is not revoked; only the devise to the ex-spouse is.

a. Separation without a divorce does not prevent a spouse from taking under the will, but the spouse may be barred by a separation agreement. Under UPC § 2-213(d) "a waiver of 'all rights' (or equivalent language)" in such an agreement bars the spouse from taking under a previously executed will.

b. UPC § 2-804 applies only to a divorce by the testator. If a will leaves property "to John and his wife Mary," Mary takes even though she divorced John and is thus no longer his "wife." *First Interstate Bank v. Lindberg,* 746 P.2d 333 (Wash. App. 1987).

c. UPC § 2-804 applies also to devises to "relatives" of a former spouse who are not also related to the testator. Many comparable statutes have no such provision and so do not affect devises to stepchildren or in-laws. *In re Estate of Kerr*, 520 N.W.2d 512 (Minn. App. 1994) (devise to stepdaughter unaffected when testator divorced her mother).

d. If the testator and spouse remarry after the divorce, the devise to the spouse is revived.

e. The statute applies even if the testator was not married at the time the will was executed.

Example: A will provided for the testator's former spouse. They later remarried and then again divorced. The devise was revoked. *Matter of Estate of Rayman*, 495 N.W.2d 241 (Minn. App. 1993).

f. The bequest is revoked unless the will expressly provides otherwise. Evidence outside the will cannot be used to prove that the testator wanted the former spouse to take.

Example: The testator and his ex-spouse cohabited after the divorce, and evidence was offered that he still wanted her to take, but this was rejected because the will did not so state. *In re Reeves*, 284 Cal. Rptr. 650 (Cal. App. 1991).

g. Property devised to the spouse passes as if the spouse had disclaimed the devise. *See* #2.110, *supra*.

2. ***Other Changes* (#5.20):** At common law, a will was revoked if the testator later married and had issue. The Wills Act of 1837 provided that marriage alone revoked a will. A few states still retain this rule, but in most states a later spouse or after-born child are protected, but the will is not revoked. *See* #3.16, 3.68, *supra*.

II. GIFTS

GIFTS

A. **General Rule (#5.21):** Ordinarily gifts, unlike wills, cannot be revoked.

B. **Exceptions:**

1. ***Ingratitude* (#5.22):** Many civil law countries allow donors to revoke gifts for "ingratitude" by the donee. Louisiana adopts this idea (though it defines ingratitude narrowly). La. Civ. Code art. 1559-60. It has not been followed in the common law.

2. ***Gifts* causa mortis (#5.23):** The common law does follow the civil law in holding that gifts *"causa mortis"* (in contemplation of death) are revocable. Such gifts are rare.

3. ***Implied conditions* (#5.24):** A donor can recover a conditional gift if the condition is not satisfied. The gift of an engagement ring is usually held to be conditional on the marriage taking place.

   Example: A man was allowed to recover an engagement ring after the engagement was broken off. Although some authorities allow this only if the donee broke the engagement, this court preferred a rule which did not require a determination of who was at fault. *McIntyre v. Raukhorst*, 585 N.E.2d 456 (Ohio App. 1989).

a. When land is conveyed to a person in return for a promise to support the transferor, failure to provide the support allows the conveyance to be rescinded, even if no condition was expressed in the deed. *Trout v. Parker,* 595 N.E.2d 1015 (Ohio App. 1991).

TRUSTS

III. TRUSTS

A. *Power to Revoke* (#5.25): In most states, a living trust is irrevocable unless the trust instrument reserves a power to revoke. *Restatement (Second) of Trusts* § 330. In a few states, trusts are presumed to be revocable. Cal. Prob. Code § 154000.

1. ***Bank account trusts* (#5.26):** *"Totten* trusts*" (see* #4.68, *supra)* are an exception to the general rule; they are presumed to be revocable. *Restatement (Second) of Trusts* § 58, comm. c.

2. ***Reformation* (#5.27):** If the settlor intended to create a revocable trust, but the power to revoke was omitted by mistake, the settlor can have the trust reformed to make it revocable. *Restatement (Second) of Trusts* § 332. However, this requires clear and convincing evidence.

3. ***Rescission for mistake* (#5.28):** A settlor who creates a trust because of a material mistake of fact can rescind it (Contrast the rule as to wills where courts disregard mistakes of fact. *See* #6.1, *infra.*

   Example: A man expecting to get a government post put assets into a trust in order to avoid any conflict of interest. When he did not get the post, he was allowed to rescind the trust. *Berger v. United States,* 487 F.Supp. 49 (W.D. Pa. 1980). *But see DuPont v. Southern Nat'l Bank,* 771 F.2d 874 (5th Cir. 1985) (rescission not allowed when expected tax benefits did not materialize because they were only an incidental purpose for the trust).

B. Method of Revocation (#5.29): Most trusts which reserve a power of revocation specify how it shall be exercised. Failure to comply with the prescribed method means that the revocation fails.

Example: A person executed a will and a trust at the same time. The latter said it could be amended by a writing delivered to the trustee. When the settlor died, neither the will nor the trust could be found. The will was revoked under the presumption described in #5.5, but not the trust, since no writing was delivered to the trustee. *Matter of Estate of Pilafas*, 836 P.2d 420 (Ariz. App. 1992).

1. ***Totten trusts* (#5.30):** "Totten trusts" have been held to be revocable by a will. *Matter of Estate of Bol*, 429 N.W.2d 467 (S.D. 1988). However, UPC § 6-213 requires that any change in a bank account must be "received by the financial institution during the party's lifetime."

INSURANCE

5

IV. INSURANCE

A. Power to Revoke (#5.31): Most insurance policies expressly allow the insured to change the beneficiary or to turn the policy in for cash.

1. ***Transfer of ownership* (#5.32):** If the insured transfers ownership of the policy, the transfer is irrevocable, like any other gift. The new owner has the right to designate the beneficiary. Such transfers of ownership are often used to remove the insurance proceeds from the insured's estate at death.

2. ***POD accounts* (#5.33):** The beneficiary designation in a POD account can be changed without the beneficiary's consent. UPC § 6-213.

B. Notice to Insurer (#5.34): Insurance policies generally state that a change of beneficiary is effective only when the insurer receives notice of it. "Substantial compliance" with such a provision is enough.

Example: The insured sent the agent a letter stating that he wanted to change the beneficiary, but he died before the forms for effectuating the change arrived. The court held that the insured had substantially complied with the policy requirements. *Bergen v. Travelers Ins. Co.*, 776 P.2d 659 (Utah App. 1989). But in a case where the insured received the forms for changing the beneficiary but never completed them, there was no substantial compliance. *Eschler v. Eschler,* 849 P.2d 196 (Mont. 1993).

JOINT TENANCY

V. JOINT TENANCY

A. Bank Accounts (#5.35): Joint bank accounts belong to the parties in proportion to their contributions unless there is clear evidence of a different intent. UPC § 6-211. Courts instates which have not adopted the UPC usually apply a similar rule.

Example: A person who had supplied all the funds in a joint account could recover funds withdrawn by the other party, since he had not intended to make a gift to the defendant. *Vitacco v. Eckberg*, 648 N.E.2d 1010 (Ill. App. 1995). Under UPC §§ 6-222, 6-226, the bank would not be liable for allowing the withdrawal in this situation, and most states have similar statutes.

1. ***Proof of contributions* (#5.36):** Absent contrary proof, spouses' contributions to an account are presumed to have been equal. UPC § 6-211(b).

2. ***Writing required* (#5.37):** Under UPC § 6-213, the form of an account may be changed by "written notice to the financial institution." Oral instructions have been held insufficient. *Estate of Wolfinger v. Wolfinger*, 793 P.2d 393 (Utah App. 1990).

3. ***Stock* (#5.38):** UPC § 6-211 applies only to bank accounts (broadly defined to include savings and loans, etc). When a person puts stock into joint tenancy, courts may find that a present gift was intended.

   Example: A woman who had stock registered in the name of herself and a friend was not allowed to have the stock put back into her own name. The court distinguished joint bank accounts, where another name is often put on the account only for the convenience of making deposits and withdrawals. *Main v. Howard,* 629 P.2d 870 (Or. App. 1981). *But see Parker v. Kokot,* 793 P.2d 195 (Idaho 1990) (applying the same rule to brokerage and to bank accounts).

5

B. Land (#5.39): A person who puts land into joint tenancy is presumed to intend a gift to the other party.

Example: A man put land into joint tenancy with his cohabitant. He later sought to have her name removed from the title. The court said he could do so only if he met the requirements for reformation, *i.e.,* showed that the deed did not conform to what the parties intended at the time because of a mistake. *See* #6.39, *supra. Schulz v. Miller*, 837 P.2d 71 (Wyo. 1992).

1. ***Severance* (#5.40):** Any party to a joint tenancy can "sever" it, turning it into a tenancy in common without any right of survivorship.

   Example: A husband, wife and son owned land as joint tenants. After a quarrel with the son, the husband executed a deed to his wife. When the husband later died, the son did not succeed to his interest by right of survivorship because of the severance (but he still retained his 1/3 interest). *Estate of Zoglauer*, 593 N.E.2d 93 (Ill. App. 1992).

   a. In California an instrument of severance must be recorded. Cal. Civ. Code § 683.2. This prevents a person from fraudulently destroying a severance deed if he survives the other tenant in order to succeed to the entire interest.

2. ***Tenancy by the entirety* (#5.41):** At common law when a husband and wife hold jointly, they hold as tenants by the entirety, and neither party can sever as long as the marriage endures. Tenancy by the entirety no longer exists in many states.

   Example: A husband and wife held land as joint tenants. She conveyed her interest to her children by a prior marriage and then died. The husband could not claim the land by right of survivorship. The legislature had implicitly abolished tenancy by the entirety when it enacted a statute defining estates without mentioning it. *Schimke v. Karlstad,* 208 N.W.2d 710 (S.D. 1973).

C. Alteration by Will

1. ***General rule* (#5.42):** UPC § 6-213(b) says that a right of survivorship "cannot be altered by will." The common law is the same. This allows the survivor to deal with the property immediately after a joint tenant dies without worrying about any will which may be probated.

2. ***Election* (#5.43):** However, a will which purports to dispose of property in joint tenancy may put the other joint tenant to an election.

   Example: A wife owned land in joint tenancy with her husband. Her will devised the land to her relatives and left the residue of her estate to her husband. By taking under his wife's will, the husband was held to have elected to let the joint tenancy land pass under his wife's will. *Citizens Nat'l Bank v. Stasell,* 408 N.E.2d 587 (Ind. App. 1980).

   a. Election applies whenever a will purports to dispose of property which the testator does not own. *See* #3.60, *supra.* However, an ambiguous will is construed to dispose only of the testator's own property. In *Citizens Bank,* for example, a devise of "all my land" would not be held to cover the land in joint tenancy.

3. ***Malpractice* (#5.44):** Lawyers who draft wills should ascertain how the testator's property is held. If a devise is ineffective because the property is held in joint tenancy, the lawyer may be liable to the intended beneficiary. *McLane v. Russell,* 512 N.E.2d 366 (Ill. App. 1987).

VI. CHANGE OF CIRCUMSTANCES

CHANGE OF CIRCUM-STANCES

A. Marriage and Birth of Issue (#5.45): In most states when a testator marries or has a child after executing a will, the child or spouse gets a share of the estate, but this does not include assets not in the probate estate, such as property held in joint tenancy. *See* #3.22, 3.69, *supra.*

B. Divorce (#5.46): In most states, divorce revokes devises in a will to the former spouse but has no effect on assets outside the probate estate.

Example: A wife was the beneficiary of her husband's insurance. They divorced and he later died. She was allowed to collect the policy proceeds. It did not matter that she was described as "wife" in the policy. *Christensen v. Sabad,* 773 P.2d 538 (Colo. 1989).

1. ***Waiver* (#5.47):** The spouse may be barred by a property settlement made in connection with the divorce.

Example: A husband designated his wife as the recipient of a death benefit under a pension plan. They later divorced and in the property settlement she waived any claim to pension benefits. This was held to bar her. *Fox Valley v. Brown,* 879 F.2d 249 (7th Cir. 1989).

2. ***UPC* (#5.48):** UPC § 2-804 (1990) now provides that divorce terminates the interest of a former spouse under a revocable provision in any "governing instrument." Even without such statutory authority, some courts have applied statutes governing wills to revocable trusts by analogy in this situation. *Clymer v. Mayo,* 473 N.E.2d 1084 (Mass. 1985).

   a. *Met. Life Ins Co. v. Hanslip,* 939 F.2d 904 (10th Cir. 1991), held that a similar statute applicable to pensions was preempted by ERISA. The comment to UPC § 2-804 argues persuasively for a contrary result.

3. ***Joint tenancy* (#5.49):** When spouses hold property in joint tenancy, many courts hold that a divorce severs the joint tenancy. *Estate of Warner,* 687 S.W.2d 686 (Mo. App. 1985). Accord, UPC § 2-804(b)(2). *But see Matter of Estate of Sander,* 806 P.2d 545 (Mont. 1991) (divorce has no effect on land held in joint tenancy).

EXTRINSIC EVIDENCE

CHAPTER SUMMARY

I.	Mistake of Fact	6-2
II.	Mistake as to Contents	6-3
III.	Ambiguity	6-4
IV.	Constructive Trusts	6-5
V.	Incorporation by Reference and Pour-over Wills	6-6
VI.	Bank Accounts	6-8
VII.	Other *Inter Vivos* Transfers	6-9

EXTRINSIC EVIDENCE

INTRODUCTION: Because wills must be in writing, courts are reluctant to admit evidence outside the will to show that the testator intended something else. This reluctance resembles the parol evidence rule governing contracts, but it is applied more strictly to wills because of the fear that perjured testimony may be offered after the testator has died. Reformation allows a mistaken contract to be corrected, but it does not usually apply to wills. However, if a will is ambiguous, courts admit extrinsic evidence to resolve the ambiguity.

Another important exception to the bar against extrinsic evidence is the constructive trust. If a devisee promised the testator to use property in a particular way and failed to fulfill the promise, a constructive trust is imposed to prevent the devisee from being unjustly enriched.

Some wills invite the reader to look outside the will to ascertain the testator's intent. They may incorporate an extrinsic document by reference. Closely related to this are "pour-over" wills which leave property to trusts created by another person or by the testator herself. These perform a valuable role in estate planning and are now validated by statute in virtually all states.

Problems of extrinsic evidence also arise with respect to will substitutes, like joint bank accounts. Most courts admit evidence that the survivor was not intended to get the account, because the printed forms supplied by banks often do not reflect the depositor's intent, *e.g.,* because the joint account was simply designed for convenience.

As to land, the Statute of Frauds requires trusts of land to be in writing, but the exception in the statute for resulting and constructive trusts allows courts to give relief to prevent unjust enrichment in cases of deeds as well as wills. Also, as to deeds, reformation is available to correct mistakes.

When extrinsic evidence is offered to contradict the terns of a writing, courts require that it must be "clear and convincing" in order to satisfy the policy behind the formal requirements for wills and trusts.

The topics covered in this chapter are discussed more fully in McGovern, Kurtz and Rein, *Wills, Trusts and Estates,* 234–270 (1988).

MISTAKE OF FACT

I. MISTAKE OF FACT

A. General Rule (#6.1): Evidence that a testator was laboring under a mistake of fact does not bar probate of a will.

Example: A codicil revoked devises to the testator's niece and nephew "since I have made gifts to them." They claimed that in fact they had not received gifts from the testator. Nevertheless, the court probated the codicil. Wills are not set aside for mistake because it is too difficult to ascertain whether the mistake affected the will. *Witt v. Rosen,* 765 S.W.2d 956 (Ark. 1989).

B. **Fraud (#6.2):** If a mistake was induced by fraud, courts give relief if the mistake was material.

Example: A wife left her estate to her daughters because she thought her husband had left his property to their sons, whereas in fact he had left it to the children equally. The wife's will was denied probate because her mistake had been induced by her daughters' misrepresentations which were made "with reckless disregard for the truth." *Matter of Estate of Vick*, 557 So.2d 760 (Miss. 1990).

1. ***Innocent devisee* (#6.3):** The usual rationale given for treating fraud differently is that the devisee should not profit from his wrong, but courts refuse to allow even an innocent devisee to take a devise which was induced by the fraud of another person.

II. MISTAKE AS TO CONTENTS

A. **General Rule (#6.4):** Courts do not usually allow wills to be reformed to correct mistakes. This difference is usually attributed to the statutory requirement that wills be in writing (even though courts allow reformation of contracts despite similar requirements in the Statute of Frauds).

Example: A will left the estate to the testator's husband if he survived but made no provision if he did not. The drafter testified that the will had originally contained a clause providing for this but a secretary had deleted it. The court refused to allow the clause to be probated. *First Interstate Bank v. Young*, 853 P.2d 1324 (Or. App. 1993).

B. **Exceptions:**

1. ***Eliminating words inserted by mistake* (#6.5):** A will which was signed by mistake (*i.e.*, the testator thought it was something else) won't be probated. The statute says that wills must be written, but it does not require that every writing which purports to be a will shall be probated. Thus words which were included in a will by mistake may be denied probate.

   Example: A codicil by mistake included a clause revoking a devise to the testator's son. The court refused to probate the clause. *Matter of Estate of Smelzer*, 818 P.2d 822 (Kan. App. 1991).

2. ***Restatement* (#6.6):** Scholars have argued that courts should be allowed to reform wills like other written instruments. *Restatement (Second) of Property, Donative Transfers* § 34.7, illus. 11, adopts this view. UPC § 2-601 (1990) says that the rules of construction of wills apply "in the absence of a finding of contrary intent." According to the comment, the drafters wished to promote "the judicial adoption of a general reformation doctrine for wills."

   a. Judicial acceptance of this more liberal view is limited, but a few cases have allowed reformation, especially where it promotes tax savings.

Example: A will was reformed to allow trusts which it created to be divided in order to maximize the exemptions given by the Internal Revenue Code for the generation skipping tax. *Matter of Estate of Branigan*, 609 A.2d 431 (N.J. 1992).

AMBIGUITY

III. AMBIGUITY

A. Latent Ambiguity (#6.7): Courts admit extrinsic evidence to resolve a latent ambiguity in a will. Three types are common.

6

1. ***Testator does not own property described in will* (#6.8):** Courts often correct mistakes in describing an asset.

   Example: A will left "all the lots that I own on Suber Street" to the testator's daughters. She did not own any lots on Suber Street, but she owned other property which was known as "the Suber property." The court awarded this property to the daughters. *Fenzel v. Floyd,* 347 S.E.2d 105 (S.C. App. 1986). *But see Estate of Greenfield,* 757 P.2d 1297 (Mont. 1988) (will said to be "unambiguous" so devisee got nothing).

2. ***Will describes a nonexistent legatee* (#6.9):** When no legatee meets the description in the will, extrinsic evidence may be allowed to show that someone else was intended.

   Example: A will left property to the "Lutheran Orphan Home, Paris, Missouri." The only Lutheran Home in Missouri was actually in another town. The court struck the word "Paris" to resolve this "latent ambiguity." *In re Estate of Beck*, 649 N.E.2d 1011 (Ill. App. 1995).

   a. If there *is* a person who meets the description in the will, evidence cannot be admitted to show that the testator intended someone else. *Vadman v. American Cancer Society,* 615 P.2d 500 (Wash. App. 1980) (devise "to National Cancer Society" goes to that organization even though it was allegedly intended for American Cancer Society).

3. ***Class gifts* (#6.10):** Some courts regard a term like "children" as ambiguous when, for example, a claim is made by an adopted child. Not all courts agree.

   Example: Did a devise to "grandchildren" include a child by adoption? The court said this was ambiguous, and thus extrinsic evidence was properly received. *Connecticut National Bank & Trust Co. v. Chadwick*, 585 A.2d 1189 (Conn. 1991). *But see Martin v. Gerdes,* 523 N.E.2d 607 (Ill. App. 1988) ("heirs of the body" includes adopted child; statute bars extrinsic evidence to show a different intent).

B. Patent Ambiguity (#6.11): Some courts do not allow extrinsic evidence when the ambiguity is "patent," *i.e.*, apparent on reading the will alone, in contrast to the ambiguity in *Beck, supra,* which was "latent," because it only was discovered when one looked outside the will.

Example: A will left "all my personal property" to the testator's aunt, and "the remainder of my property, both real and personal" to charities. The court excluded extrinsic evidence because this ambiguity was patent. *Breckner v. Prestwood,* 600 S.W.2d 52 (Mo. App. 1980). Commentators see no policy reason for this distinction, and many states reject it.

C. **Circumstances vs. Declarations of Intent (#6.12):** Some courts allow evidence of the circumstances surrounding the testator, but not of the testator's declarations.

Example: A will was unclear as to how much income from a trust the testator's wife was supposed to get. Evidence of the testator's instructions to the drafter was excluded, but evidence of how much he had given her while he was alive was allowed. *Estate of Utterback,* 521 A.2d 1184 (Me. 1987).

1. ***Rationale*** **(#6.13):** Statements allegedly made by a testator may be misremembered or misreported by witnesses. Proof of relevant circumstances is usually clearer, but their bearing on the testator's intent is not always clear.

D. **Procedural Consequences**

1. ***Summary judgment*** **(#6.14):** When a court finds that a will is unambiguous, it may decide questions of construction by summary judgment. *Martin v. Gerdes,* #6.10, *supra. Compare Hancock v. Krause,* 757 S.W.2d 117 (Tex. App. 1988) (error to grant summary judgment where will was ambiguous because extrinsic evidence was admissible).

2. ***Scope of review*** **(#6.15):** Ordinarily in construing wills, appellate courts do not defer to the views of the trial court. *Estate of Edwards,* 250 Cal.Rptr. 779 (Cal. App. 1988). But when a trial court has heard extrinsic evidence because the will was ambiguous, its decision will be affirmed if there is substantial evidence to support it. *Matter of Estate of Klein,* 434 N.W.2d 560 (N.D. 1989).

IV. CONSTRUCTIVE TRUSTS

CONSTRUCTIVE TRUSTS

A. **Promise by Devisee (#6.16):** If a devisee promised to give the devised property to someone else, the promise will be enforced by imposing a constructive trust. Such a promise can be inferred from silence if the testator tells the devisee what to do with the property.

Example: A mother left property to her daughter, Emily, telling her that she should share it with her incompetent sister, Mary. When Emily refused to do so, the court imposed a constructive trust on her. *Kauzlarich v. Landrum,* 274 N.E.2d 915 (Ill. App. 1971). The result would have been the same if the mother had died intestate or had left an existing will unchanged in reliance on Emily's promise. *Restatement (Second) of Trusts* § 55, comm. c.

1. ***Semi-secret trusts* (#6.17):** Cases like *Kauzarlich* are often called "secret trusts" because the will does not disclose them. In a "semi-secret" trust, the will indicates that the devisee is not supposed to keep the property himself, but the terms of the trust are not revealed.

   Example: A will directed the executor to distribute the estate "in accordance with verbal guidelines given by me." The court refused to allow evidence as to the contents of these "verbal guidelines." *Matter of Reiman's Estate,* 450 N.E.2d 928 (Ill. App. 1983).

   6

   Rationale: In a secret trust, a constructive trust is necessary to prevent the devisee from being unjustly enriched. In a semi-secret trust, there is no risk of unjust enrichment since there will be a resulting trust to the estate if the terms of the trust cannot be proved. Nevertheless, *Restatement (Second) of Trusts* § 55, comm. b, contrary to the holding in *Reiman,* gives the intended beneficiary the property in bothsecret and semi-secret trusts.

2. ***Communication to legatee* (#6.18):** No trust is imposed if the testator's intent was not communicated to the devisee while the testator was alive, because in this situation the devisee is not regarded as having done anything wrong. *Restatement (Second) of Trusts* § 55, *comm. f.*

3. ***Procedural safeguards* (#6.19):** Constructive trusts seem to violate the policy behind the requirement that wills be in writing. Courts try to safeguard this policy in various ways.

   a. Many formal requirements imposed by the law, like the parol evidence rule, arise from distrust of a jury's ability to ascertain who is telling the truth. These rules do not apply in equity where there is no jury. However, modern cases tend to blur the historic distinctions between courts. *See In re Will of Artope*, 545 N.Y.S.2d 670 (N.Y. Surr. 1989) (probate court enforces a constructive trust to avoid multiplicity of suits).

   b. Courts impose a trust only if the evidence is "clear and convincing."

B. **Force and Fraud (#6.20):** If a person by force or fraud prevents a testator from making a will, courts impose a constructive trust for the benefit of the intended legatee. *Latham v. Father Divine,* 85 N.E.2d 168 (N.Y. 1949). If force or fraud causes a will to be executed, the will is denied probate, so a constructive trust is not necessary. *See* #6.2, *supra, and* #7.2, *infra*.

INCORPORATION BY REFERENCE AND POUR-OVER WILLS

V. INCORPORATION BY REFERENCE AND POUR-OVER WILLS

A. **Incorporation by Reference (#6.21):** A will can incorporate a document by reference. This allows the document to be probated even though it is not signed or attested.

   Example: A will duly executed in 1977 referred to an unsigned document dated 1969 which was attached to the will by a paper clip. The attached paper was admitted to probate as having been incorporated by reference in the will. *In re Estate of McGahee,* 550 So.2d 83 (Fla. App. 1989).

1. ***Compared with integration* (#6.22):** When a will consists of several pages, and only the last one is signed, the other pages can be probated on the theory that they were integrated with the signature page if all the pages were present when the witnesses attested the will. This requirement does not limit incorporation by reference.

2. ***Description of writing* (#6.23):** The will must "describe the writing sufficiently to permit its identification" and manifest an intent to incorporate it by reference. UPC § 2-510.

   Example: A duly executed "codicil to will" was insufficient to incorporate an unattested will which was found stapled to it. The testator had executed several wills so the identification was not sufficiently clear. *Matter of Estate of Norton,* 410 S.E.2d 484 (N.C. 1991).

3. ***Future document* (#6.24):** The writing must have been in existence when the will was executed. UPC § 2-510.

   Example: A will left property to a trust which was to be created. A trust was later drawn up, but the devise failed because it was not in existence when the will was executed. *Tierce v. Macedonia United Meth. Church,* 519 So.2d 451 (Ala. 1987).

   a. A document written after the will was executed can be incorporated if the will is thereafter republished by a codicil. *Clark v. Greenhalge,* 582 N.E.2d 949 (Mass. 1991).

4. ***List of tangible personalty* (#6.25):** UPC § 2-513 permits a testator to refer in the will to a list of tangible personal property which can be written before or after the execution of the will. The list must be signed by the testator. (There is no such requirement as to other documents which are incorporated by reference).

   Rationale: Since tangible personal property is usually of little value, it was thought unnecessary to require execution of a new will or codicil whenever a testator wishes to change the disposition of an item of furniture, for example.

B. **Pour-over Wills (#6.26):** Many wills leave property to a trust which the testator or someone else has created. Such a "pour-over" bequest is valid even though the will itself does not contain the terms of the trust, if they are set forth in a written instrument. UPC § 2-511. This is derived from a Uniform Testamentary Additions to Trusts Act which many states have adopted. The original Act required that the trust instrument be executed before or concurrently with the will, but the UPC now allows the trust to be executed later.

1. ***Rationale* (#6.27):** Since the terms of the trust are contained in a written instrument, there is little danger of perjury or fraud. Also, there are good reasons for using this device. If the testator or another member of the family has already created a trust, it may be more efficient to add property to the existing trust rather than to create a separate trust for the same persons.

2. ***Pour-over to testamentary trust* (#6.28):** Often both spouses want their property to be held in trust for their children after they both die. Typically, *H*'s will pours his estate into a trust created by *W*'s will or *vice versa*. The order in which the two wills were executed does not matter.

3. ***Amendments to trust* (#6.29):** Because of the prohibition against incorporating future documents by reference (*see* #6.24, *supra*), courts used to hold that a pour-over was invalid if the trust was amended after the will was executed. However, UPC § 2-511 specifically allows this.

   Example: A wife's will left property to a trust for her daughter as provided in her husband's will. The husband later amended the terms of the trust. The wife's assets were administered under the trust as amended. *Matter of Will of Daniels*, 799 P.2d 479 (Kan. 1990).

4. ***Trust not incorporated into will* (#6.30):** When a will pours property into a living trust, the trust is not incorporated into the will. Thus the terms of the trust can remain secret, even though wills become public documents when they are probated.

C. **Facts of Independent Significance (#6.31):** Some wills require resort to facts outside the will in order to be carried out. This is permissible if the facts have significance apart from the will. UPC § 2-512.

   Example: A will leaves property "to my children" without naming them. Extrinsic evidence is admissible to identify the children, because the fact that the testator was their parent has significance apart from giving them an interest under the will.

   1. ***Future facts* (#6.32):** Facts of independent significance can involve events which occur after the will was executed, such as an after-born child in the foregoing example.

BANK ACCOUNTS

VI. BANK ACCOUNTS

A. **Admissibility of Evidence (#6.33):** Under UPC § 6-212 (1990), a multiple party account passes to the survivors when one dies, but, according to the comment, not if the court "finds that the account was opened solely for the convenience of a party who supplied all the funds . . . [who] intended no present gift or death benefit for the other party." Most courts apply a similar rule.

   Example: A father put virtually all his assets into a joint account with one daughter. After he died, her siblings were awarded an equal share based on evidence that the father had set up the joint account only for convenience. *Matter of Estate of Savage,* 631 N.E.2d 797 (Ill. App. 1994).

1. ***Comparison with wills* (#6.34):** Because of the care with which most wills are executed, claims that they do not represent the testator's intent are suspect. In creating a joint account, on the other hand, the depositor typically signs a fine-print form prepared by the bank. A claim that this form does not reflect the depositor's intent is quite plausible.

2. ***Conclusive presumption* (#6.35):** In some states the terms of the account are conclusive.

   Example: An account was awarded to the designated surviving joint tenants even though there was evidence they had been put on the account only for convenience. A statute made the terms of the account conclusive, absent fraud or undue influence, which were not alleged. Nor would the court impose a constructive trust, since no wrongdoing was alleged. *Baker v. Leonard*, 843 P.2d 1050 (Wash. 1993).

3. ***Clear evidence* (#6.36):** Courts usually say that to overcome the presumption created by the terms of an account, the evidence must be clear.

4. ***Time* (#6.37):** Intent at the time the account is created is controlling, but courts admit evidence of earlier and later statements as throwing light on this intent.

OTHER INTER VIVOS *TRANSFERS*

VII. OTHER *INTER VIVOS* TRANSFERS

A. **Parol Evidence Rule (#6.38):** *Inter vivos* transfers are not governed by the wills act, but courts often exclude parol evidence when interpreting a written instrument.

   Example: A living trust provided for certain named nieces and nephews of the settlor and for "grandnieces and grandnephews." The court held that this was not limited to the children of the named nieces and nephews. Since the instrument was "unambiguous," parol evidence was inadmissible. *Matter of Huxtable Living Trust*, 757 P.2d 1262 (Kan. 1988).

B. **Reformation (#6.39):** But deeds and living trusts, unlike wills, can be reformed to correct mistakes.

   Example: A father deeded land to his children "for $10 and affection." The legal description was omitted by mistake, and the father, who had quarreled with the donees, refused to execute a new deed. The court granted reformation to supply the omission. Although a donee cannot ordinarily get reformation, there was sufficient consideration here to warrant it. *Snyder v. Peterson*, 814 P.2d 1204 (Wash. App. 1991). (Some courts allow a donee to have a deed reformed without regard to the lack of consideration. *Kolkovich v. Tosolin,* 311 N.E.2d 782 [Ill. App. 1974].)

1. ***Mutuality* (#6.40):** The intention of only one of the parties to a deed is not controlling.

   Example: A man executed a deed which conveyed land to his niece. He later tried to revoke it, claiming he thought he was signing a will. The court denied relief because there was no evidence also the niece also thought the document was a will. *Felonenko v. Siomka,* 637 P.2d 1338 (Or. App. 1981). *Contra, Restatement (Second) of Trusts* § 333, comm. e (unless the donee has changed her position in reliance on the gift).

6

2. ***Negligence* (#6.41):** Courts sometimes deny relief if the donor was negligent, *e.g.*, signed the deed without reading it. *Henkle v. Henkle*, 600 N.E.2d 791 (Ohio App. 1991).

C. **Mistake of Fact (#6.42):** Courts do not give relief for a mistake of fact.

   Example: A father gave land to his son. Gas was later discovered under the land. A daughter claimed that if the father had known this, she would also have received a share. The court rejected her claim because it rested on "speculation." *Thomas v. Reid,* 608 P.2d 1123 (N.M. 1980). However, relief may be given if the mistake was induced by fraud. *Hinson v. Hinson,* 343 S.E.2d 266 (N.C. App. 1986); #6.2, *supra.*

D. **Fraud in the Execution (#6.43):** A deed can be voided for fraud in the execution, *i.e.,* when the signer was led to believe he was not signing a deed. *Pedersen v. Bibioff,* 828 P.2d 1113 (Wash. App. 1992) (son induced father with limited knowledge of English to sign a deed without realizing it).

E. **Delivery (#6.44):** Normally a deed is not effective unless it is delivered. #4.40, *supra.* Courts sometimes invoke this rule if extrinsic evidence indicates that a person who executed a deed did not in fact intend to make a gift. *Johnson v. Ramsey,* 817 S.W.2d 200 (Ark. 1991) (intention to pass title is essential to delivery).

F. **Constructive Trusts (#6.45):** When *A* conveys land to *B* with the understanding that *B* is to hold the land for *A* or for a third person, courts may impose a constructive trust on *B* in order to prevent unjust enrichment, despite the parol evidence rule and the Statute of Frauds.

1. ***Comparison with wills* (#6.46):** This is very similar to the case where *A* *devises* property to *B* with the understanding that *B* will convey it to another. *See* #6.16, *supra.* However, when the transfer is by deed, a constructive trust is imposed only in cases of fraud or breach of a confidential relationship. *Restatement (Second) of Trusts* §§ 44, 45. The distinction between wills and deeds is odd because the law usually requires more formalities for wills than for *inter vivos* transfers.

2. ***Fraud* (#6.47):** A grantee who never intended to perform is guilty of fraud. Courts sometimes infer such a fraudulent intent from the mere fact that

the grantee failed to perform the promise. *But see Nessralla v. Peck,* 532 N.E.2d 685 (Mass. 1989) (refusal to infer fraud from defendant's failure to perform). English courts always give relief by imputing fraud to the donee.

3. ***Confidential relationship* (#6.48):** Courts also impose a constructive trust if there was a confidential relationship between the parties.

   a. If this is interpreted broadly, the Statute of Frauds becomes meaningless; if *A* trusted *B* to perform, he must have had confidence in *B*, and so all oral trusts would be enforceable.

   b. Some courts find a confidential relationship only if there is inequality between the parties. *Mattes v. Olearain,* 759 P.2d 1177 (Utah App. 1988).

   c. Other courts find a confidential relationship whenever the parties are members of the same family. *Matter of Estate of McKim*, 807 P.2d 215 (N.M. 1991) (deed between spouses).

4. ***Later promise* (#6.49):** The promise must be made by the grantee at the time of the transfer. A later promise is insufficient. *Walsh v. Walsh*, 841 P.2d 831 (Wyo. 1992).

G. **Purchase Money Resulting Trust (#6.50):** When *A* pays for land but title is conveyed to *B,* courts presume that the parties intended that *B* was to hold the land in trust for *A*. *Restatement (Second) of Trusts* § 440. This trust is enforceable despite the Statute of Frauds.

1. ***Comparison with constructive trust* (#6.51):** In this situation, it is not necessary to prove fraud or a confidential relationship because the circumstances are said to indicate that a trust was intended, whereas when *A* conveys to *B*, the circumstances are said to indicate an intent to make a gift to *B*. This distinction seems questionable, but it is not very significant since it is relatively easy to prove fraud or a confidential relationship necessary for a constructive trust.

2. ***Relationship between A and B* (#6.52):** According to *Restatement (Second) of Trusts* § 442, the presumption of a trust does not arise if *B* is "a wife, child or other natural object" of *A*'s bounty; in such cases, courts presume that *A* intended to make a gift to *B*.

   Example: A daughter paid for a home but title was taken in the name of her mother. Her claim to a resulting trust was upheld. There was no presumption of a gift when a child paid for land put into a parent's name. *Boatwright v. Perkins*, 894 P.2d 1091 (Okl. 1995). *Contrast Durward v. Nelson,* 481 N.W.2d 586 (N.D. 1992) (no resulting trust when parents paid for land deeded to son and his wife).

   a. Some courts have rejected the Restatement's distinction between husbands and wives as inconsistent with modern notions of sexual equality. *Lollis v. Lollis,* 354 S.E.2d 559 (S.C. 1987).

3. ***Rebutting the presumption* (#6.53):** Whether a gift or a trust is presumed, evidence is admissible to show the actual intent of the parties. *Restatement (Second) of Trusts* § 443; *Hilliard v. Hilliard*, 844 P.2d 54 (Mont. 1992) (resulting trust imposed when father pays for land deeded to son, since presumption of gift was rebutted).

4. ***Sale on credit* (#6.54):** When land is bought on credit, if *A* does not actually pay the price but agrees to do so at the time of the purchase, the presumption of a trust arises.

   Example: A son agreed to buy a house with the understanding that his mother would make all the payments and would own the house even though it was put in his name. The court treated imposed a resulting trust in the mother's favor. *Watkins v. Watkins,* 351 S.E.2d 331 (N.C. App. 1986).

5. ***Partial payment* (#6.55):** Someone who pays part of the price may be awarded part of the land. The proportions are not necessarily the same as the contributions. *Bassett v. Bassett*, 798 P.2d 160 (N.M. 1990) (land divided equally in accordance with understanding even though contributions were unequal).

H. **Evidence Required (#6.56):** For reformation, or for a constructive or resulting trust, the evidence must be clear and convincing.

1. ***Circumstances* (#6.57):** Although statements of intent are admissible (*cf.* #6.12, *supra*), courts frequently rely on circumstantial evidence.

   Example: A father deeded land to his son, who for the next thirty years divided the profits with his sister. He later denied that his sister had an interest in the land, but the court held for the sister, because the father had equal affection for both children, and the son had acted for so long as if his sister owned a share of the land. *Levin v. Smith, 513* A.2d 1292 (Del. 1986).

2. ***Uncommunicated intent* (#6.58):** Intent which is not communicated at the time of a transfer is irrelevant.

   Example: A husband deeded land to himself and his wife as joint tenants. Although he larer said that he never intended her to have an interest, the court rejected his claim. The presumption of a gift could only be rebutted by clear expressions of contrary intent at the time the deed was executed. *Graham v. Graham,* 760 P.2d 772 (Nev. 1988).

3. ***Statute of limitations* (#6.59):** The statute of limitations does not staart to run until the trustee repudiates the trust. *Granado v. Granado,*760 P.2d 148 (N.M. 1988).

I. **Clean Hands (#6.60):** Often title to property is put into the name of someone who is notintended to be the beneficial owner in order to deceive third persons. Courts may refuse to impose a constructive or resulting trust because the plaintiff has "unclean hands." *Restatement (Second) of Trusts* § 444.

1. ***Balancing* (#6.61):** On the other hand, the clean hands defense is often rejected on the ground that it is outweighed by the policy against unjust enrichment.

2. ***Discretion* (#6.62):** Trial courts have discretion on this issue.

   Example: A convicted felon bought a bar and had title put into his father's name to avoid legal restrictions on felons holding liquor licenses. His children were allowed to enforce a resulting trust because *they* were not guilty of any wrong. Also, the legislature had relaxed the restrictions which indicated that the policy involved was relatively unimportant. *Granado v. Granado,* 760 P2d 148 (N.M. 1988).

6

J. **Third Persons (#6.63):** Constructive and resulting trusts are usually enforceable against third persons who derive title from the trustee unless they are bona fide purchasers. *Restatement (Second) of Trusts* § 284.

   Example: In *Granado,* #6.62, *supra,* the father had conveyed the bar to his daughter. She was held subject to the trust. She would have been protected as a bona fide purchaser only if she had not known of the trust *and* had paid value. However, if she had changed her position, *e.g.*, by improving the property, she might have been protected by estoppel. *Restatement (Second) of Trusts* § 292.

1. ***Creditors* (#6.64):** Creditors of the trustee can enforce their claims against the trust property if they extended credit in reliance on the trustee's apparent ownership and the beneficiary knew this. *Restatement (Second) of Trusts* § 313. Otherwise the claims of the trustee's creditors are subject to the rights of the beneficiary. *Amendaris Water Dev. Co. v. Rainwater*, 781 P.2d 799 (N.M. App. 1989).

2. ***Bankruptcy* (#6.65):** If the trustee goes bankrupt, the bankruptcy trustee will hold free of trust for the benefit of the trustee's creditors. Bankruptcy Act of 1978, §§ 544, 558.

Notes

INCAPACITY AND UNDUE INFLUENCE

CHAPTER SUMMARY

I.	Incapacity	7-2
II.	Undue Influence	7-4
III.	*Inter Vivos* Transfers	7-5
IV.	Ethical Problems	7-7

INCAPACITY AND UNDUE INFLUENCE

INTRODUCTION: Wills are often challenged on the ground that the testator lacked mental capacity. This is often linked with a claim that the testator was unduly influenced in making the will. These issues are becoming more important, since more wills are executed by elderly persons as life spans increase. This chapter discusses incapacity and undue influence both as to wills and as to *inter vivos* gifts, since the rules are similar.

This chapter also covers some ethical problems faced by attorneys in estate planning. Many of these are associated with claims of undue influence, for example when an attorney drafts a will under which the attorney receives a bequest.

The topics covered by this chapter are also discussed in McGovern, Kurtz and Rein, *Wills, Trusts* and *Estates* 272–96 (1988).

INCAPACITY

I. INCAPACITY

A. Age (#7.1): In most states, a person must be eighteen years of age or older in order to make a will. UPC § 2-501.

B. Mental Capacity (#7.2): A will is invalid if the testator lacked the mental capacity to know he was making a will or the extent of his property or the natural objects of his bounty. The same test applies to the revocation of wills. *Wood v. Bettis*, 880 P.2d 961 (Or. App. 1994) (will probated even though destroyed by the testator when he lacked capacity).

Example: A testator who denied that he had a son did not know the natural objects of his bounty, and so his will was denied probate. *Estate of Record,* 534 A.2d 1319 (Me. 1987). *But see Bland v. Graves,* 620 N.E.2d 920 (Ohio App. 1993) (testator's not knowing the names of her second cousins did not show lack of capacity).

1. ***Conservatorship* (#7.3):** The fact that a testator has been adjudicated incompetent and is under conservatorship does not preclude finding that she had the capacity to make a will, since less capacity is required for making a will than for transacting business. *Estate of Ioupe,* 878 P.2d 1168 (Utah App. 1994). But in *Wood,* #7.1, *supra*, the appointment of a guardian for the testator was held to create a rebuttable presumption of incapacity).

C. Evidence

1. ***Burden of proof* (#7.4):** Most states put the burden on the contestants of a will to prove lack of capacity. UPC § 3-407.

2. ***Question of fact* (#7.5):** Capacity is a question of fact, so the finding of a jury or trial court will be affirmed if there is evidence to support it. Nevertheless, directed verdicts on this issue are not uncommon because courts fear that juries may reject a will out of sympathy for the heirs who were disinherited. *Morse v. Volz,* 808 S.W.2d 424 (Mo. App. 1991) (jury finding of incapacity reversed).

3. ***Testimony* (#7.6):**

   a. Medical experts frequently testify on the question of capacity. They may do so on the basis of medical records even though they never saw the testator. *Succession of Hamiter,* 519 So.2d 341 (La. App. 1988).

   b. Lay persons can also testify as to the testator's capacity. Courts give great weight to testimony by the subscribing witnesses because they were present when the testator actually executed the will. *Lucero v. Lucero*, 884 P.2d 527 (N.M. App. 1994) (medical experts testified for contestants but will upheld because witnesses to will said testator "knew what she was doing").

4. ***Time to which testimony relates* (#7.7):**

   a. The relevant time for determining capacity is when the will was executed.

      Example: The testator's alcoholism does not matter if he was sober when he signed the will. *Estate of Elam,* 738 S.W.2d 169 (Tenn. 1987).

   b. But evidence relating to a time before or after execution is admissible, if it is not too remote. *Estate of Berry*, 524 N.E.2d 689 (Ill. App. 1988) (error to exclude evidence of incapacity four and a half months prior to execution).

D. **Insane Delusion (#7.8):** Even if the testator had the capacity to transact ordinary business, if the will was produced by an insane delusion, it will not be probated.

   Example: The testator's grandson put her in a hospital on advice from her doctor. She accused him of trying to "put her away" and executed a new will which disinherited him. A jury finding of incapacity was upheld, even though everyone agreed that "in a general sense the testator was sane." *Spruance v. Northway,* 601 S.W.2d 153 (Tex. Civ. App. 1980).

   1. ***Distinguished from mistake* (#7.9):** If there is some basis for the testator's belief, it is not an insane delusion. *Akers v. Hodel,* 871 F.2d 924 (10th Cir. 1989) (even if testator's belief he was not the father of a child was false it was not unreasonable, so will is probated). *See* #6.1, *supra.*

   2. ***Causation* (#7.10):** An insane delusion is relevant only if it had an effect on the will. The existence of other, rational grounds for the will may defeat the challenge. *Goodman v. Zimmerman,* 32 Cal. Rptr. 2d 419 (Cal. App. 1994) (claim of insane delusion rejected because other reasons for will).

UNDUE INFLUENCE

II. UNDUE INFLUENCE

A. Comparison with Incapacity (#7.11): A will may also be denied probate because the testator signed under duress or undue influence. This claim is usually joined with a claim that the testator lacked capacity. The two ideas are linked because a weak mind is particularly susceptible to influence.

Example: A finding of undue influence was affirmed partly because the testator was susceptible to such influence through alcohol abuse. *Boehm v. Allen*, 506 N.W.2d 781 (Iowa App. 1993). Conversely, a finding of undue influence was reversed because the testator was "strong minded." *Matter of Estate of Webb*, 863 P.2d 1116 (Okl. 1993).

1. ***Effect on part of a will* (#7.12):** Normally when a testator lacks capacity, the whole will is invalid. Sometimes undue influence affects only part of the will. If so, the rest is probated. *Estate of Lane,* 492 So.2d 395 (Fla. App. 1986).

2. ***Character of the influence* (#7.13):** Influence exerted on the testator is not necessarily "undue."

   Example: The court refused to find undue influence from the fact that the testator had discussed her will with her sons. In advising her they had acted as "dutiful sons." *Carter v. Carter,* 526 So.2d 141 (Fla. App. 1988). But a court found undue influence in a lawyer's advice to the testator which violated the Code of Professional Responsibility. *Estate of Dankbar,* 430 N.W.2d 124 (Iowa 1988).

3. ***Influence by others* (#7.14):** Influence may be undue even if it is not exerted by the devisee. *Matter of Estate of Maheras*, 897 P.2d 268 (Okl. 1995) (devise to church voided because of undue influence by its pastor).

4. ***Naturalness of will* (#7.15):** Both as to incapacity and undue influence, courts and juries are often influenced by whether the will seems "natural." Therefore, a statement by the testator of the reasons for an apparently unnatural provision can help to defeat a challenge to the will. *Estate of Rothenberg,* 530 N.E.2d 1148 (Ind. App. 1988) (recital in will that daughter had received gifts from testator).

B. Proof

1. ***Question of fact* (#7.16):** Undue influence is a question of fact, and the burden of proof is generally on the contestants. UPC § 3-407.

2. ***Circumstantial evidence* (#7.17):** Direct evidence of undue influence is often unavailable, since the testator is dead and the influencer is likely to deny it. Therefore, it is often inferred from circumstances.

C. Presumption Arising from Confidential Relationship (#7.18): If a person in a confidential relationship with the testator participated in preparing the will, a presumption arises that the will was the product of undue influence.

Example: The court relied on this presumption in *Maheras,* #7.14, *supra*, saying there was a confidential relationship between the testator and her pastor, who had chosen the lawyer who prepared the will.

1. ***Confidential relationship*** **(#7.19):**

   a. Certain relationships are deemed confidential by nature, *e.g.*, attorney/client, guardian/ward, or doctor/patient. The granting of a power of attorney creates a confidential relationship between the principal and agent.

   b. Kinship does not necessarily create a confidential relationship for this purpose. *Compare* #6.48, *supra*. The key factor is dominance by one person over the other rather than intimacy between them.

   Example: The testator's daughter drafted the will which gave her all the estate. A claim of undue influence was rejected because the parent/child relationship was not a confidential one. *Estate of Jones v. Jones,* 759 P.2d 345 (Utah App. 1988). Wills produced by the influence of the testator's spouse are usually upheld. *Morse v. Volz*, 808 S.W.2d 424 (Mo. App. 1991) (will leaving all to spouse upheld, since spouses can properly influence each other).

2. ***Participation*** **(#7.20):** The more the beneficiary participates in preparation of the will, the stronger the presumption. To forestall challenges, the drafter should talk with the testator outside the presence of the beneficiaries, and they should be out of the room when the will is executed.

3. ***Rebutting the presumption*** **(#7.21):** The presumption can be rebutted by showing that the testator received independent advice. The lawyer who drafts the will can play a crucial role, assuming he or she is independent of the devisee. *Higgs v. Estate of Higgs*, 892 S.W.2d 284 (Ark. App. 1995) (rejecting claim of undue influence on the basis of testimony by the lawyer who drafted will).

III. *INTER VIVOS* TRANSFERS

INTER VIVOS *TRANSFERS*

A. Comparison with Wills (#7.22): Deeds, trusts, and other *inter vivos* conveyances can also be challenged for undue influence or incapacity. Courts usually apply the same rules in the two situations.

1. **Adjudication of incompetency (#7.23):** A person who has been adjudicated incompetent may still have the capacity to make a will. *See* #7.3, *supra*. But in many states, such an adjudication renders all subsequent gifts invalid.

   Example: A conservator appointed for a woman could recover property which she later deeded to others, since the establishment of the conservatorship was an adjudication that she was incapacitated. *O'Brien v.*

Dudenhoeffer, 19 Cal. Rptr. 2d 826 (Cal. App. 1993). The result would be similar under UPC § 5-419, which gives the conservator upon appointment title to all the conservatee's property.

2. ***Time of suit* (#7.24)**: In most states, a will can be contested only after the testator dies. *See* #12.1, *infra*. Gifts may be challenged during the donor's lifetime by the donor or a conservator. *E.g., Bedree v. Bedree,* 528 N.E.2d 1128 (Ind. App. 1988) (donor voids deed for undue influence).

3. ***Protection of bona fide purchasers* (#7.25):** Even if a transfer is voidable for incapacity or undue influence, a bona fide purchaser from the donee can retain the property.

   Example: *A* conveyed a ranch to *B* who later mortgaged it to a bank. *A* then sued to set aside the deed, alleging incapacity and undue influence. The court held for the bank. Since there had been no prior adjudication of incapacity, the deed was only voidable. A mortgagee was like a bona fide purchaser. *First Interstate Bank v. First Wyoming Bank,* 762 P.2d 379 (Wyo. 1988).

   a. In this situation damages may be recovered from *B*.

      Example: An alcoholic sold land to the defendant at a bargain price. The defendant, who had resold the land, was required to pay damages based on the difference between the price he paid and the value of the land. *Barshak v. Buccheri*, 547 N.E.2d 23 (Mass. 1989)

4. ***Ratification* (#7.26):** Although conveyances by a minor are voidable, they may be ratified by failure to take action within a reasonable time after the minor comes of age. *Restatement (Second) of Property (Donative Transfers)* § 34.4(1).

B. Gifts by Guardians and Agents

1. ***Wills* (#7.27):** A guardian or conservator cannot make a will for the ward. UPC § 5-407(b).

2. ***Substituted judgment* (#7.28):** Conservators can make gifts of the ward's property. In such cases, the court substitutes its judgment for that of the ward, *i.e.*, tries to determine what the ward would have done if competent.

   Example: A court allowed a conservator to use the ward's property to create charitable trusts. The ward had no will and no heirs, so her property would otherwise escheat to the state when she died. *Matter of Jones,* 401 N.E.2d 351 (Mass. 1980).

   a. UPC § 5-424 allows conservators to make gifts not exceeding 20% of the income of the ward's estate without court approval. A court can authorize larger gifts. UPC § 5-407(c).

Example: A conservator changed the beneficiary of insurance on the conservatee's life. This was ineffective because no prior court approval had been obtained. *Matter of Estate of Leone*, 860 P.2d 973 (Utah App. 1993).

3. ***Agents* (#7.29):** All states now allow "durable" powers of attorney under which an agent's powers continue even though the principal becomes incompetent. UPC § 5-501. Such powers may avoid the need for court approval generally required for conservators, but only if the terms of the power are broad enough to authorize making gifts.

   Example: Gifts of the principal's property under a durable power were ineffective. Such powers should be narrowly construed. Language in the power about "doing anything I could do" was not sufficient. *Estate of Casey*, 948 F.2d 895 (4th Cir. 1991). *But see Estate of Bronston,* T.C. Memo 1988-510 (gifts under a power of attorney upheld).

C. **Change of Status (#7.30):** Succession to an estate may be affected by a marriage or adoption since spouses and adopted children are heirs. An adoption or marriage may be challenged for incapacity, but attack on a marriage may be barred after one of the spouses has died.

   Example: A son sued to annul his father's marriage after his death for lack of mental capacity. The court dismissed the suit because a relative can sue for an annulment only while the spouse is alive. *Hall v. Nelson,* 534 N.E.2d 929 (Ohio App. 1987).

   A marriage cannot be challenged for undue influence. *Hoffman v. Kohns,* 385 So.2d 1064 (Fla. App. 1980).

ETHICAL PROBLEMS

IV. ETHICAL PROBLEMS

A. **Conflict of Interest (#7.31):** If a lawyer drafts a will from which the lawyer receives a benefit, the will may be challenged for undue influence because of the confidential relationship which exists between lawyer and client. *See* #7.19, *supra.* In addition, the lawyer may be disciplined for unethical conduct.

   Example: A lawyer was suspended from practice for drafting a will in which he was a beneficiary in violation of Rule 1.8(c) of the Model Rules of Professional Conduct: "[A] lawyer shall not prepare an instrument giving the lawyer or a person related to the lawyer as parent, child, sibling, or spouse any substantial gift from a client, including a testamentary gift, except where the client is related to the donee." *Discip. Proceeding against Gillingham*, 896 P.2d 656 (Wash. 1995).

   1. ***Code of Professional Responsibility* (#7.32):** The relevant provisions of the Code of Professional Responsibility are less clear, but they have also been used to discipline lawyers in this situation. *E.g. Cleveland Bar Association v. Kelley,* 642 N.E.2d 611 (Ohio 1994).

2. ***Gifts* (#7.33):** Although the Model Rule speaks only of "preparing an instrument," the comment suggests that a lawyer may accept gifts from a client only if they "meet general standards of fairness." *Cf. Matter of Smith,* 572 N.E.2d 1280 (Ind. 1991) (lawyer suspended for taking gifts from mentally incompetent client).

3. ***Relatives* (#7.34):** Despite the exception "where the client is related to the donee," drafting a will which gives the drafter more than her intestate share seems questionable, *e.g.*, a lawyer who was one of four children drafting a will which gave her the entire estate.

4. ***Designation of fiduciary* (#7.35):** Clients often ask lawyers for advice in naming an executor or trust. A lawyer's recommendation of himself may be unethical under EC 5-6 of the Code of Professional Responsibility, but the Model Rules have no comparable provision.

B. **Lawyer as Witness (#7.36):** Lawyers frequently testify in will contests as to the testator's capacity and freedom from undue influence. A lawyer's credibility as a witness may be impaired if she also appears as an advocate. Therefore, a lawyer who can reasonably expect to be called as a witness should not serve in a contest.

Example: A lawyer who drafted a will was banned from acting as attorney for the estate because he was expected to testify as to undue influence. *Estate of Seegers,* 733 P.2d 418 (Okl. App. 1986); DR 5-102. Model Rule 3.7 is similar, but the disqualification does not bar another member of the lawyer's firm from acting.

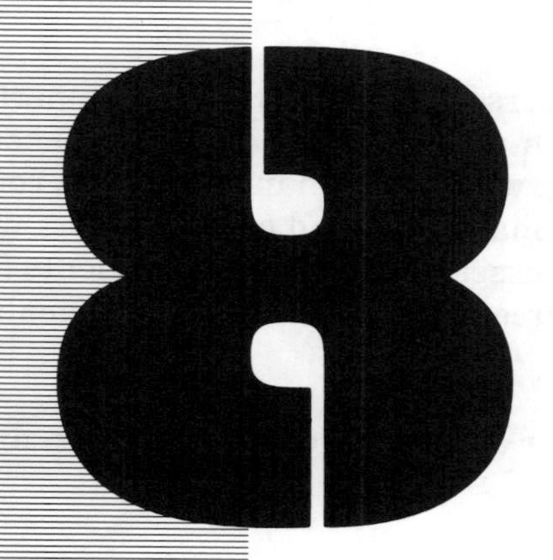

CONTRACTS TO MAKE WILLS

CHAPTER SUMMARY

I.	Formal Requirements	8-2
II.	Remedies	8-4
III.	Disadvantages of Contractual Wills	8-5

CONTRACTS TO MAKE WILLS

INTRODUCTION: Claims that a person promised to leave property to the plaintiff by will are frequently litigated. Such a promise is enforceable even if it was not made with the formalities prescribed for a will, but in many states the contract must be in writing. However, courts have traditionally enforced oral contracts when there has been part performance. This chapter discusses the formal requirements for contracts to make wills, the remedies available to enforce them, and why knowledgeable estate planners advise against their use.

These matters are covered in greater detail in McGovern, Kurtz, and Rein, *Wills, Trusts and Estates,* 384–96 (1988).

FORMAL REQUIREMENTS

I. FORMAL REQUIREMENTS

A. Statutes

1. ***Statute of Frauds* (#8.1):** All states have copied the requirement in the Statute of Frauds that contracts to sell land must be in writing. Contracts to devise land are covered by this provision.

2. ***UPC § 2-514* (#8.2):** Many states, like UPC § 2-514, require that all contracts to make a will (or not to revoke a will or to die intestate) be in writing and signed, even if the contract covers only personal property.

B. Joint and Mutual Wills

1. ***Joint wills* (#8.3):** Many couples execute a joint will which disposes of the property of both spouses. Some courts presume that persons who execute a joint will have agreed not to revoke it.

   Example: *H* and *W* executed a joint will. After *H* died, *W* executed a new will. The new will could not be admitted to probate because it was inconsistent with the implied contract between the spouses. *In re Estate of Kaplan,* 579 N.E.2d 963 (Ill. App. 1991).

   a. UPC § 2-514, on the other hand, says the "the execution of a joint will ... does not create a presumption of a contract not to revoke the will."

2. ***Mutual wills* (#8.4):** Many couples execute separate wills at the same time with reciprocal provisions, *e.g., H* leaves his estate to *W* if she survives him and *vice versa,* followed by a devise to third person(s), if the other spouse does not survive. Courts do not infer the existence of a contract from mutual as distinguished from joint wills. *See Estate of Maher,* 606 N.E.2d 46 (Ill. App. 1992).

3. ***Does the will satisfy the writing requirement?* (#8.5):** If a will is executed pursuant to an alleged contract (and then revoked), some courts hold that the will itself satisfies the writing requirement. But under UPC

§ 2-514, this is true only if the will states the material provisions of the contract or expressly refers to it.

4. ***Lost writing* (#8.6):** The statute does not prevent enforcement of a contract if the only written copy was lost. *Baker v. Mohr*, 826 P.2d 111 (Or. App. 1992).

C. Part Performance

1. ***Statute of Frauds* (#8.7):** Courts have held that part performance can satisfy the sale-of-land provision in the Statute of Frauds, even though the statute itself did not say so. Courts frequently invoke this exception in contracts to make wills.

   Example: *H* and *W* executed mutual wills which provided for *H*'s children by a prior marriage after both spouses were dead. *H* died, and *W* took his estate under his will. She then made a new will. *H*'s children produced oral evidence that the mutual wills were made pursuant to a contract. The court held that one "who has accepted benefits of such an agreement will not be permitted to rescind." *Woelke v. Calfee*, 608 P.2d 606 (Or. App. 1980).

2. ***UPC § 2-514* (#8.8):** This provision contains no part-performance exception, but some courts have held that one who receives benefits under an oral contract is "estopped" from invoking the statute. *Juran v. Epstein,* 28 Cal. Rptr. 2d 588 (Cal. App. 1994).

   a. The comment to UPC § 2-514 says it does not "preclude recovery in quantum meruit for the value of services rendered the testator."

   Example: A father promised his son that if he worked for the family business the father would leave him a share of the company. The son was allowed to recover for the value of his services, and the value of the promised share in the company was evidence of this. *Slawsby v. Slawsby,* 601 N.E.2d 478 (Mass. App. 1992).

3. ***Executory contracts* (#8.9):** Unlike ordinary contracts, many courts hold that either party to a contract to make a will can repudiate it before there has been any part performance, even if the contract is in writing. *Boyle v. Schmitt*, 602 So.2d 665 (Fla. App. 1992). *Contra, In re Estate of Johnson,* 781 S.W.2d 390 (Tex. App. 1989).

D. Consideration (#8.10): A promise to devise property, like other contracts, is unenforceable without consideration. *In re Estate of Casey*, 583 N.E.2d 83 (Ill. App. 1991).

REMEDIES

II. REMEDIES

A. **Jurisdiction (#8.11):** Most courts probate a will even if it was executed in breach of a contract on the grounds that probate courts have no jurisdiction to enforce contracts. *Perino v. Eldert,* 577 N.E.2d 807 (Ill. App. 1991). But see Mich. Stat 700.22(c) (probate court has concurrent jurisdiction to enforce contracts to make wills).

B. Timing

8

1. ***Anticipatory breach* (#8.12):** Although the contract is not broken until the testator dies, courts often allow suit when a promisor repudiates the agreement while still living.

   Example: A father sold land which he had contracted to devise to his son. The son was allowed to have a trust imposed on the proceeds even though his father was alive. *Dickie v. Dickie,* 769 P.2d 225 (Or. App. 1989).

2. ***Statute of Limitations* (#8.13):** However, the promises can wait until the promisor dies to sue; only then does the statute of limitations start to run.

C. Relief

1. ***Specific performance* (#8.14):** The relief normally given is equivalent to specific performance; courts impose a trust on the property for the benefit of the beneficiary. Hence there is no right to jury trial. *Walton v. Walton,* 36 Cal. Rptr. 2d 901 (Cal. App. 1995).

2. ***Quasi-contractual relief* (#8.15):** If the promise is indefinite, the plaintiff may be restricted to quasi-contractual relief.

   Example: A man promised his secretary that "he would take care of her when he died." The secretary recovered the reasonable value of the services she had performed in reliance on the promise. *Restaino v. Vannah,* 483 N.E.2d 847 (Mass. App. 1985). *Cf. Story v. Hargrave,* 369 S.E.2d 669 (Va. 1988) (error to limit plaintiffs' recovery to the value of their services since they had been promised the entire estate).

D. Third Parties

1. **Inter vivos *transfers* (#8.16):** An *inter vivos* transfer from the promisor may constitute a breach even if the contract literally only covers wills.

   Example: *H* and *W* executed a joint will. After *H* died, *W* put most of their assets into joint tenancy. The court held that this property was subject to the contract. The promisor could use the property and make "reasonable gifts" and the case was remanded to determine if the gifts were reasonable. *Powell v. American Charter Fed. S.& L.,* 514 N.W.2d 326 (Neb. 1994). *Compare Blackmon v. Estate of Battock,* 587 N.E.2d 280 (N.Y. 1991) (creation of Totten trust did not breach contract).

2. ***Spouse of promisor* (#8.17):** Some courts give the rights of the promisor's spouse precedence over the contract.

   Example: *H* and *W* had contractual wills. *H* remarried after *W* died. When he later died, his second wife was able to claim as a pretermitted spouse despite the claims of the beneficiaries of the contractual will. *Putnam v. Via,* 638 So.2d 981 (Fla. App. 1994). The community property interest of the second spouse in property acquired during that marriage is protected.

   a. Some courts, however, limit the rights of the promisor's spouse on the ground that the promisor's estate is "encumbered" with the contractual claims. *Gregory v. Estate of Gregory,* 866 S.W.2d 379 (Ark. 1993).

DISADVANTAGES OF CONTRACTUAL WILLS

III. DISADVANTAGES OF CONTRACTUAL WILLS: Knowledgeable estate planners recommend against the use of contractual wills. A trust is a better way to accomplish the goals of the parties.

A. Tax Consequences (#8.18): Contracts to make wills may have adverse tax consequences.

Examples: When couples use contractual wills, they may lose the federal estate tax marital deduction on the ground that the surviving spouse, being contractually bound to leave property in a certain way at death, has only a terminable interest. *Bartlett v. Commissioner,* 68 AFTR 2d # 149,039 (7th Cir. 1991). Also, the surviving spouse may be deemed to have made a taxable gift when the first spouse dies. *Grimes v. Commissioner*, 851 F.2d 1005 (7th Cir. 1988).

B. Inflexibility (#8.19): A contract may preclude changes in an estate plan when circumstances change after the contract was made.

Example: A couple agrees that after they die, their property should go to their children. *H* dies, and one child becomes especially needy. The contract may preclude *W* from leaving a larger share of the estate to the needy child or from disinheriting a child who had been cruel to her. A trust with a special power given to *W* to appoint among the children would probably better reflect what the couple wanted.

C. Uncertainty (#8.20): The rights of the promisor over the property are not clear.

Example: What exactly does it mean to say that the promisor "may make reasonable" gifts? Powell, #8.16, *supra.* A well-drafted trust, supplemented by the rules of trust law, gives clearer guidance.

D. **Enforceability (#8.21):** If a promisor is insolvent, the beneficiary may have no effective remedy. The beneficiary may be also be subject to the rights of bona fide purchasers and the promisor's spouse.

1. ***Comparison with trust*** **(#8.22):** Trustees may post bond to secure performance of their obligation; they account periodically and keep the trust assets "earmarked" so they can be identified. See #12.75, *infra*. These requirements make it more likely that the beneficiaries will actually receive the property intended for them.

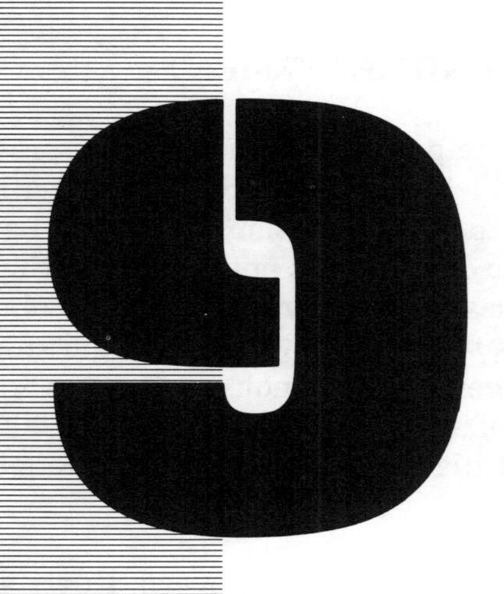

ADEMPTION AND ABATEMENT

CHAPTER SUMMARY

I.	Ademption	9-2
II.	Abatement	9-5
III.	Payment of Taxes	9-7

ADEMPTION AND ABATEMENT

INTRODUCTION: It is sometimes impossible to carry out the provisions of a will because the testator, after executing the will, transferred property which was specifically devised in the will. This may lead to an "ademption" (from the Latin *adimere,* to take away), which means that the specific devisee gets nothing. Sometimes the estate is insufficient generally to pay all the devises and some must therefore abate. This chapter covers ademption and abatement. As to both problems, the legal rules may turn on the classification of devises as specific," "general," "demonstrative," or "residuary." Contrary to what you might think, a legacy of a specific amount, *e.g.,* $1,000, is considered to be general rather than specific. A specific devise is one which refers to an identified asset, like "my house."

The topics in this chapter are fully discussed in McGovern, Kurtz and Rein, *Wills, Trusts and Estates*, 397–420 (1988).

ADEMPTION

I. ADEMPTION

A. **General Rule (#9.1):** When property that is specifically devised is not in the testator's estate, the devise is often held to be "adeemed," and the devisee gets nothing.

Example: A will devised a savings account at a bank. The testator later withdrew the funds in the account and used them to buy certificates of deposit. The court held that the devise was adeemed. *Estate of Mayberry v. Mayberry*, 886 S.W.2d 627 (Ark. 1994).

1. ***Intent*** **(#9.2):** Although courts often say that ademption occurs regardless of the testator's intent, *Wasserman v. Cohen,* 606 N.E.2d 901 (Mass. 1993), under UPC § 2-606 (1990) there is no ademption "unless the facts and circumstances indicate that an ademption of the devise was intended by the testator."

   Example: A will devises "any residence owned by me at my death to my spouse." If the testator later sells his house and moves into an rented apartment, the devise would be adeemed even under the UPC.

2. ***Classification*** **(#9.3):** Ademption applies only to specific devises. A bequest of "$1,000" is not "specific" because it can be satisfied with any property.

   a. A bequest of "100 shares of IBM stock" is usually classified as general. Therefore, the executor would buy the stock for the legatee if the testator did not own 100 shares of IBM at death. *Soles' Estate,* 304 A.2d 97 (Pa. 1973).

   b. A bequest of *"my* 100 shares of IBM stock," on the other hand, is specific. *Estate of Wales,* 727 P.2d 536 (Mont. 1986).

   c. A third type of bequest, called "demonstrative," is not subject to ademption.

Example: A will left $8,000 to a granddaughter, to be paid from the testator's account at a named bank. There was only $1,339 in the account when the testator died, but the granddaughter was awarded the balance of the $8,000 from other assets of the estate. *Leaver v. McBride,* 506 S.W.2d 141 (Tenn. 1974).

3. ***Sale on credit* (#9.4):** If specifically devised property is sold on credit, UPC § 2-606(a)(1) provides that the devisee gets "any balance of the purchase price" owed to the testator at death.

   Example: A testator executed a will devising certain stock. He later sold it for $275,000 plus a note for $75,000, which was unpaid at death. Under the UPC the devisees would be entitled to the $75,000 note under § 2-606(a)(1). They would also be entitled to the value of the stock (less the $75,000) under § 2-606(a)(5) if the facts or circumstances did not show an intent to adeem.

4. ***Change of form* (#9.5):** A "mere change of form" does not cause ademption.

   Examples: If a will devises "my home" and the testator later sells her home and buys another, the devisee gets the new home. If a will devises a business which is later incorporated, some courts give the devisee the stock of the corporation. *Creed's Estate,* 63 Cal. Rptr. 80 (Cal. App. 1967). In *Mayberry,* #9.1 *supra,* the trial court found that the switch from a bank account to certificates of deposit was just a change in form, but the appellate court disagreed.

B. **Involuntary Transfers (#9.6):** If a testator ceases to own property for reasons over which he had no control, no intent to adeem can be imputed to the testator. Therefore, in many states there is no ademption in such cases.

1. ***Mergers* (#9.7):** Under UPC § 2-605, a specific devisee of securities gets "securities of another entity owned by the testator as a result of a merger, consolidation, or reorganization." Many courts reach the same result without a statute.

   a. This does not apply to cash received in a merger.

   Example: A will devised the testator's Houston Natural Gas stock. Most of this was later converted to cash as a result of a merger. The devise was held to be adeemed as to the cash even though it was traceable in the estate. *Opperman v. Anderson,* 782 S.W.2d 8 (Tex. App. 1989). The result would be the same under UPC § 2-605, but the devise might be saved under the general presumption against ademption in § 2-606(a)(5).

2. ***Stock splits* (#9.8):** UPC § 2-605 also gives the devisee any additional securities of the same company acquired by the testator after the will was executed by reason of action initiated by the company.

Example: A will left "100 shares of Citizens Bankshares." The stock split four for one after the will was executed. The court awarded the devisee 400 shares. *Watson v. Santalucia*, 427 S.E.2d 466 (W.Va. 1993).

a. Otherwise, the devise would be seriously diminished because the price of each share drops after a stock split to reflect the fact that each share now represents a smaller share of the pie.

b. This reasoning does not apply so much to stock dividends because they are based on the company's earnings. Some courts therefore hold that stock dividends paid prior to the testator's death do not go to the specific devisee. However, UPC§ 2-605 gives the devisee both splits and stock dividends (but not *cash* dividends).

c. Some courts give the legatee the benefit of a stock split only if the legacy is specific. But the court in *Watson, supra,* refused to distinguish between specific and general legacies. (The legacy in that case was arguably general. *See* #9.3, *supra.)*

3. ***Casualty* (#9.9):** If property is destroyed by accident and insurance proceeds have not been paid to the testator at death, the devisee of the property gets the insurance under UPC § 2-606(a)(3).

a. UPC § 2-606(a)(3) does not apply if the insurance is paid to the testator before death, but some courts have awarded the insurance to the devisee even in this case on the theory that there could have been no intent to adeem if the loss was accidental. *Estate of Kolbinger,* 529 N.E. 2d 823 (Ill. App. 1988).

b. If the loss is not covered by insurance, the devisee is not protected. Arguably, however, damages recovered from a tortfeasor should also go to the devisee. UPC § 2-606(a)(2) gives the devisee the condemnation award paid after the testator dies if the property is taken by eminent domain.

4. ***Sale by conservator* (#9.10):** Under UPC § 2-608(b), if the property is sold by a conservator, the specific devisee gets a general devise equal to the net proceeds of sale. Many courts reach the same result on the ground that a sale could not reflect an intent to adeem if it occurred when the testator was incompetent.

a. Some courts give the sale proceeds to the devisee only if they can be traced in the estate. This is not true under the UPC, however.

b. Many courts reach a similar result when a conservator takes action that affects a will substitute.

Example: Although a conservator had closed a joint account which the conservatee had established for her niece and nephew, the court held that the money withdrawn should go to them since closing the account was beyond the conservator's powers. *Matter of Estate of Briley*, 825 P.2d 1181 (Kan. App. 1992). Under UPC § 5-426 a conservator in making withdrawals for support must "take into account any estate plan" of the conservatee.

c. Many persons today avoid conservatorship by executing durable powers of attorney which allow an agent to act even after the principal has become incompetent. *See* #10.32, *infra.* UPC § 2-606(b) (1990) also avoids ademption in the case of a sale by "an agent acting within the authority of a durable power of attorney for an incapacitated principal." The result is unclear in many states.

Example: The devise of a house was held to be adeemed when it was sold by an attorney under a durable power. This was different from a sale by a conservator since there was no finding that the testator was incompetent at the time of the sale. *Chapman v. Chapman*, 577 A.2d 775 (Me. 1990). Under UPC § 2-606(e), it would be presumed that the testator was incapacitated at the time of the sale.

C. **Other Construction Problems (#9.11):** Specific devises often give rise to litigation as to their scope. A devise of a house "and its contents" creates problems.

Example: A devise of land "and its contents" was held not to include a safe with $30,000 in it. *Matter of Clark*, 417 S.E.2d 856 (S.C. 1992). *But see In re Estate of Rothko*, 352 N.Y.S.2d 574 (Surr. 1974) (multimillion dollar art collection included in devise of "contents" of home).

1. ***Devises of "money"* (#9.12):** A bequest of "cash" may be held to include certificates of deposit. *Estate of Mitchell,* 519 So.2d 430 (Miss. 1988).

2. ***Drafting* (#9.13):** Most well-drafted wills make few if any specific devises since usually the testator's objectives can be better accomplished by either a pecuniary devise or a share of the residue.

II. ABATEMENT

ABATEMENT

A. **Statement of the Problem (#9.14):** Sometimes a will makes devises which exceed the amount of property in the testator's estate.

Example: A will leaves $10,000 to *A*, $5,000 to *B*, and the residue of the estate to *C*. The testator's estate only contains $12,000. A similar problem is presented if the testator has assets worth $30,000 but there are $18,000 in claims against the estate, because claims must be paid before legacies.

B. **Hierarchy of Devises (#9.15):** Residuary devises abate before general devises and general devises abate before specific devises. Within each class, abatement is pro-rata. UPC § 3-902. Thus, in the foregoing example, *C* would get nothing since her devise was residuary. *B* and *C* would split the $12,000 proportionately, $8,000 to *A* and $4,000 to *B*. If the will had also devised "my home" to *D, D* would get the home unabated because his devise was specific.

Rationale: In most estates, the residuary estate has enough to pay all claims with a substantial amount left over for the residuary devisees. It is administratively convenient to pay all claims out of the residue because attempting to allocate an appropriate portion to each general and specific devise would raise questions of valuation.

1. ***Classification* (#9.16):** It is sometimes not clear how a particular devise should be classified.

   Examples: A will left certain land to two nieces and "all personal property" to various relatives. The latter devise was held to be residuary and thus subject to the claims against the estate. *Estate of Brannan v. LaSalle State Bank*, 569 N.E.2d 104 (Ill. App. 1991). A devise of "a sum equal to 10% of the value of my estate" was general and thus not subject to debts. *Williams v. Faucett,* 579 So.2d 572 (Ala. 1989). The result would probably have been different if the will had said "10% of my *net* estate."

2. ***Contrary intent* (#9.17):** Under UPC § 3-902(b), if "the express or implied purpose of the devise" would be defeated by the usual order of abatement, devises abate so as "to give effect to the intention of the testator." Many courts, however, follow the order of abatement rigidly.

   Example: A will left the testator's farm to his son and "an equal portion of my estate" to his daughter. There was not enough in the estate to give the daughter an equal portion after the son got the farm. Her devise was held to be general and it abated. The son's did not because it was specific. *Matter of Estate of Hale,* 704 S.W.2d 725 (Tenn. App. 1985). The testator's apparent purpose to treat his two children equally was not carried out.

C. Other Factors

1. ***Type of property* (#9.18):** In a few states, devises of personal property abate before devises of land. But under UPC § 3-902, there is no priority as between real and personal property.

2. ***Legatee* (#9.19):** In Iowa, devises to a spouse abate last. Iowa Code § 633.436. The text of UPC § 3-902 contains no such provision, but the comment states, "[I]t is commonly held that, even in the absence of a statute, general legacies to a wife, or [children] are to be preferred to other legacies in the same class."

3. ***Exoneration* (#9.20):** At common law, if property specifically devised was subject to a mortgage, the devisee was entitled to have the property exonerated; i.e., require the executor to use other assets of the estate to pay off the mortgage. But UPC § 2-607 says that "a specific devise passes subject to any mortgage without right of exoneration."

   a. A similar problem arises when mortgaged property is held in joint tenancy. The surviving joint tenant may take subject to the mortgage by analogy to a statute like UPC § 2-607. *Bonner v. Arnold,* 676 P.2d 290 (Or. 1984).

b. A manifestation of contrary intent in the will controls, *e.g.,* if the will devises land "free of encumbrances." *Matter of Estate of Brown,* 764 P.2d 373 (Colo. App. 1988). But a general direction in the will to pay the testator's debts does not show an intent to exonerate specific devises. UPC § 2-607.

c. The mortgagee is not affected by this question. If the testator was personally liable, the mortgagee may have the debt paid out of the estate. If this happens, the mortgage will be assigned to the executor, and the devisee will take subject to it under UPC § 3-814.

4. ***Pretermitted heirs* (#9.21):** A child who is not mentioned in a will may be able to get an intestate share of the estate. *See* #3.16, *supra.* In some states, all devisees contribute pro-rata to satisfy the child's claim. Cal. Prob. Code § 6573. However, under UPC § 2-302(d), the devises abate in the same order prescribed for other claims.

5. ***Elective share* (#9.22):** In most states, a surviving spouse can elect a share of the estate regardless of the terms of the will. *See* #3.27, *supra.* Under UPC § 2-209, the spouse's claim to an elective share "is equitably apportioned among the recipients" of the estate. However, some states follow the normal order of abatement for the elective share. Fla. Stat. § 732.209.

D. **Nonprobate Assets (#9.23):** In many states, assets not in the probate estate, such as property held in joint tenancy or a revocable trust, are not subject to claims by thedecedent's creditors. *See* #11.5, 11.16, *infra.* UPC § 6-215 allows creditors to reach assets in a multiple party account, but only "if other assets of the estate are insufficient." Thus such assets are more privileged than devises under a will.

III. PAYMENT OF TAXES

PAYMENT OF TAXES

A. **Introduction (#9.24):** In larger estates, the biggest single claim is often death taxes. In some states this claim, like any other, is paid first from the residue, then from general, then from specific devisees. But in many situations the tax burden is prorated among all the beneficiaries of the estate.

B. **Internal Revenue Code (#9.25):** Federal law calls for such apportionment as to insurance, property subject to a general power of appointment, and property included in the estate because the decedent reserved a life interest. Int. Rev. Code §§ 2206, 2207, 2207B. Other questions are left to state law.

C. **State Apportionment Statutes (#9.26):** State law controls this question except where it conflicts with a specific provision of the Internal Revenue Code. Many states have general apportionment statutes which require all beneficiaries of the estate to pay a pro-rata share of taxes. *E.g.,* UPC § 3-916.

1. ***Probate vs. nonprobate* (#9.27):** Some states distinguish between probate and nonprobate assets; taxes attributable to the latter are prorated, but all taxes attributable to the probate estate come from the residue.

Rationale: Since nonprobate assets often constitute the bulk of the decedent's property, imposing the whole tax burden on the probate estate may wipe it out. Preresiduary legacies, on the other hand, are usually a small portion of the probate estate. It is administratively convenient to have small claims paid out of the residue of the probate estate. *See* #9.15, *supra.*

2. ***Income interests* (#9.28):** Under UPC § 3-916(e), income interests are not subject to apportionment; the burden falls on the remainderman. Thus when a widow was left a life estate in a residence, she was not charged with any of the tax attributable to her interest. *Matter of Estate of Hamilton,* 869 P.2d 971 (Utah App. 1994).

3. ***Contrary intent* (#9.29):** UPC § 3-916 requires apportionment "unless the will otherwise provides." Similarly, the Internal Revenue Code provisions cited in #9.25, *supra,* can be overcome by a manifestation of contrary intent. There is much litigation over this question since many provisions on the subject are ambiguous.

   Example: A will said that debts and taxes were to be paid as soon as practicable. The court construed this as a direction against apportionment since the testator wanted taxes and other debts treated the same way. *Lynchburg College v. Central Fidelity Bank,* 410 S.E.2d 617 (Va. 1991). Many courts on similar language go the other way, saying that apportionment should apply unless there is a clear manifestation of contrary intent. *E.g., Wright v. Union Nat. Bank,* 819 S.W.2d 698 (Ark. 1991).

   a. A will may show an intent to have only partial apportionment, *e.g.,* only taxes attributable to the probate estate paid from the residue. *Estate of Fleischman,* 776 P.2d 684 (Wash. App. 1989) (direction to pay "estate taxes attributable to bequests" from residue). *Compare Estate of Tovrea v. Nolan,* 845 P.2d 494 (Ariz. App. 1992) (direction to pay all taxes from residue includes taxes attributable to insurance policy).

   b. In some cases a court must reconcile conflicting provisions in two documents.

      Example: A will directed that all estate taxes be paid from the residue. A living trust of the testator said the trustee should pay its share of the taxes. The latter provision was held to control, since it was the later expression of intent. *Matter of Estate of Pickrell,* 806 P.2d 1007 (Kan. 1991). *Compare Matter of Estate of Roe,* 426 N.W.2d 797 (Mich. App. 1988) (ignoring trust language because statute requires contrary intention to appear in "the will").

D. **Marital and Charitable Devises (#9.30):** If a devise to a spouse or a charity has to pay a portion of the estate tax, the federal estate tax marital or charitable deduction is reduced. Int. Rev. Code §§ 2055(c), 2056(b)(4). UPC § 3-916(e) expressly exempts such devises from paying a share of taxes.

1. ***Contrary intent* (#9.31):** This provision is also subject to a contrary provision in the will.

   Example: A will provided that all taxes were to be paid from the residue. The residue was left partly to charities, partly to individuals. The charities had to pay a pro-rata share of the taxes. *Matter of Estate of Atkinson,* 539 N.Y.S.2d 112 (App. Div. 1989). However, other courts have held that such a provision was not clear enough to override the exemption. *Estate of Phillips*, 90 T.C. 797 (1988).

2. ***Elective share* (#9.32):** The spouse's elective share is generally computed on the basis of the net estate, after the payment of claims (see #3.31, *supra*), but most courts exonerate it from the tax burden. *Tarbox v. Palmer,* 564 So.2d 1106 (Fla. App. 1990).

3. ***QTIP trusts* (#9.33):** A QTIP trust is one which qualifies for the marital deduction because the trust is taxed in the spouse's estate even though the spouse has no power over the assets. The tax attributable to a QTIP trust is paid from the trust assets, unless the spouse's will specifically directs otherwise. Int. Rev. Code § 2207. A general direction in the spouse's will to pay all taxes from the residue is not construed to apply to a QTIP trust. *Maurice F. Jones Trust v. Barnett Bank,* 637 N.E.2d 1301 (Ind. App. 1994).

E. Other Taxes

1. ***Gift taxes* (#9.34):** Gift taxes are charged to the donor. If the donor fails to pay the tax before death, the taxes are paid like other claims and are not apportioned. *Estate of Brannan v. LaSalle State Bank*, 569 N.E.2d 104 (Ill. App. 1991).

2. ***State inheritance taxes* (#9.35):** Some states impose an inheritance tax based on the amount received by each heir or devisee rather than on the total size of the estate. Inheritance taxes are almost always apportioned, but a will may provide otherwise. *Matter of Estate of Herz*, 651 N.E.2d 1251 (N.Y. 1995) (direction to pay all death taxes from residue exonerates pecuniary devise from German inheritance tax).

F. Planning (#9.36): A will should make it clear how taxes should be paid. Relevant factors to consider are the size and liquidity of the various parts of the estate, and the maximizing of any marital or charitable deduction.

Example: A woman who has put most of her assets into a revocable trust should probably specify that the trustee should pay the estate tax. Specific devisees may not have the money needed to pay their share of the taxes without having to sell the property, whereas the trust may have liquid funds, like insurance proceeds. Any share of the trust which is designed to get the marital or charitable deduction should be exempted from having to pay a share of the taxes.

Notes

PURPOSES OF TRUSTS

CHAPTER SUMMARY

I.	Historical Uses of Trusts	10-2
II.	Avoiding Probate	10-2
III.	Tax Advantages of Trusts	10-4
IV.	Management of Property	10-7
V.	Discretionary Trusts	10-8
VI.	Modification of Trusts	10-10
VII.	Charitable Trusts	10-13

PURPOSES OF TRUSTS

INTRODUCTION: The formalities needed to create a trust were covered in Chapter 4, and revocation of trusts in Chapter 5. The present chapter is concerned with the reasons people create trusts. (The person who creates a trust is usually called the "settlor.")

Different types of trust are used for different purposes. Trusts created by will are called testamentary trusts. Others created by living settlors are called "living" or *"inter vivos"* trusts. Living trusts are often used to avoid probate, but the assets of a testamentary trust are part of the settlor's probate estate. Testamentary trusts, like wills, are revocable until the testator dies, but living trusts may be either revocable or irrevocable. Irrevocable living trusts have tax advantages which do not apply to revocable trusts.

10

A trust is a device for managing property. This chapter compares trusts with alternatives such as guardianship, agency, and custodianship under the Uniform Transfers to Minors Act.

The subjects covered in this chapter are discussed in detail in McGovern, Kurtz, and Rein, *Wills, Trusts, and Estates,* 297-338 (1988).

HISTORICAL USES OF TRUSTS

I. HISTORICAL USES OF TRUSTS

A. **Devises of Land (#10.1):** Before 1540, land could be devised only by putting it in "use." The use is the ancestor of the modern trust. Today property can be devised without using a trust.

B. **Protecting Married Women (#10.2):** At common law, a husband acquired his wife's personal property when they married. Married women could not make gifts or wills. These restrictions were evaded by creating trusts for married women which kept the assets out of her husband's control and gave her power to dispose of them. Trusts became unnecessary for this purpose with the enactment of Married Women's Property Acts in the nineteenth century.

AVOIDING PROBATE

II. AVOIDING PROBATE

A. **Reasons to Avoid Probate (#10.3):** Many persons wish to avoid probate. A few years ago a book entitled *How to Avoid Probate!* became a national bestseller. Strictly speaking, probate is the procedure for proving the validity of a will, a rather simple matter. The real problem is administration of an estate, which is expensive and time-consuming. Modern statutes like the UPC have simplified administration, but there are still advantages in avoiding it.

1. ***Cost* (#10.4):** Administration is expensive. The most important cost is the fee charged by the executor or administrator and by the attorney for the estate. In some states, these fees are based on the size of the probate estate and thus can be reduced by avoiding probate. *See* #12.47, *infra.* On the other hand:

a. Many states now give the executor and attorney a "reasonable" fee, based on the time spent and other factors not limited to the size of the estate.

b. Often a family member serves as executor and does not charge a fee.

c. Fees of the executor or attorney are deductible for tax purposes, so part of the cost is in fact borne by the government.

2. ***Delay*** **(#10.5):** A common complaint about administration is that the heirs or devisees must wait so long before they get the property. Distribution is much quicker for assets outside the probate estate.

3. ***Publicity*** **(#10.6):** Wills become public documents when they are admitted to probate; a living trust does not. For most people this is not important since their will excites no public interest. However, wills are more likely to be contested than nonprobate transfers because heirs are usually notified when a will is offered for probate. *See* #12.7, *supra.*

4. ***Claims of spouse and creditors*** **(#10.7):** In some states, the spouse's elective share does not extend to assets outside the probate estate. *See* #3.32, *supra.* A testator's creditors can reach property in the probate estate, but their ability to reach nonprobate assets is limited. *See* #11.16, *infra.*

   a. The UPC reduces the importance of this distinction by allowing a spouse a share of the "augmented" estate. *See* #3.33, *supra.* The UPC also allows creditors to reach some nonprobate assets. UPC § 6-215.

B. Advantages of Probate

1. ***Cost of preparing trust*** **(#10.8):** Attorneys may charge more for drafting a living trust than for a will. This cost is generally not tax deductible, unlike the expenses of administering an estate.

2. ***Time limit on will contests*** **(#10.9):** Most states impose short time limits for contesting a will. *See* #12.9, *infra.* These do not apply to nonprobate transfers.

C. Alternative Ways to Avoid Probate (#10.10): A living trust is not the only way to avoid probate. Commonly used alternatives are joint tenancy and the designation of a beneficiary of death benefits under a pension or insurance policy, POD bond, or bank account. These methods are typically employed without legal advice and are therefore cheap, but they have drawbacks.

1. ***Outright ownership by survivor*** **(#10.11):** A surviving joint tenant or insurance beneficiary may be incapable of managing the property. A trust can provide for management for an incompetent beneficiary.

2. ***Inclusion in survivor's estate* (#10.12):** If the beneficiary of a nonprobate transfer receives assets outright, they will be included in her taxable (and probate) estate when she dies (unless she consumes them). This can be avoided by keeping the property in trust for her life, with a remainder at her death to a designated beneficiary.

3. ***Joint tenancy as a present gift* (#10.13):** If *A* puts property into joint tenancy with *B*, this may be regarded as a present gift. *See* #5.40, *supra.*

10

   a. If the parties have a falling out, *B* may be allowed a share of the property. A well-drafted trust can avoid this problem by making it clear that the settlor can revoke the trust.

   b. Creditors of the noncontributing party are sometimes allowed to reach assets in joint tenancy.

TAX ADVANTAGES OF TRUSTS

III. TAX ADVANTAGES OF TRUSTS

A. Income Taxes (#10.14): A person who owns income-producing property may reduce taxes by shifting the income to a family member who is in a lower tax bracket.

1. ***Spouse* (#10.15):** Such income-shifting between spouses is unnecessary because spouses can file a joint income tax return.

2. ***Minor children* (#10.16):** Shifting income to children is less advantageous than it once was because unearned income of a child under fourteen is taxed in the parents' bracket under Int. Rev. Code § 1(g).

3. ***Restrictions* (#10.17):** In order for a trust to shift income from the settlor for tax purposes, the trust must be irrevocable. There are other restrictions, too complex to be covered in this outline, which must be followed in drafting a trust with this objective.

4. ***Sprinkling trusts* (#10.18):** Giving a trustee discretion to distribute income among a group can save taxes because the trustee can distribute income to those persons who are in lower tax brackets.

   a. If the trustee has power to distribute the income to herself, the income will be attributed to the trustee. Int. Rev. Code § 678.

   b. The possible income tax savings from trusts were curtailed by the reduction in the number of tax brackets in 1986. Today, all the members of a family may be in the same bracket.

   c. Accumulating income in a trust was once advantageous, but it no longer is. Such income is taxed to the trust as an entity and the trust is usually in a higher bracket.

5. ***Outright gifts* (#10.19):** It is not necessary to use a trust to give income-producing property to someone in a lower tax bracket, but if the potential donees are minors or otherwise incompetent to handle property, a trust is usually desirable.

B. Estate Tax Savings (#10.20): Irrevocable trusts are also used to reduce taxes on the settlor's estate at death. The creation of an irrevocable trust may require paying a gift tax. Gifts are taxed at the same rate as transfers at death, but they can save taxes.

1. ***Annual exemption* (#10.21):** There is an annual gift tax exemption of $10,000 for each donor and donee. Thus a husband and wife with three children could give a total of $60,000 to the children every year without making a taxable gift.

2. ***Valuation* (#10.22):** A gift is valued as of the date of the gift. If property appreciates before the owner dies, the gift tax on its present value will be lower than an estate tax on its higher value when the owner dies, even though the rate is the same.

   a. The saving in estate taxes by making gifts may be offset by the loss of the step-up in basis of property which is included in an estate at death. There is no similar step-up in basis when a gift is made; the donee usually takes over the old basis. Basis is used to determine how much capital gain is realized if property is later sold by the donee or devisee.

   b. An insurance policy is often a good asset to give away. Since insurance proceeds are not generally taxed as income, the step-up in basis is unimportant.

3. ***Inclusion in taxable estate* (#10.23):** If the settlor of a trust reserves the income for life or a power to revoke, the trust assets are included in the settlor's taxable estate at death. Int. Rev. Code §§ 2036, 2038.

C. Risks of Irrevocable Trusts (#10.24): Balanced against the tax advantages of irrevocable trusts are possible disadvantages. The settlor might fall on hard times and need the assets later or repent of his choice of beneficiaries, like King Lear.

Example: A father gave stock in a family business to his son in order to save taxes. When the son later used the stock to drive his father out of the business, the father attempted to rescind the gift but was not allowed to. *Pascale v. Pascale*, 549 A.2d 782 (N.J. 1988).

D. Bypass Trusts (#10.25): Trusts can allow a beneficiary to enjoy income without having the assets which produce the income included in the beneficiary's probate or taxable estate.

Example: *H* leaves his estate in trust for *W* for life, the assets to be distributed to their issue when she dies. When *W* dies, the trust assets will not be included in her taxable or probate estate.

1. ***Marital deduction* (#10.26):** If *H* wants to qualify the trust for the estate or gift-tax marital deduction, the trust assets must be includable in *W*'s estate when she dies; a trust cannot qualify for the marital deduction and also bypass the spouse's estate. Many wills create two trusts: one to qualify for the marital deduction, and the other as a bypass trust.

2. ***Generation-skipping tax* (#10.27):** The tax avoidance possibilities of bypass trusts led Congress to enact a generation-skipping tax.

   Example: *S* creates a trust for her daughter for life, remainder to the daughter's issue. The trust assets are not in the daughter's estate because she had only a life interest, but a generation-skipping tax may be imposed, usually when the daughter dies.

   a. There is a $1 million exemption for the generation-skipping tax, so bypass trusts continue to be advantageous.

   b. The generation-skipping tax applies only if the settlor and the income beneficiary are in different generations. A trust created for *S's* husband for life, remainder to their children, would not incur a generation-skipping tax since spouses are deemed to be in the same generation.

3. ***Legal life estates* (#10.28):** It is not necessary to use a trust to bypass a person's estate. *H* might give or devise property to *W* for life, remainder to their issue without using a trust. Such legal life estates are usually less desirable than a trust, however.

   a. Many questions arise with legal life estates. Can the life tenant sell the property? If so, do the remaindermen get the proceeds? Must the life tenant post a bond to protect the remaindermen? Such questions are more clearly answered by the law of trusts.

      Example: A will left land to the testator's daughter for life, "with full power to sell or dispose of it." The daughter deeded the land to her daughter. In litigation which went up to the highest court of the state, the deed was held invalid. *Childs v. Hutson*, 545 A.2d 43 (Md. 1988). Had the daughter been designated as a trustee of the property, the answer would be clearer: she would have had an implied power to sell, but not to give the property away. *See* #12.66, 12.71, *infra.*

   b. Some persons are deterred from using trusts because of trustees' fees. However, a family member, such as the income beneficiary, may serve as trustee without charge.

IV. MANAGEMENT OF PROPERTY

MANAGEMENT OF PROPERTY

A. Introduction (#10.29): Trusts are often created to handle property for persons who are incapable of managing it. They may be legally incompetent (minors or adjudicated incompetents), or they simply may not be able to handle property, in the settlor's opinion. For example, many nineteen-year-olds are legally adults but not mature enough to manage large amounts of property.

B. Alternatives

1. ***Guardianship*** **(#10.30):** All states have a mechanism for handling the property of a legally incompetent person, generally known as guardianship or conservatorship. It is less desirable than a trust for several reasons.

   a. Guardianship terminates when a minor comes of age (usually eighteen), although many persons are not actually able to handle property at that age. Trusts can last until the beneficiary reaches any age.

   b. An adult can be adjudicated incompetent, but this is an expensive and embarrassing experience that family members usually wish to avoid.

   c. Most states supervise guardians and conservators much more strictly than trustees. For example, the investments which guardians and conservators can make are often restricted. *See* #12.78, *infra.*

   d. A trustee can make unequal distributions among children whose needs differ from time to time.

   Example: Child *A* is about to go to college and needs money for her tuition. Her brother *B* is still in grammar school. A trustee could use the trust funds for *A* (perhaps in later years making compensating distributions to *B*). A guardian must treat the property of each child separately.

2. ***Custodianship under the Uniform Transfers to Minors Act*** **(#10.31):** Virtually all states have enacted some form of this act. Under the Act, property is held by a "custodian" who manages the property for the minor's benefit very much like a trustee.

   a. By registering property in a custodianship, the donor incorporates the terms of the Act by reference, so it is not necessary to draft a trust instrument. This makes custodianship attractive for small gifts which do not justify the costs of drafting a trust.

   b. Custodians are free from court supervision, but they suffer from other disadvantages of guardians. The custodianship ends when the minor reaches twenty-one. Also, a custodian, unlike a trustee, cannot sprinkle distributions among several children.

3. ***Agency* (#10.32):** An agent often manages property for a principal. An agent, like a trustee, custodian, or guardian, is a fiduciary. Many banks act both as trustees and as agents. Agents take directions from the principal, whereas trustees are not ordinarily subject to control by the beneficiary.

   a. Many living trusts are used to avoid probate. *See* #10.3, *supra.* An agency cannot be used for this purpose because it terminates when the principal dies.

   b. Traditionally an agency also ended if the principal became incompetent. However, virtually all states now allow "durable" powers of attorney which continue to operate despite the principal's incapacity. See UPC § 5-501. Durable powers are used in lieu of a trust by persons who want to avoid the need for a conservatorship in case they become incompetent later in life.

   c. Trust law confers many implied powers on trustees, but an agent only has such powers as are expressly conferred in the power of attorney, and courts tend to construe these strictly.

   Example: A woman gave a power of attorney to her son which gave him "full power to deal with any of my property." After the mother became incompetent, the son tried to take advantage of the annual gift tax exclusion by making gifts of her property to her children and grandchildren. *See* #10.21, *supra.* The gifts were held to be invalid because the power did not authorize them. *Estate of Casey v. Commissioner*, 948 F.2d 895 (4th Cir. 1991).

4. ***Insurance options* (#10.33):** The owner of an insurance policy can select an option under which the insurer holds the proceeds when the insured dies and makes periodic payments to the beneficiary. In this situation, the insurer acts much like a trustee, but insurers do not exercise discretion in distributing the proceeds among a group of beneficiaries. Therefore, it is usually better to have insurance proceeds paid to a trust.

DISCRE-TIONARY TRUSTS

V. DISCRETIONARY TRUSTS

A. Introduction (#10.34): Trustees can be given discretion to alter the distribution of benefits from time to time as circumstances change. Most trusts authorize the trustee to invade principal if the income is insufficient for the support of the income beneficiary. Many also allow the trustee to "sprinkle" income among a group of beneficiaries or accumulate it.

1. ***Uniform Statutory Will Act* (#10.35):** A Uniform Statutory Will Act (USWA) provides a form for drafters who wish to create discretionary trusts. A trust gives the testator's spouse the income and allows the trustee to pay the "spouse and issue of the testator amounts of principal the trustee deems advisable" for their "needs for health, education, support or maintenance." USWA § 6(b). This language is typical of a well-drafted trust.

a. If the testator is survived by children under age twenty-three and no spouse, the trustee is to pay income and principal to "one or more of the issue of the testator in amounts the trustee deems advisable" for their support needs. Any unpaid income is added to principal. USWA § 8. A direction to pay all the income to minor children would be inadvisable, since it would have to be paid to a guardian in the child's behalf.

B. Judicial Review of Trustees' Decisions

1. ***"Sole discretion" of trustee* (#10.36):** Although many trusts contain language which seems to make the trustee's decisions final, courts review for an "abuse of discretion" by the trustee.

Example: A trust gave an annuity of $100 a month to the testator's sister "and such additional sums as may be required for any emergency or need in the sole discretion of my trustee." The trustee was surcharged for paying the sister $1,000 a month. This was an abuse of discretion, even though the trustee did not act in bad faith. *Austin v. U.S. Bank of Washington*, 869 P.2d 404 (Wash. App. 1994).

2. ***Deference to trustee* (#10.37):** Courts usually defer to the trustee's decisions.

Example: An order directing a trustee to use principal for a beneficiary was reversed because the appellate court found no abuse of discretion by the trustee in refusing to do so. *Nationsbank of Virginia v. Estate of Grandy*, 450 S.E.2d 140 (Va. 1994).

3. ***Considering beneficiary's other resources* (#10.38):** In *Nationsbank, supra,* the trustee took into account the fact that the beneficiary had property of her own which could satisfy her needs. The trust in USWA § 6, *supra*, expressly allows the trustee to give "reasonable consideration to other resources available to the distributee." Where the instrument is silent on this issue, some courts hold that the trustee should not consider the beneficiary's other resources. *Matter of Estate of Lindgren,* 885 P.2d 1280 (Mont. 1994).

a. In a bypass trust, it is often desirable to have the beneficiary use her own resources first because they will be taxed in her estate at death, whereas the trust assets will not be. However, the beneficiary's estate may not be large enough to incur an estate tax. Also, the beneficiary's assets may not be easily convertible into cash. Thus it is desirable to give the trustee discretion on this point.

b. State welfare benefits may be a resource which a trustee can consider.

Example: A trustee was directed to use income and principal in her discretion for the support of the testator's daughter. The daughter was disabled and living in a nursing home. Nevertheless, the trustee's decision not to pay her anything from the trust was upheld, because "the testator did not intend for the trust funds to be used as a substitute for public assistance." *Lineback v. Stout*, 339 S.E.2d 103 (N.C. App. 1986).

4. ***Station in life*** **(#10.39):** In determining what is "necessary for support," the trustee should take into account the beneficiary's station in life.

   Example: It was an abuse of discretion for a trustee to pay the beneficiary only $700 a month when the settlor was "clearly well to do," lived in a house with eight acres of land, and "had several domestic servants." *Gulf Nat'l Bank v. Sturtevant,* 511 So.2d 936 (Miss. 1987).

5. ***Lack of a standard*** **(#10.40):** If the trust instrument contains no standard like "support" by which to measure the trustee's decisions, judicial review is more limited. *Restatement (Second) of Trusts §* 187, comment d.

C. **Conflict of Interest (#10.41):** If a beneficiary is named trustee or cotrustee of a discretionary trust, some courts do not allow her to make distributions to herself. *First Union Bank v. Cisa,* 361 S.E.2d 615 (S.C. 1987). Usually, however, a trustee's decisions will not be overturned simply because of a conflict of interest, since the settlor would have been aware of the conflict and assumed the trustee would nevertheless act fairly.

   Example: A remainderman was the trustee of a trust which authorized the use of principal for the income beneficiary. The court held that the trustee had not abused her discretion in refusing to invade the principal. *Matter of Damon*, 419 N.Y.S.2d 742 (App. Div. 1979).

1. ***Estate tax consequences*** **(#10.42):** If a trustee can make distributions to herself, the trust assets will be taxable in her estate unless the power is restricted by a standard related to "support or education." Int. Rev. Code § 2041.

   Example: A trustee was to pay himself income and principal as necessary for his "support, welfare, and general happiness." When he died, the trust assets were included in his taxable estate. *Estate of Lille*, 87 T.C. 599 (1986). The problem could have been avoided either by naming a disinterested trustee, such as a bank, or by using a standard like that in USWA § 6, *supra.*

2. ***Income tax consequences*** **(#10.43):** If the trustee can distribute income or principal to herself, she will be taxed on trust income even if it is actually paid to someone else. Int. Rev. Code § 678.

MODIFICATION OF TRUSTS

VI. MODIFICATION OF TRUSTS

A. **Settlor (#10.44):** In most states a settlor can modify a trust only if the power to do so is reserved in the instrument, *see* #5.25, *supra,* or with the consent of all the beneficiaries.

1. ***Consent of all beneficiaries* (#10.45):** In most trusts some beneficiaries are minors, or unborn, or unascertainable and so obtaining their consent is impossible.

   Example: A settlor had a testamentary power of appointment over a trust with a gift in default of appointment to her descendants. She was not allowed to terminate the trust because her descendants were beneficiaries and she did not have their consent. *Cooper v. Trust Company Bank*, 357 S.E.2d 582 (Ga. 1987).

10

2. ***Proof that further children are impossible* (#10.46):** Some courts accept proof that no further beneficiaries will come into being.

   Example: A trust was to end when all the settlor's grandchildren reached thirty. The living grandchildren were thirty and the settlor's children had surgery, rendering further children impossible. The court allowed termination. *Korten v. Chicago City Bank and Trust Co.,* 533 N.E.2d 102 (Ill. App. 1988). *See also Restatement (Second) of Trusts* § 340, comment e.

   a. An argument against this result is that anyone can *adopt* a child.

   b. Even if a person can have no more children, if an interest is given to her "issue," her children are usually capable of producing more issue who are potential beneficiaries.

3. ***"Heirs" of the settlor* (#10.47):** A provision for distribution to the settlor's "heirs" may be construed not to give them an interest but rather to leave the settlor a reversion. *Restatement (Second) of Trusts* § 127, comment b; N.Y.E.P.T.L. § 7-1.9(a). In California, the consent of those heirs "who are reasonably likely to take" suffices to terminate a trust. Cal. Prob. Code § 15404(c).

   Example: If the gift in default of appointment in *Cooper,* #10.45, *supra,* had been to the settlor's "heirs," and she had adult children who would probably be her heirs and who consented, the trust could have been terminated.

4. ***Consent by guardian* (#10.48):** Guardians can consent on behalf of minor or unborn beneficiaries if this is consistent with their fiduciary duty to preserve the ward's property. In Wisconsin a guardian can consent on the basis of a "general family benefit accruing to living members of the beneficiary's family." Wis. Stat. § 701.12(2).

   a. Courts will not overrule a guardian's refusal to consent to a modification if the decision appears rational. *Matter of Schroll*, 297 N.W.2d 282 (Minn. 1980).

   b. Even if a guardian appointed to represent unborn and minor beneficiaries consents to a modification, the guardian cannot consent on behalf of adult contingent beneficiaries who object. *Barber v. Barber*, 837 P.2d 714 (Alaska 1992).

5. ***Partial termination* (#10.49):** If some beneficiaries do not consent, a modification that does not affect them may be possible.

   Example: A trust required payment of an annuity to one beneficiary. All the other beneficiaries wanted to terminate the trust. The court allowed termination, but left enough property in the trust to pay the annuity. *Matter of Boright,* 377 N.W.2d 9 (Minn. 1985).

6. ***Administrative provisions* (#10.50):** Courts distinguish between distributive and administrative provisions. For example, if a trust directs the trustee to retain an asset, a court may order it sold if a change in circumstances makes this necessary. *See* #12.70, *infra.*

B. **Purposes of the Settlor (#10.51):** Even if all the beneficiaries consent, most courts will not modify a trust if the settlor does not agree, *e.g.,* because the settlor is dead, if the purposes of the trust have not been accomplished.

   Example: A trust called for distribution of the assets to the settlor's son when he reached age thirty. The son could not terminate the trust when he reached twenty-four even though he was the only beneficiary. *Claflin v. Claflin,* 20 N.E. 454 (Mass. 1889). Most American states follow the "Claflin rule" established by this case.

   1. ***English rule* (#10.52):** England and a few American states do not follow *Claflin,* on the theory that the wishes of the beneficiaries (if competent) should prevail over those of the settlor.

   2. ***Determination of trust purpose* (#10.53):** A court may find that the purpose of a trust has been accomplished even though the time designated for termination has not arrived.

      a. Extrinsic evidence may show what the purposes of a trust were.

         Example: A settlor created a trust to keep the funds away from her daughter's husband. After the husband died, the daughter was allowed to terminate the trust. *Matter of Harbaugh's Estate,* 646 P.2d 498 (Kan. 1982).

      b. Courts often look to the presence or absence of a spendthrift provision (*see* #11.21, *infra*) in determining whether the settlor's purpose would be defeated by modifying a trust.

         Example: A trust required the payment of an annuity to the settlor's children, and a remainder at their death to named grandchildren. The beneficiaries got an order for the immediate payment of principal to the grandchildren. All the beneficiaries were adults and the trust had no spendthrift provision. *In re Trust of Lane*, 592 A.2d 492 (Md. 1991). *Compare Mahan v. Mahan,* 577 A.2d 70 (Md. 1990) (modification of a spendthrift trust by consent of all beneficiaries was ineffective).

3. ***Position of the trustee* (#10.54):** A trustee's interest in collecting fees is not a valid reason for refusing to terminate a trust. However, the trustee has standing to appeal if a lower court orders the trust terminated.

4. ***Settlements* (#10.55):** Will contests and other controversies involving estates are often settled by an agreement which calls for a different distribution from that provided in a will. UPC § 3-1101 authorizes such settlements even if the effect is to modify a spendthrift trust.

5. ***Small trusts* (#10.56):** A small trust is uneconomical if there is a professional trustee. Some statutes allow small trusts to be terminated with immediate distribution to the beneficiaries. *E.g.*, Cal. Prob. Code § 15408.

VIII. CHARITABLE TRUSTS

A. **Special Rules (#10.57):** The rules governing charitable trusts differ somewhat from those applicable to private trusts. Private trusts must have definite beneficiaries, but since charitable trusts serve the public interest, they can be enforced by the attorney general. There are special exceptions in the Rule Against Perpetuities for charitable trusts. Charitable trusts qualify for deductions under the estate and gift tax and the income tax.

B. **Definition of "Charitable" (#10.58):** Charitable purposes include the relief of poverty, advancement of education, religion, health, governmental, and "other purposes... beneficial to the community." *Restatement (Second) of Trusts* § 368.

1. ***Eccentric ideas* (#10.59):** Courts treat a trust as charitable even if they do not agree with the settlor's objectives, unless the scheme is too eccentric.

   Examples: A trust to publish the settlor's book was held to be charitable despite testimony that the book was "without aesthetic merit." *Rosser v. Prem,* 449 A.2d 461 (Md. App. 1982). On the other hand, an English court held that a trust created by George Bernard Shaw to reform the alphabet to make it phonetic was not charitable. *In Re Shaw,* [1957] 1 All E.R. 745.

2. ***Limited beneficiaries* (#10.60):** A trust may be charitable even though the benefits are confined to a small group, but not if the group is *too* small, such as a trust for the education of the settlor's descendants.

   a. The beneficiaries may be limited to members of one sex or religion, such as a rest home "for Christian women." *Zahn's Estate,* 93 Cal. Rptr. 810 (Cal. App. 1971). But in *In re Certain Scholarship Funds*, 575 A.2d 1325 (N.H. 1990) a limitation in a trust for scholarships to "Protestant boys" was removed as contrary to state policy.

   b. Racial restrictions are valid as a matter of trust law, but if a governmental institution serves as trustee, a racial restriction is invalid as a denial of equal protection under the Fourteenth Amendment.

Example: A testator left land to a city to use as a park for white people only. This was held unconstitutional. *Evans v. Newton,* 382 U.S. 296 (1966).

c. Racially restrictive trusts are denied a charitable deduction for tax purposes. *Bob Jones University v. United States,* 461 U.S. 574 (1983).

3. ***Political causes* (#10.61):** A trust to promote a change in the law is charitable, but not one to support a political party. *Restatement (Second) of Trusts* § 374, comments j, k.

4. ***Profit-making* (#10.62):** Even an institution devoted to health or education is not charitable if it makes a profit, unless the profits are devoted to charity. Charging fees for services does not disqualify a charity, however. *Restatement (Second) of Trusts* § 376.

5. ***"Benevolence"* (#10.63):** A famous old case held that a trust for "benevolent" purposes was broader than charitable and hence invalid. *Morice v. Bishop of Durham,* 32 E.R. 656 (1805). However, modern cases tend to treat "benevolent" as synonymous with charitable. *Wilson v. Flowers,* 277 A.2d 199 (N.J. 1971).

6. ***Mixed trusts* (#10.64):** When a trust designates charitable purposes along with others, courts may cut out the noncharitable purpose in order to save the trust.

   Example: A trust for "worthy charities, institutions, and individuals" was construed to be a charitable trust. In case of doubt, a construction should be chosen which validates the will. *Newick v. Mason*, 581 A.2d 1269 (Me. 1990).

7. ***Honorary trusts* (#10.65):** Even if a trust is not charitable, it may be valid as an "honorary" trust. This means that the trustee may carry out the trust terms. If the trustee fails to do so, there is a resulting trust for the settlor's estate. *Restatement (Second) of Trusts* § 124. Typical examples are trusts to maintain a tomb or to care for a pet.

   a. Honorary trusts often run afoul of the Rule Against Perpetuities, since they do not qualify for the exemption for charities. However, UPC § 2-907 (1990) validates trusts for pets, and many jurisdictions have special statutes allowing limited amounts to be maintained for the upkeep of tombs.

C. Standing to Enforce

1. ***Attorney General* (#10.66):** The state attorney general can enforce a charitable trust, even when established charitable institutions are designated as beneficiaries.

   Example: A suit over the fees charged by the attorney for an estate left to charities was settled by the designated charities. The attorney general was allowed to challenge the settlement on appeal. *Estate of Laas,* 525 N.E.2d 1089 (Ill. App. 1988).

2. ***Donor* (#10.67):** Settlors have no standing to enforce the trust.

 Example: A suit by Howard Hughes's administrator involving a charitable foundation created by Hughes was dismissed on the ground that only the attorney general had standing. *Wier v. Howard Hughes Medical Institute,* 407 A.2d 1051 (Del. Ch. 1979).

 a. However, the settlor (or her successor) can sue to recover trust assets if a charitable trust fails. *Evans v. Abney,* 396 U.S. 435 (1970).

3. ***Cotrustee* (#10.68):** A cotrustee can sue to challenge actions by the other trustees. *Takabuk v. Ching,* 695 P.2d 319 (Haw. 1985).

4. ***Other persons* (#10.69):** Other persons are usually denied standing to sue on the ground that this would open the doors to vexatious litigation. *Restatement (Second) of Trusts* § 391. However, persons with a "special interest" in the trust have been allowed to sue. The meaning of "special interest" is unclear.

 Example: Land was given to a village "for public purposes." When the village proposed to sell the land, neighbors were permitted to sue to stop this, even though the attorney general had approved the sale. *Matter of Village of Mount Prospect,* 522 N.E.2d 122 (Ill. App. 1988).

 a. Any private person can bring suit in the name of the attorney general, but the attorney general has control over the conduct of the suit. *Restatement (Second) of Trusts* § 391, comment a.

 b. Many have argued that the rules about standing should be liberalized because the attorney general is so busy that many violations of charitable trusts are overlooked.

D. Restrictions in Charitable Gifts (#10.70): Restrictions in charitable gifts are enforceable, whether or not the gift is in trust. *Restatement (Second) of Trusts* § 348, comment f.

1. **Cy pres (#10.71):** Courts remove restrictions in a charitable gift which have become impracticable. This doctrine is known as *cy pres,* from the French *si près,* meaning "as near," because the court seeks to stay as near as possible to the settlor's intent when it alters the terms of the trust.

 Example: A will left $150,000 to erect a hospital for tuberculosis patients. This was insufficient to build a hospital, and moreover tuberculosis today is usually treated on an outpatient basis. The court modified the trust but refused to allow the money to be used for the treatment of other diseases. *Matter of Estate of Craig,* 848 P.2d 313 (Ariz. App. 1992).

a. *Cy pres* has also been used when money is left to a charitable organization which has gone out of existence, or when the designated purpose has been accomplished.

   Example: When a will left money to promote the abolition of slavery, the money was applied *cy pres* after the Thirteenth Amendment was enacted. *Jackson v. Phillips,* 96 Mass. 539 (1867).

b. Courts refuse to alter the terms of a trust simply because they think they can improve on the settlor's scheme.

   Example: A charitable trust was created to provide scholarships for students. The students had to be chosen from specified high schools on a rotating basis. Members of the family of a school board member were excluded. The trustee sought to remove these limitations under *cy pres*, but the court refused because there was no showing that they frustrated the purpose of the trust. *Matter of Estate of Murdock*, 884 P.2d 749 (Kan. App. 1994).

c. Even if the result is a failure of the gift, courts do not apply *cy pres* unless the settlor had a "general" charitable intent, as distinguished from an intent to benefit a particular entity.

   Example: Money was raised to finance a bone marrow transplant, but the patient died before the operation could be performed. A claim for the funds by the Leukemia Foundation was rejected, and the funds were returned to the donors. Their intention had been just to benefit the particular patient. *Matter of Gonzales*, 621 A.2d 94 (N.J. Super. 1992)

d. In some cases, but not in others, a transferee of a charity to which property is devised will take the devise.

   Examples: A will left money to the Lutheran Orphan Home, which ceased to operate and transferred its assets to Lutheran Family and Childrens Services. The transferee did not get the devise. *In re Estate of Beck*, 649 N.E.2d 1011 (Ill. App. 1995). But a devise to provide scholarships for students at the "Academy of Our Lady" passed to a school into which the Academy merged. *Colgan v. Sisters of St. Joseph*, 604 N.E.2d 989 (Ill. App. 1992).

e. Courts are more willing to apply *cy pres* if a trust has been in existence for a long time, since in this case the settlor's successors have only a remote connection with the settlor. *Restatement (Second) of Trusts* § 399, comment i. A famous example is a trust established under the will of Benjamin Franklin in 1790 which lasted 200 years and was often modified under *cy pres.*

f. In most states, application of *cy pres* does not require the settlor's consent. *Restatement (Second) of Trusts* § 399, comment g. Under the Uniform Management of Institutional Funds Act § 7 (adopted in about half the states), the settlor's consent alone suffices to remove any restriction in a charitable trust.

g. Courts are not bound to follow the views of the trustee or of the attorney general in applying *cy pres*. Trustees should not deviate from the terms of the trust under *cy pres* without court approval.

Notes

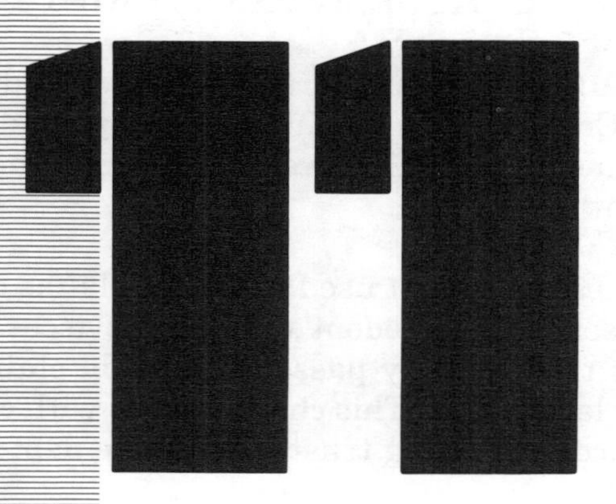

RIGHTS OF CREDITORS; SPENDTHRIFT TRUSTS

CHAPTER SUMMARY

I.	Fraudulent Conveyances	11-2
II.	Joint Tenancy	11-2
III.	Insurance	11-4
IV.	Trusts	11-5
V.	Spendthrift Provisions	11-6
VI.	Claims against Probate Estate	11-9
VII.	Liability of Beneficiaries, Heirs and Devisees	11-12

RIGHTS OF CREDITORS; SPENDTHRIFT TRUSTS

INTRODUCTION: A transfer of property may affect creditors of both the transferee and the transferor. Creditors can reach all property which the debtor owns, but not property owned by someone else. However, creditors of the donor may be able to attack a gift as a fraudulent conveyance.

A decedent's probate estate is first used to satisfy claims of the decedent's creditors. Only what is left passes to the decedent's heirs or devisees. Property which is not in the probate estate has traditionally passed free from claims, but this has been changed in many states by legislation. This chapter deals with creditors' rights against joint tenancy, life insurance, and living trusts, while the debtor is alive and after he dies.

Donors often want to give property in a form which will make it exempt from claims by creditors of the donee. A spendthrift trust is commonly used for this purpose. Similar protection is provided for pensions, Social Security, and insurance by both federal and state legislation.

The matters covered in this chapter are discussed in greater detail in McGovern, Kurtz, and Rein, *Wills, Trusts, and Estates,* 339–53, 366–68 (1988).

FRAUDULENT CONVEY-ANCES

I. FRAUDULENT CONVEYANCES (#11.1)

A. Creditors of a donor can set aside a gift if it is fraudulent as to them. A conveyance which renders the conveyor insolvent is fraudulent without regard to intent.

Example: A mother conveyed land to her daughter. A creditor of the mother was allowed to attack it as fraudulent. Transfers for consideration are excepted, but the defendant had the burden of proving that the transfer was for consideration. *Cardiovascular & Thoracic Surgery v. DiMazzio,* 524 N.E.2d 162 (Ohio App. 1987).

There is a Uniform Fraudulent Transfer Act. The common law is substantially similar. Trustees in bankruptcy can also challenge fraudulent conveyances under federal law.

JOINT TENANCY

II. JOINT TENANCY

A. While Parties Are Alive

1. ***Bank accounts; contributions test* (#11.2):** UPC § 6-211 presumes that joint bank accounts belong to the parties in proportion to the amounts each has contributed. Courts generally apply this rule even without a statute.

   Example: A son put his mother's name on a bank account, but he was the sole contributor. A creditor of the mother was not allowed to reach the account because she had no ownership interest in it. *Yakima Adjustment*

Service, Inc. v. Durand, 622 P.2d 408 (Wash. App. 1981). Creditors of the son, on the other hand, could have levied on the entire account.

a. UPC § 6-211 allows "clear and convincing evidence of a different intent." Thus, if the son had intended to make a gift to his mother, she would be deemed an owner even though she had contributed nothing.

b. Some courts presume that all the money in the account belongs to the debtor unless there is evidence to the contrary. *Traders Travel Int'l, Inc. v. Howser,* 753 P.2d 244 (Haw. 1988). UPC § 6-211(b) presumes that the contributions are equal if the parties are married to each other.

11

2. ***Land* (#11.3):** When land is put into joint tenancy, a gift to the noncontributing party is usually presumed. *See* #5.40, *supra.* Creditors of either party can reach their debtor's interest.

Example: A mother bought land, taking title in the name of herself and her two sons. A creditor of one of the sons was allowed to reach his interest. *Remax of Blue Springs v. Vajda & Co. Inc.,* 708 S.W.2d 804 (Mo. App. 1986). The result would be different if the proof showed that no gift was intended and so the son held in trust for his mother. *See* #6.63, *supra*.

3. ***Tenancy by the entireties* (#11.4):** If the tenants are married to each other, in many states they hold the land as tenants by the entirety, and creditors of one spouse cannot reach it while both spouses are alive.

B. After Tenant Dies

1. ***Common law* (#11.5):** At common law, creditors of a deceased joint tenant cannot reach the property to satisfy their claims.

Example: A federal statute allowed states which had furnished Medicaid assistance to get reimbursement from the recipient's "estate" after he died. This did not include property that was in joint tenancy, since this was not part of the estate. *Citizens Action League v. Kitzer*, 887 F.2d 1003 (9th Cir. 1989), cert. den., 110 S.Ct. 1524 (1990).

a. A mortgage by one joint tenant may sever the tenancy (*See* #5.41, *supra*) so that the mortgagee's interest survives the death of the mortgagor. *Hutchinson Nat'l Bank & Trust Co. v. Brown,* 753 P.2d 1299 (Kan. 1988). *But see Kalk v. Security Pacific Bank Washington,* 894 P.2d 559 (Wash. 1995) (pledge to bank by joint tenant ineffective after pledgor's death).

2. ***UPC § 6-215* (#11.6):** The UPC allows creditors of the owner of a joint bank account to reach it after the debtor dies if the debtor's probate estate is insufficient to satisfy claims.

INSURANCE

III. INSURANCE

A. **Creditors of the Insured (#11.7):** In many states, life insurance policies are totally or partially exempt from claims by creditors of the insured, both during life and after the insured dies.

Example: *H* was insured under a policy which named *W* as beneficiary. A creditor sought to reach the policy. During the proceedings, *H* died. The creditor failed because by statute insurance payable to a spouse or dependent relative was exempt from claims. *Dock v. Tuchman,* 497 N.E.2d 945 (Ind. App. 1986).

1. ***Bankruptcy*** **(#11.8):** Bankruptcy Code § 522(d)(8) has a limited exemption of insurance for debtors in bankruptcy, but they can elect the more liberal exemptions which are often provided by state law.

2. ***Probate estate*** **(#11.9):** The insurance exemption is lost when the proceeds are paid to the insured's probate estate.

   Example: A wife was the beneficiary of insurance on her husband's life. She murdered him and so was disqualified from getting the proceeds. *See* ???, *supra.* Because he had designated no alternate beneficiary, the proceeds were payable to the husband's estate and became available to his creditors. *Estate of Chiesi v. First Citizens Bank*, 613 N.E.2d 14 (Ind. 1993).

3. ***Divorce settlements*** **(#11.10):** Promises are often made in a divorce settlement that a spouse or child will be the beneficiary of an insurance policy. These promises may be enforced despite the exemption of insurance from general creditors.

   Example: In a divorce settlement, *H* promised to maintain his children as beneficiaries of his insurance. Nevertheless, he named his new wife as beneficiary. She was held to take the proceeds under a constructive trust for the children even though she was unaware of her husband's obligation. *Perkins v. Stuemke,* 585 N.E.2d 1125 (Ill. App. 1992).

   a. If the insurance was issued to an employee of the federal government under a special policy controlled by statute, the exemption from creditors' claims applies even in cases like *Perkins*, supra. *Dean v. Johnson,* 881 F.2d 948 (10th Cir. 1989).

B. **Creditors of Beneficiary (#11.11):** Most state exemption statutes do not apply to creditors of a beneficiary.

Example: The designated beneficiary of an insurance policy was bankrupt when the insured died. The proceeds were not exempt because the relevant state statute only covered creditors of the insured. *Matter of Heins,* 83 B.R. 504 (S.D. Ohio 1988).

1. ***Bankruptcy* (#11.12):** However, if the beneficiary was a dependent of the insured, Bankruptcy Code § 522(d)(11) exempts the proceeds to the extent that they are "reasonably necessary for the support of the debtor."

IV. TRUSTS

TRUSTS

A. Creditors of the Settlor (#11.13): The creation of a trust may be subject to attack as a fraudulent conveyance. *See* #11.1, *supra; Territorial Sav. & Loan Ass'n v. Baird,* 781 P.2d 452 (Utah App. 1989) Creditors of the settlor may have other rights against the trust assets as well.

1. ***Settlor's interest* (#11.14):** If the settlor retains an interest, such as a right to the income, creditors can reach this interest.

2. ***Discretionary trust* (#11.15):** Even if the trustee has discretion over distributions to the settlor, her creditors may be able to reach the trust.

   Example: By the terms of a trust, the trustee had discretion to use income and principal for the support of the settlor. Creditors of the settlor were allowed to reach the trust. *State v. Hawes*, 564 N.Y.S.2d 637 (App. Div. 1991).

3. ***Revocable trust* (#11.16):** If the settlor only has a power to revoke the trust, his creditors cannot reach the assets according to *Restatement (Second) of Trusts* § 330, comment o (1959). However, many states have changed this rule by statute. In California, for example, creditors of the settlor of a revocable trust can reach the trust assets while the settlor is alive and after he dies. Calif. Prob. Code §§ 18200, 19001.

4. ***Who is the settlor?* (#11.17):** A person may be deemed to be the settlor of a trust even if it was technically created by another.

   Examples: A father created a trust for his son which was to terminate in 1988 unless the son elected to extend it. When the son did so, he was deemed to be the settlor thereafter. *Hartsfield v. Lescher*, 721 F.Supp 1052 (E.D. Ark. 1989). Money received in settlement of a child's tort claim was put into a trust. The child's guardian claimed he was the settlor, but the court held that the child was the settlor. *Forsyth v. Rowe*, 629 A.2d 379 (Conn. 1993). *But see Kegel v. State,* 830 P.2d 563 (N.M. App. 1992).

B. Creditors of Beneficiaries

1. ***Remedies* (#11.18):** Creditors of a trust beneficiary can get an order directed to the trustee to pay their claims from the beneficiary's interest as it falls due, *e.g.,* as the income is payable. Alternatively, courts may order a sale of the beneficiary's interest use the sale proceeds to satisfy claims unless the interest "is so indefinite or contingent that it cannot be sold with fairness" because no buyer would pay an adequate price. *Restatement (Second) of Trusts* § 162.

Example: Under a trust, income is payable to *A* for life, remainder at *A*'s death to her issue. A court might order a sale of *A*'s income interest for the benefit of *A*'s creditors to expedite payment of their claims but might refuse to order a sale of the interest of *A*'s grandchild, whose interest might be worthless, *e.g.*, if his parent (*A*'s child) survived *A*. *See* #2.1, *supra*.

2. ***Discretionary trusts* (#11.19):** If the trustee has discretion whether or not to make payments to the debtor, the debtor is often held to have no interest in the trust which his creditors can reach (unless the debtor is the settlor of the trust — *see* #11.15, *supra*). But the trustee cannot make payments to the debtor after being served with process in a suit by the creditor. *Restatement (Second) of Trusts § 155; Wilcox v. Gentry,* 867 P.2d 781 (Kan. 1994).

   a. If the trustee is directed to use income or principal for the support of a beneficiary, creditors who have supplied the beneficiary with support can get reimbursement from the trust on the theory that it would be an abuse of discretion for the trustee not to pay. *Button by Curio v. Elmhurst Nat. Bank*, 522 N.E.2d 1368 (Ill. App. 1988).

   b. This creates a distinction between "support" and "discretionary" trusts which ishard to apply in many cases. *E.g., Chenot v. Bordeleau,* 561 A.2d 891 (R.I. 1989) (trustee had "sole discretion" to use income and principal to support beneficiary).

3. ***Statutory spendthrift trusts* (#11.20):** In some states, creditors' rights are limited by a statute which makes all trusts spendthrift trusts. *E.g.*, Rev. Code Wash. § 6.32.250. As to spendthrift trusts, *see* #11.21*, et seq., infra.*

SPENDTHRIFT PROVISIONS

V. SPENDTHRIFT PROVISIONS

A. Validity (#11.21): In most states the settlor of a trust can include a provision which restricts creditors of beneficiaries from reaching their interest. Such trusts are called "spendthrift" trusts, although this word is not used in the trust instrument.

Example: "No interest in the principal or income of this trust shall be assigned, or encumbered, or subject to any creditor's claim prior to its actual receipt by the beneficiary."

1. ***History* (#11.22):** Spendthrift trusts were first held valid by American courts in the latter part of the nineteenth century. England does not allow them. A few American states follow the English view, but their number is diminishing. Rhode Island, for example, once rejected spendthrift trusts but now allows them. R.I. Gen. Laws § 18-9.1-1.

2. ***Protective trusts* (#11.23):** England allows "protective trusts" under which a beneficiary's interest is forfeited if his creditors try to reach it. This provision defeats creditors but does not allow the beneficiary to enjoy benefits from a trust while his creditors remain unpaid.

3. ***Statutory limits* (#11.24):** In some states, creditors can reach the income of a spendthrift trust to the extent that it exceeds the amount "necessary for the education and support of the beneficiary." *E.g.,* Calif. Prob. Code § 15307. Many states, however, do not limit the amount which can be put under a spendthrift provision.

4. ***Bankruptcy* (#11.25):** Bankruptcy Code § 541(c) makes spendthrift trusts effective in bankruptcy if they are valid under the law of the relevant state.

5. ***Principal* (#11.26):** In a few states, spendthrift provisions are valid as to income, but not as to principal. In most states, however, they are valid as to both. *Restatement (Second) of Trusts* § 153(1).

B. **Legal Interests (#11.27):** Traditionally, restraints on the alienation of a legal interest were invalid. Spendthrift trusts are distinguishable because the restraint is imposed on an equitable interest. Property is not "tied up" because the trustee can sell the assets and reinvest the proceeds. This is also true of assets held in a pension plan, even if it is not strictly a trust.

1. ***Pensions* (#11.28):** The Federal Employee Retirement Income Security Act of 1974 (ERISA), which covers most pensions, makes benefits under the plan unassignable. Social Security benefits are also unassignable by statute. In fact, these statutes impose greater limits on creditors than a spendthrift trust.

C. **After Payment**

1. ***Income* (#11.29):** Creditors can reach money from a spendthrift trust after it has been distributed to the beneficiary. In this respect, spendthrift trusts differ from Social Security payments.

   Example: A creditor could garnish money in a bank account which contained money received from the debtor's pension, but not deposits from Social Security. The pension was like a spendthrift trust, whereas the Social Security Act was more protective. *Brosamer v. Mark,* 561 N.E.2d 767 (Ind. 1990).

2. ***Principal* (#11.30):** When principal becomes payable, creditors can reach it, even before it is distributed to the beneficiary.

   Example: A spendthrift trust gave each child of the settlor a share of the principal when they reached age forty. Creditors were allowed to reach the share as soon as a child reached forty even though it had not yet been distributed. *Brent v. State Cent. Collection Unit*, 537 A.2d 227 (Md. 1988).

D. **Alimony and Child Support (#11.31):** In most states, claims for alimony and child support can be satisfied from a spendthrift trust.

Rationale: This exception is sometimes said to rest on the settlor's intent and sometimes on public policy because otherwise these claimants might burden state welfare programs. Also, unlike ordinary creditors, children claiming support have not voluntarily extended credit to the beneficiary. *Council* v. *Owens,* 770 S.W.2d 193 (Ark. 1989).

1. ***Court discretion* (#11.32):** The court can order such claims to be only partially satisfied from the trust in order to assure the beneficiary's own support. *Restatement (Second) of Trusts* § 157, comment b.

2. ***Pensions* (#11.33):** Statutes which exempt pensions from claims usually provide a comparable exception for alimony and child support. *E.g., Albertson v. Ryder*, 621 N.E.2d 480 (Ohio App. 1993) (proper to order child support payments from an ERISA plan).

E. Necessaries (#11.34): Creditors who have supplied necessaries to a beneficiary can get reimbursement from the trust despite a spendthrift provision. Otherwise they might refuse to supply the beneficiary, and this would be contrary to the settlor's wishes. *Restatement (Second) of Trusts* § 157(b); *Sisters of Mercy Health v. First Bank*, 624 N.E.2d 520 (Ind. App. 1993) (health care).

F. Tort Claims (#11.35): Commentators have argued that tort claimants should be able to reach a spendthrift trust since they did not voluntarily extend credit to the beneficiary. However, ERISA makes no exception for tort claims. *Ellis Nat'l Bank v. Irving Trust Co.,* 786 F.2d 466 (2d Cir. 1986).

G. Breach of Trust (#11.36): If a beneficiary is also a trustee and commits a breach of trust, his interest in the trust can be reached to satisfy claims of the trust against him despite a spendthrift provision on the theory that the settlor would probably have sointended. *Restatement (Second) of Trusts §* 257, comment f.

1. ***Pensions* (#11.37):** A similar attempt to reach pension benefits of the trustee of a pension plan who had embezzled money from the plan was rejected in *Guidry v. Sheet Metal Workers Nat. Pen. Fund,* 493 U.S. 365 (1990).

H. Taxes (#11.38): Claims by state and federal governments for taxes can be asserted against a beneficiary's interest in a trust despite a spendthrift provision. *Restatement (Second) of Trusts* § 157(d).

I. Self-settled Trusts (#11.39): Spendthrift provisions are invalid with respect to any interest reserved by the settlor of the trust. *Restatement (Second) of Trusts* § 156.

Example: A person settled a personal injury claim by getting an annuity which provided that it could not be reached by process. Nevertheless, a creditor of the annuitant was allowed to garnish it, because this was equivalent to a self-created spendthrift trust. *Wilson v. Dixon*, 598 N.E.2d 158 (Ohio App. 1991). As to who is deemed to be the settlor of a trust, *see* #11.17, *supra.*

1. ***Insurance and pensions* (#11.40):** The treatment of self-settled trusts is anomalous, since most states exempt insurance even when the debtor paid

for it. *See* #11.7, *supra*. This is also true of pensions, for which employees generally pay directly or indirectly.

Example: An Individual Retirement Account was not subject to garnishment under a state statute even though it was created by the debtor. A statute barring spendthrift trusts for the settlor did not apply. *Greening Donald v. Okl. Wire Rope Prod.,* 766 P.2d 970 (Okl. 1988).

J. Voluntary Transfers (#11.41): Most spendthrift provisions also bar the beneficiary from alienating her interest voluntarily.

Example: A spendthrift trust gave the income to the settlor's daughter for life, the remainder to her sons. One of the sons assigned his interest in the remainder while the daughter was alive. The assignment was ineffective because of the spendthrift provision. *Knight v. Knight*, 589 N.Y.S.2d 195 (App. Div. 1992).

1. ***Disclaimer* (#11.42):** Under UPC § 2-801 and many other statutes a disclaimer is effective despite a spendthrift provision. As to disclaimers, *see* #2.104, *et seq., supra.*

2. ***Effect of assignment* (#11.43):** The assignment of an "unassignable" interest is not without effect; the trustee can honor it by distributing income to the assignee, but the assignor can revoke the assignment. A contract to assign the interest is enforceable. *Restatement (Second) of Trusts* § 152, comments i, k.

VI. CLAIMS AGAINST PROBATE ESTATE

CLAIMS AGAINST PROBATE ESTATE

A. Survival (#11.44): Most claims survive death and can be asserted against the debtor's estate, or by the estate of the creditor. There are a few exceptions to this rule.

1. ***Punitive damages* (#11.45):** In many states, claims for punitive damages do notsurvive the death of either the tortfeasor or the victim. *Doe v. Colligan,* 753 P.2d 144 (Alaska 1988).

2. ***Personal contracts* (#11.46):** Some contracts do not survive death. For example, if an employee dies during the term of employment, her estate is not liable for damages. *Restatement (Second) of Contracts* § 262.

B. Insolvent Estates (#11.47): If an estate does not have enough assets to pay all claims, the personal representative must pay claims in a prescribed order. For example, under UPC § 3-805 expenses of administration are paid first, then funeral expenses, etc. Claims within each class are paid pro rata.

C. Statute of Limitations (#11.48): When a debtor dies, the creditors have no one they can sue until administration of the estate begins. Therefore, UPC § 3-802 suspends statutes of limitations for four months following the decedent's death.

D. Nonclaim Statutes (#11.49): Creditors must file claims against an estate promptly. For example, under UPC § 3-801, a personal representative can publish a notice to creditors "to present their claims within four months... or be forever barred."

1. ***Notice* (#11.50):** Notice by publication is insufficient under the Constitution to bar claims which are "reasonably ascertainable" by the personal representative. *Tulsa Professional Collection Services, Inc. v. Pope,* 485 U.S. 478 (1988). Therefore, UPC § 3-801(b) also authorizes the personal representative to notify creditors by mail.

   a. A creditor whom the personal representative did not discover despite a diligent search is barred even though he received no notice. *In re Estate of Thompson*, 484 N.W.2d 258 (Minn. App. 1992). So is a creditor who had actual knowledge of the estate proceedings, even if he received no formal notice of them. *Venturi v. Taylor,* 41 Cal. Rptr. 2d 272 (Cal. App. 1995).

   b. Even if a claimant received no notice, the claim must be filed within a year of the decedent's death. UPC § 3-803(a)(1); *Matter of Estate of Dire*, 851 P.2d 271 (Colo. App. 1993).

2. ***Comparison with statute of limitations* (#11.51):** Nonclaim statutes differ from statutes of limitations. The statute of limitations on a debt does not start to run until it is due, but claims which are not yet due can be barred under a nonclaim statute. UPC § 3-803(a).

   a. Statutes of limitations are usually longer for contracts than for torts, but the nonclaim statutes apply the same limit to both.

   b. To satisfy the statute of limitations, the plaintiff must file a complaint, but sending a statement to the personal representative satisfies UPC § 3-804. Perhaps for this reason, provisions tolling statutes of limitations often do not extend to nonclaim limitations. *In re Estate of Allen*, 843 P.2d 781 (Mont. 1992) (claimant in prison).

3. ***Purpose* (#11.52):** Nonclaim statutes are designed to let personal representatives know the total amount of claims against the estate so they can pay them and distribute the balance of the estate promptly to the heirs and devisees.

4. ***Claims to property* (#11.53):** Nonclaim statutes do not apply to claims to property.

   Example: A claim that property had been fraudulently conveyed to the decedent was allowed even though the claim was not filed in time. *Gorham State Bank v. Seliens,* 772 P.2d 793 (Kan. 1989).

   a. Claims secured by a mortgage need not be presented unless the mortgagee wishes to reach other assets of the debtor because the mortgage is insufficient.

5. ***Governmental claims* (#11.54):** Statutes differ as to whether claims by the state are covered. Claims by the federal government are not affected by state nonclaim statutes.

6. ***Insurance* (#11.55):** UPC § 3-803(d), like many statutes, excepts claims covered by liability insurance since they do not deplete the assets of the estate.

7. ***Set-off* (#11.56):** In most states a claim which is not filed in time can still be used as a set-off against claims asserted by the estate. *Estate of Ruehl v. Ruehl*, 623 N.E.2d 741 (Ohio Prob. 1993).

8. ***Bequests* (#11.57):** Bequests are not subject to the nonclaim statutes, but a general direction in the will to pay debts does not make debts bequests for this purpose.

9. ***Contingent claims* (#11.58):** Even contingent claims, like a guarantee of another's debt, must be filed under most statutes. UPC § 3-803. The claimant may be paid its present value from the assets of the estate "taking any uncertainty into account," or an arrangement may be made for future payment, such as getting a bond from the distributees to assure payment if the claim becomes due after the estate is distributed. UPC § 3-810.

E. Liability for Improper Payment (#11.59): A personal representative may be surcharged for paying an invalid claim or for ignoring the established priorities.

1. ***Court approval* (#11.60):** Some states require that claims be allowed by the court before they can be paid, but UPC § 3-807 permits personal representatives to "pay any just claim which has not been barred, with or without formal presentation."

   Example: An administrator was surcharged for claims he paid which were not filed in time under the nonclaim statute, but not for those paid before the nonclaim period expired, even though the claims had not been formally presented. *Estate of Sturm*, 246 Cal. Rptr. 852 (Cal. App. 1988).

2. ***Charitable pledges* (#11.61):** UPC § 3-715(4) allows personal representatives to satisfy written charitable pledges of the decedent even if they are not "binding obligations...in the judgment of the personal representative the decedent would have wanted the pledges completed."

F. Claims Arising during Administration

1. ***Common law* (#11.62):** At common law, personal representatives are personally liable on contracts they make on behalf of the estate. The same applies to torts and to trustees.

a. Fiduciaries can get reimbursement from the estate or trust for this liability if they were acting properly when they incurred the liability.

Example: A trustee employed a manager for a farm held by the trust. Persons injured by a truck driven by the manager recovered a judgment against the trustee, but he was allowed to use trust assets to satisfy it. *Cook v. Holland,* 575 S.W.2d 4 (Ky. App. 1978). This right of reimbursement may be inadequate if the claim exceeds the trust assets, but the trustee can get protection by insurance.

b. Claimants can reach the trust assets via the trustee's right of reimbursement but this right is limited by any liability the trustee has to the trust. *Restatement (Second) Trusts* § 268.

2. ***Statutes*** **(#11.63)**: Many statutes treat personal representatives and trustees like agents who are not personally liable on contracts which they make on behalf of the principal. Under UPC § 7-306, "a trustee is not personally liable on contracts properly entered in his fiduciary capacity...unless he fails to reveal his representative capacity and identify the trust estate in the contract." A similar rule applies to personal representatives (3-808) and to conservators (5-428).

a. Personal representatives, trustees, and conservators are not liable for torts committed in the course of administration unless they are "personally at fault." UPC §§ 3-808(b), 5-428(b), 7-306(b).

b. Such claims can be asserted directly against the trust or estate. UPC §§ 7-306(c), 3-808(c), 5-428(c).

LIABILITY OF BENEFICIARIES, HEIRS, AND DEVISEES

VII. LIABILITY OF BENEFICIARIES, HEIRS, AND DEVISEES

A. **Trusts (#11.64):** Beneficiaries of a trust are not personally liable on contracts or torts of the trustee. *Restatement (Second) of Trusts* § 275-276. In this respect trustees differ from agents.

B. **Estates (#11.65):** Heirs and devisees are not personally liable on claims against a decedent, unless they have agreed to assume such liability in order to avoid administration.

1. ***UPC*** **(#11.66):** UPC §§ 3-312 et. seq. allow the heirs of an intestate or residuary devisees of a testator to accept the estate assets without administration by assuming responsibility for discharging claims. This system is common in the civil law. Similarly, Cal. Prob. Code § 13500 allows a decedent's surviving spouse to take property without administration. A spouse who invokes this procedure becomes liable for the decedent's debts to the extent of the property received from the decedent.

PROBATE AND ADMINISTRATION

CHAPTER SUMMARY

I.	Probate	12-2
II.	Necessity for Administration	12-5
III.	Ancillary Administration	12-6
IV.	Choice of Fiduciary	12-6
V.	Fees and Other Costs	12-10
VI.	Sales by Fiduciaries	12-13
VII.	Investments	12-14
VIII.	Self-dealing	12-17
IX.	Remedies against Fiduciaries	12-19
X.	Allocations between Principal and Income	12-22
XI.	Distribution	12-24

PROBATE AND ADMINISTRATION

INTRODUCTION: A will must be "probated" in order to be effective, *i.e.,* its validity must be proved in a special court which in most states is called the probate court (from the Latin *probare*, to prove). This is a relatively summary procedure, often occurring without notice. Therefore, most states allow a will to be contested even after it is admitted to probate. The first part of this chapter deals with procedural questions raised by probate and will contests.

An estate must be administered, whether or not the decedent left a will. Since administration is supervised by the probate court, the term probate is often used to cover administration, even though administration of an intestate estate does not involve any probate, strictly speaking. The balance of this chapter deals with administration.

This chapter also covers administration of trusts. Many people today avoid probate through the use of living trusts. However, even the administration of a living trust may involve court proceedings, *e.g.,* if a beneficiary seeks to have the trustee removed or surcharged for improper conduct, such as an imprudent sale or investment. Since the rules governing trustees, executors, and other fiduciaries are similar, they are treated together here.

PROBATE

I. PROBATE

A. *Ante-mortem* Probate (#12.1): It is easier to determine a testator's capacity and freedom from undue influence while she is still alive. Nevertheless, most states do not allow actions for a declaratory judgment as to the validity of a will while the testator is alive because the judgment would become moot if the testator later revoked the will or died without an estate.

Example: A judgment declaring wills executed by living conservatees were invalid for incapacity was reversed; since the testators were still living, the court had no jurisdiction. *In re Conservatorship of Bookasta*, 265 Cal. Rptr. 1 (Cal. App. 1989).

1. ***Exceptions* (#12.2):** A few states provide for *ante-mortem* probate. *E.g.,* Ohio Rev. Code § 2107.081.

B. Time Limits on Probate (#12.3): Under UPC § 3-108 probate proceedings must be commenced within three years of the decedent's death (with exceptions). Some states allow wills to be probated at any time. *In re Estate of Schafroth*, 598 N.E.2d 479 (Ill. App. 1992) (testator died in 1982, will probated in 1990).

C. Jurisdiction and Venue (#12.4): Under UPC § 3-201 a will can be probated where the testator was domiciled at death, or if the decedent was domiciled in another state, where the decedent had property.

Example: It was error to refuse to probate the will of an Arizona domiciliary in Wisconsin because he had property there. *Matter of Estate of Warner*, 468 N.W.2d 736 (Wis. 1991). But Oregon refused to probate the will of a Massachusetts domiciliary. Although the testator owned a note secured by mortgage on Oregon land, the note was deemed to be located at the testator's domicile. *West v. White*, 758 P.2d 424 (Or. App. 1988).

1. **In rem (#12.5):** Probate is *in rem, i.e.,* it binds persons who reside in other states and would not be subject to an action *in personam*.

2. ***Foreign land* (#12.6):** At common law, probate of a will in one state has no effect on land in another state.

   Example: A will which had been probated in California, where the testator resided, could be contested in Wyoming, where the testator owned land. The California decree was not *res judicata* as to the Wyoming land. *Estate of Reed*, 768 P.2d 566 (Wyo. 1988).

   a. Many states have changed this rule by statute. Under UPC § 3-408, a decree admitting the will in the state of the testator's domicile is conclusive.

12

D. Notice (#12.7): Historically wills could be probated "in common form" without notice to the interested parties. UPC § 3-306 retains this "informal probate" as an option, but the personal representative, who is appointed when a will is probated, must notify the testator's heirs and devisees within thirty days. UPC § 3-707.

E. Will Contests (#12.8): In most states a will can be contested even after it has been admitted to probate. UPC § 3-401 allows a will which has been informally probated to be set aside in "formal testacy proceedings."

1. ***Time limits* (#12.9):** Most states require that will contests must be brought within a short period after a will is probated. *E.g.,* Ohio Rev. Code § 2107.76 (four months except for persons under disability).

   a. In *Matter of Estate of Wilson,* 610 N.E.2d 851 (Ind. App. 1993) an heir who had not been notified that a will had been probated argued that a five-month limit on will contests after probate was unconstitutional by analogy to *Tulsa,* #11.50, *supra.* The claim was rejected on the ground that heirs who were disinherited by a will had only an "expectancy," not a property interest.

   b. There are divergent views as to whether an attempt to probate a later will which revokes earlier wills is a "contest" of the earlier will within the meaning of such limits. *Compare Matter of Estate of Brown,* 587 N.E.2d 686 (Ind. App. 1992) (later will barred) *with Cousee v. Estate of Efston,* 633 N.E.2d 815 (Ill. App. 1994) (later will not barred).

   c. These time limits do not affect suits to construe a will. *Hall v. Eaton,* 631 N.E.2d 805 (Ill. App. 1994) (claim that a will provision was against public policy can be asserted after the time limit on contests has expired).

2. ***Standing* (#12.10):** A will can only be contested by someone who has a financial interest in setting it aside. The testator's heirs have standing because if the will is invalid the estate will go to them by intestacy. Devisees under an earlier will of the testator also have standing.

   a. If a testator left several wills, an heir who seeks only to challenge the last one lacks standing if she was also disinherited by earlier wills. *Miller v. Todd*, 447 S.E.2d 9 (W. Va. 1994).

   b. Fiduciaries have standing on behalf of persons whom they represent. For instance, an administrator can contest a will on behalf of the heirs. However, the fiduciary's desire to earn a fee does not of itself confer standing.

   Example: A will created a trust for a charity. The testator later executed a codicil which gave the same amount to the charity directly. A trustee named in the will was not allowed to challenge the codicil since it did not affect the charity. *Matter of Estate of Getty*, 149 Cal. Rptr. 656 (Cal. App. 1978).

3. ***Jury trial* (#12.11):** Because historically the ecclesiastical courts probated wills and they did not use trial by jury, there is no constitutional right to it in probate proceedings. However, many state statutes give a right to jury trial in will contests. *E.g.,* UPC § 1-306.

F. Forfeiture Clauses (#12.12): Many wills provide that any devisee who challenges the will forfeits the devise. If the will is found invalid, this clause fails along with the other provisions. If the will is upheld, the effect of the clause is more doubtful.

1. ***Validity* (#12.13):** In a few states, such clauses are void. Ind. Code § 29-1-6-2. In most, however, they are enforceable unless the contestant had "probable cause" for contesting the will. UPC § 3-905; *Matter of Estate of Campbell*, 876 P.2d 212 (Kan. App. 1994) (unsuccessful claim that testator lacked capacity did not cause a forfeiture because there was probable cause).

2. ***Coverage* (#12.14):** Forfeiture clauses (sometimes called "*in terrorem*" provisions) are strictly construed. For example, they are held not to cover claims that property did not belong to the testator. *Estate of Richter*, 16 Cal. Rptr. 2d 108 (Cal. App. 1993) (widow's claim that property was community property was not a will contest within the meaning of a forfeiture clause).

G. Settlements (#12.15): Many will contests are settled. UPC § 3-1101-02 facilitates such settlements by allowing parents to represent minor children and fiduciaries to represent beneficiaries if the court finds the settlement is "just and reasonable."

Example: A will contest was settled by giving some of the estate to the heirs. The settlement was binding on minor beneficiaries of a trust created by the will because they were represented by the trustee. *Fifth Third Bank v. Fifth Third Bank*, 602 N.E.2d 325 (Ohio App. 1991).

II. NECESSITY FOR ADMINISTRATION

NECESSITY FOR ADMINIS-TRATION

12

A. **Purpose (#12.16):** Administration is designed to assure the orderly collection of claims against a decedent. If claimants sued the heirs and devisees directly, this would be inconvenient when there are many claims, or many heirs and devisees.

1. ***Insolvency*** **(#12.17)**: When the claims against an estate exceed the assets, the personal representative acts like a trustee in bankruptcy. Some claims, such as expenses of administration and funeral expenses, must be paid before others. Creditors in the same class are paid pro-rata. *E.g.,* UPC § 3-805. The heirs and devisees get nothing, but they are not personally liable. *See* #11.65, *supra.*

2. ***Practical necessity*** **(#12.18):** In solvent estates the claims are usually paid quickly, but administration is still necessary to collect and sell assets.

   Example: A suit by the decedent's children against a person who owed money totheir father was dismissed because only the personal representative has standing to sue on behalf of the decedent. *McGill v. Lazzaro*, 416 N.E.2d 29 (Ill. App. 1980).

B. **Avoiding Administration**

1. ***Small estates*** **(#12.19):** Under UPC § 3-1201, successors to an estate of less than $5,000 can collect the assets without administration by executing an affidavit that they are entitled to the property.

   a. A person owing money to the decedent (*e.g.,* a bank or employer) can pay the person executing the affidavit without being liable to claimants with a better right. UPC § 3-1202.

      Example: A widow collected money owed to a decedent by Big Heart Pipe Line, filing an affidavit stating she was his sole heir. In fact, his collateral relatives were also heirs. They could recover their share from her, but not from Big Heart. *Clark v. Unknown Creditors*, 782 P.2d 1384 (Okl. 1989).

   b. In some states, the amount which can be collected by affidavit is much larger. *E.g.,* Cal. Prob. Code § 13100 ($60,000).

   c. The rationale for these provisions is that the expense of administration is particularly burdensome when the estate is small. Also, creditors of the decedent have little to lose from the lack of administration, since small estates are usually exempt from creditors claims.

2. ***Nonprobate property* (#12.20):** Property not included in the probate estate is not usually subject to administration, but it may be in some states when this is necessary to pay claims. *See* #11.16, *supra*.

ANCILLIARY ADMINISTRATION

III. ANCILLARY ADMINISTRATION

A. Necessity (#12.21): When a decedent owned property in more than one state, ancillary administration may be necessary because at common law a personal representative appointed in one state has no power to act outside its boundaries.

12

Example: An administrator appointed by a California court for a California decedent could not sue to recover assets of the decedent in Missouri, unless he alleged that the assets were taken from the administrator's possession. Missouri had jurisdiction to appoint an administrator for this property. *Matter of Estate of Widmeyer*, 741 S.W.2d 758 (Mo. App. 1987).

1. ***Statutes* (#12.22):** Many states have modified the rule by statute. UPC § 4-205 allows foreign personal representatives appointed by the decedent's domicile to exercise all the powers of a local appointee if there is no local administration pending. *Cf. Allen v. Amoco Production Co.,* 833 P.2d 1199 (N.M. App. 1992) (sale by Colorado executor of land in New Mexico was invalid because decedent died before the effective date of the UPC).

3. ***Trustees* (#12.23):** The bar against foreign personal representatives does not apply to trustees. Therefore, it may be advisable to put out-of-state property into a living trust in order to avoid ancillary administration.

B. Distribution of Ancillary Assets (#12.24): After an ancillary administrator has collected the decedent's assets in a state, courts may either order the ancillary administrator to distribute the assets to the domiciliary representative, or directly to the heirs or devisees of the decedent.

Example: An Oklahoma court approved a distribution of the Oklahoma assets of a Texan to his widow over the objection of his Texas executor on the ground that Oklahoma law should govern since land was involved. *Miller v. Estate of Miller*, 768 P.2d 373 (Okl. App. 1988).

CHOICE OF FIDUCIARY

IV. CHOICE OF FIDUCIARY

A. Types (#12.25): There are various types of fiduciary, such as executors, trustees, guardians, conservators, etc. There are similarities among them, but also certain differences.

1. ***Executors* (#12.26):** A person designated in a will to carry out its provisions is called an executor. Normally the court appoints the executor named in the will.

2. ***Administrators* (#12.27)**: If a person dies without a will, the court appoints an administrator to handle the estate. An administrator is also ap-

pointed if a will fails to name an executor, or if the executor named is unable or unwilling to act. In the latter case, the administrator is often called an administrator "with will annexed" or *cum testamento annexo* (*c.t.a.*).

a. Priorities for the choice of an administrator are established by statute. Under UPC § 3-203(a), for example, preference is given (1) to the testator's spouse if a devisee, (2) other devisees if there is a will. On intestacy, preference is given to (1) the spouse, (2) other heirs. A creditor of the decedent may also be chosen.

b. A court may depart from this order in certain circumstances, *e.g.,* if the estate is insolvent.

c. If a minor is entitled to appointment, his guardian may nominate another person to act in his behalf. UPC § 2-203(d). *Compare Courtney v. Lawson,* 631 A.2d 102 (Md. App. 1993) (decedent's sister appointed administrator when his heirs were minor children).

3. ***Personal representatives* (#12.28):** The generic term for executors and administrators is "personal representative."

4. ***Trustees* (#12.29)**

a. Most trust instruments designate a trustee. If they do not, or if the designated trustee refuses or is unable to act, a court appoints one. *Restatement (Second) of Trusts* § 108 (1959).

b. Testamentary trustees are usually appointed by the probate court, but the designated trustee of a living trust usually acts without any court appointment.

c. The settlor may act as trustee of a living trust. A beneficiary can also serve as trustee.

d. Often the same person or institution acts as executor of a will and trustee of trusts created by the will. Their distinct roles should not be confused. Thus the approval of a person's accounts as executor does not preclude surcharging him for misconduct as trustee. *Kemper v. Kemper*, 532 N.E.2d 1126 (Ill. App. 1988).

5. ***Guardians and conservators* (#12.30)**: The UPC uses "conservator" for persons appointed to manage the property of minors and incapacitated adults. UPC § 5-401. Some states use different terminology. California uses the term "guardian of the estate" for minors; "conservator" is only used for adults. Cal. Prob. Code §§ 1500, 1800.

a. Like personal representatives, guardians and conservators are appointed by a court, and are subject to closer court supervision than trustees.

6. ***Agents*** **(#12.31):** Agents are also fiduciaries. In recent years the appointment of an agent under a durable power is frequently used to avoid conservatorship. *See* #10.32, *supra*.

7. ***Custodians*** **(#12.32):** Custodians under the Uniform Transfers to Minors Act operate very much like trustees. *See* #10.31, *supra*.

B. **Removal (#12.33):** Courts sometimes refuse to appoint or remove a fiduciary who qualifies under the foregoing rules. UPC § 3-203(f) says no one shall serve as a personal representative "whom the Court finds unsuitable." However, courts are more reluctant to remove a fiduciary designated by a settlor or testator. Trial courts have wide discretion on removal.

1. ***Conflict of interest*** **(#12.34)**

   a. A conflict of interest may be disqualifying.

   Example: A court refused to appoint a spouse as administrator because she was claiming part of the estate as her community property. *Ayala v. Marinez*, 883 S.W.2d 270 (Tex. 1994). But if a fiduciary has been designated by a testator or settlor despite an obvious conflict of interest, removal may be denied. *Schildberg v. Schildberg*, 461 N.W.2d 186 (Iowa 1990) (trustee).

   b. Sometimes a special administrator is appointed to avoid a conflict on a particular matter.

   Example: A special administrator was appointed to handle a claim because the executor was a partner of the lawyer for the defendant. *Sauter's Estate*, 615 P.2d 875 (Mont. 1980).

2. ***Hostility*** **(#12.35):** Hostility between the fiduciary and the beneficiaries of the estate or trust is disqualifying only in extreme cases.

   Example: Where litigation had generated ill will between beneficiaries and a trustee who had broad discretion in allocating benefits, it was error to dismiss a suit to remove the trustee. *Waits v. Hamlin,* 776 P.2d 1003 (Wash. App. 1990).

   Some trusts by their terms allow beneficiaries to remove a trustee and designate another.

3. ***Misconduct*** **(#12.36):** Fiduciaries are sometimes removed for breach of duty. However, removal is not appropriate for minor wrongs.

4. ***Nonresidence*** **(#12.37):** Some states prohibit a nonresident from serving as personal representatives. Such statutes have been challenged as unconstitutional with mixed results. *Compare Munford v. Maclellan,* 373 S.E.2d 368 (Ga. 1988) (refusal to remove nonresident designated as *trustee*).

C. **Resignation (#12.38):** No one can be appointed as trustee or personal representative involuntarily. Once accepted, however, the office cannot be resigned without court approval or the consent of all the beneficiaries. *Restatement (Second) of Trusts* § 106 (1959).

1. ***Exceptions* (#12.39):** Some statutes make it easier for trustees to resign without court proceedings. *E.g.,* Cal. Prob. Code § 15640(a)(3) (consent of adult beneficiaries suffices). Many trusts have similar provisions designed to avoid the cost of judicial proceedings.

D. **Successors**

1. ***Multiple fiduciaries* (#12.40)**: Under many statutes, if two or more fiduciaries are designated and one ceases to act, the remaining ones can act without a replacement. UPC § 3-718 (personal representatives); Uniform Trustees' Powers Act § 6 (trustees).

2. ***Designation of successor* (#12.41)**:

   a. Many wills and trusts designate successor fiduciaries, or provide a way to select one — *e.g.,* the beneficiaries can choose.

   b. In the absence of such provision, courts have discretion in choosing a successor trustee. The wishes of the beneficiaries (and the settlor if still living) are considered, but are not determinative. *Restatement (Second) of Trusts* § 108, comment i (1959).

3. ***Powers of successor* (#12.42):** A successor fiduciary has the same powers as the original one unless a power is deemed "personal." Under UPC § 3-716, this occurs only when the power is "expressly made personal to the executor named in the will." But a court may infer an intent to make a power conferred on a trustee personal from the circumstances, *e.g.,* if the original trustee was a near relative of the settlor. *Restatement (Second) of Trusts* § 196, comment f (1959).

   Example: A will gave the executor a power of sale. After the executor died, a new personal representative was appointed. A sale by the successor was authorized by the power. *Matter of Estate of Webb*, 832 P.2d 27 (Okl. App. 1991).

E. **Multiple Fiduciaries (#12.43):** Wills and trusts often designate two or more persons to act as executors or trustees. This may be desirable to avoid conflicts of interest and to utilize the special skills of different persons.

1. ***Taxes* (#12.44):** A trustee who has power to distribute to himself may be taxed on the trust income even if he does not receive it. Int. Rev. Code § 678. This can be avoided by naming a co-trustee.

2. **Unanimity (#12.45):** At common law, all the trustees had to agree to exercise their powers (except for charitable trusts where there are often numerous trustees). *Restatement (Second) of Trusts* § 194 (1959). UPC § 3-717 is similar as to personal representatives. However, many trust instruments and statutes provide for majority rule. *E.g.,* Uniform Trustees' Powers Act § 6.

FEES AND OTHER COSTS

12

V. FEES AND OTHER COSTS

A. **Personal Representatives (#12.46):** Under UPC § 3-719, "a personal representative is entitled to reasonable compensation for his services." Various factors are considered in determining what is reasonable. Trial courts have broad discretion in weighing the relevant factors.

1. ***Size of the estate*** **(#12.47):** The size of the estate is relevant because the greater the value of the property involved, the greater the responsibility. Also, custom is relevant, and fiduciaries have customarily based their fees on the size of the estate. Some states fix the fee at a percentage of the estate, but in others this cannot be the sole criterion.

   Example: It was error to award personal representatives a $96,000 fee for the administration of a $2.3 million estate. Given the time required, this amounted to $561 an hour, which was excessive. *Ford v. Peoples Trust and Sav. Bank*, 651 N.E.2d 1193 (Ind. App. 1995).

2. ***Time spent*** **(#12.48):** The time required for the job is relevant, but this does not justify inefficient use of time.

   Example: Fees claimed by an executor were reduced because some of the time used as the basis for the fee represented unnecessary work. *In re Estate of Wallace*, 829 S.W.2d 696 (Tenn. App. 1992). There is a difference of opinion as to whether time devoted to justifying the fee is itself compensable.

3. ***Breach of duty*** **(#12.49)**: A fee may be denied or reduced because of improper conduct by the fiduciary. However, misconduct does not always lead to a denial of compensation.

4. ***Number*** **(#12.50)**: In some states when there is more than one personal representative the compensation is apportioned among them. Cal. Prob. Code § 10805. In other states, the fee may be multiplied. N.Y. Surr. Ct. Proc. Act § 2307(5).

B. **Trustees (#12.51):** In some states, trustees are entitled to "reasonable compensation." In others, there is a sliding scale based on the size of the trust. Usually trustees get a percent of the income as well as a percent of the corpus. *E.g.,* Md. Estates & Trusts Code § 14-103.

1. ***Periodic and termination fees* (#12.52):** Since trusts last a long time, trustees generally collect a periodic fee, and another fee at termination. *Matter of Trusts under Will of Dwan*, 371 N.W.2d 641 (Minn. App. 1985) (approving a 2% termination fee).

C. **Contract**

1. ***Specified fee in instrument* (#12.53)**: If the will or trust specifies a fee, the fiduciary may be limited to that fee. *Lehman v. Irving Trust Co.*, 432 N.E.2d 769 (N.Y. 1982). However, some courts allow higher compensation if the work was more onerous than anticipated.

   a. UPC § 3-719 allows a personal representative to renounce a provision for compensation in a will and claim reasonable compensation, unless there was a contract between the fiduciary and the decedent governing compensation.

2. ***Waiver* (#12.54)**: Family members often serve without compensation. This may actually be advantageous to them since a fee is taxable income whereas a bequest is not. On the other hand fiduciary fees are deductible for purposes of the estate tax.

D. **Agents (#12.55):** Fiduciaries can be reimbursed from the estate or trust for hiring an agent, such as a broker to sell property. However, a trustee cannot be reimbursed for hiring agents "to do acts which the trustee ought personally to perform." *Restatement (Second) of Trusts* § 188, comment c (1959).

1. ***UPC* (#12.56):** UPC § 3-715(21) allows personal representatives to employ "auditors or investment advisors." Similar language appears in the Uniform Trustees' Powers Act § 3. However, it would normally be improper for a professional fiduciary to pay an investment advisor, since this should be covered by the fiduciary's regular fee.

E. **Attorneys (#12.57):** Normally personal representatives hire an attorney whose fee is paid from the estate. In some states they get a percentage of the estate. Cal. Prob. Code § 10810. In others they get a "reasonable" fee, based on factors like those used in determining the fiduciary's fee.

1. ***Model Rules of Professional Conduct* (#12.58):** Rule 1.5 says "a lawyer's fee shall be reasonable," and lists eight factors to be considered. DR 2-106(B) of the Code of Professional Responsibility is similar. These rules are frequently cited by courts in determining the reasonableness of attorney fees. *E.g., Duggan v. Keto,* 554 A.2d 1126 (D.C. App. 1989).

2. ***Attorney-executor* (#12.59):** When the executor is an attorney, some courts allow compensation in both capacities. In some states the executor must elect between an attorney fee or an executor's fee. Miss. Code § 91-7-281.

a. This situation involves a conflict of interest; in effect, the executor hires herself. Ordinarily such self-dealing is prohibited, but there may be savings in having the same person do both jobs.

3. ***Fiduciary not entitled to attorney fees* (#12.60):** A fiduciary is not allowed attorney fees incurred in the fiduciary's own interest, *e.g.,* in unsuccessfully opposing a suit for a surcharge.

F. Bond

1. ***Personal representatives* (#12.61):** In most states, personal representatives must file a bond with sureties to protect the beneficiaries if the personal representative causes a loss to the estate and is unable to pay damages. The premium on the bond is charged against the estate. *E.g.,* Cal. Prob. Code §§ 8480, 8486.

   a. In keeping with its effort to reduce the cost of administration, UPC § 3-603 does not require a bond unless one is demanded by a person interested in the estate.

   b. Bonds are usually not required for corporate fiduciaries since they have the wherewithal to pay claims.

2. ***Waiver* (#12.62)**: Many wills waive bond in order to save the expense. This is usually effective, but a court "may for good cause require that a bond be given" despite the waiver. Cal. Prob. Code § 8481.

3. ***Other fiduciaries* (#12.63)**: Normally bonds are not required of trustees of living trusts or custodians under the Uniform Transfers to Minors Act § 15(c). They are often required of trustees of testamentary trusts, but under UPC § 7-304, a trustee does not have to provide a bond "unless required by the terms of the trust, reasonably requested by a beneficiary or found by the Court to be necessary to protect the interests of beneficiaries."

   a. Guardians/conservators must provide bonds. UPC § 5-410. Agents do not.

G. Appraisal (#12.64): Many states require that estates be appraised by a court-appointed official who gets a fee based on the size of the estate. *E.g.,* Cal. Prob. Code §§ 8900 et seq.

1. ***UPC* (#12.65):** UPC § 3-707 makes the employment of an appraiser optional. In many estates this expense is unnecessary, *e.g.,* because the estate consists of nationally traded securities whose value can be determined from the newspaper.

VI. SALES BY FIDUCIARIES

SALES BY FIDUCIARIES

A. Statutes (#12.66): Many statutes give fiduciaries power to sell property in an estate or trust. UPC § 3-715, for example, authorizes personal representatives to dispose of assets in the estate if "acting reasonably for the benefit of the interested persons." Uniform Trustees' Powers Act § 3(c) confers a similar power on trustees.

1. ***Restrictive statutes*** **(#12.67):** Many statutes, however, are more restrictive. Sales of land by personal representatives often require court confirmation. *E.g.*, Cal. Prob. Code § 10308.

B. Provisions of the Instrument (#12.68): Many wills and trusts confer broad powers to sell on executors or trustees. Conversely, some direct that certain assets be retained. Normally such provisions operate to expand or contract the fiduciary's powers.

1. ***Purpose of sale*** **(#12.69):** Even with an apparently unlimited power, a sale without a proper purpose may be improper.

   Example: A will gave the executor a power of sale, but it was held improper to sell property which was specifically devised, since the sale was not needed to pay debts of the estate. *Maier v. Henning,* 578 A.2d 1279 (Pa. 1990). See also UPC § 3-906(a)(1) (specific devisee normally entitled to distribution in kind).

   a. A sale may be required in order to avoid the inconvenience of dividing an asset among several distributees.

      Example: If a house was distributed to one child, there would not be enough assets left to effectuate the equal distribution intended by the testator. Therefore, a sale was proper. *Estate of Barthelmess*, 243 Cal. Rptr. 832 (Cal. App. 1988).

   b. A sale may be necessary because property does not produce income or is speculative. *In re Estate of McCool*, 553 A.2d 761 (N.H. 1988) (executor surcharged for failing to sell stock of a company in precarious condition); *Restatement (Second) of Trusts* § 190, comment d (1959); #12.82, *infra.*

2. ***Prohibition on sale*** **(#12.70):** A prohibition on sale by an executor or trustee is valid, but it may be overruled if a change of circumstances makes a sale necessary.

   Example: A farm was left in trust. The trust did not permit a sale, but the court authorized one because changing land uses made the land worth $473,000, whereas it was producing only $3,000 a year as a farm. *Ex parte Guarantee Bank & Trust Co.*, 177 S.E.2d 358 (S.C. 1970).

12

C. Terms of Sale

1. ***Credit* (#12.71)**: A power to sell does not necessarily include a power to sell on credit.

   Example: Trustees contracted to sell stock with the price to be paid in installments. The court enjoined this because the settlor contemplated that any sale would be for cash. *In re Gould's Will*, 234 N.Y.S.2d 825 (App. Div. 1962).

   a. However, UPC § 3-715(6) authorizes personal representatives to sell property "for cash or on credit." Uniform Trustees' Powers Act § 3(7) is the same.

2. ***Price* (#12.72)**: A fiduciary can be surcharged for selling an asset at too low a price. *Cf. Mest v. Dugan,* 790 P.2d 38 (Or. App. 1990) (trustees surcharged for leasing trust property for less than its rental value).

   a. In states where court confirmation of sales is required, it may be denied if a higher bid for the property is received. *Matter of Estate of Rozell*, 886 P.2d 1004 (Okl. App. 1994).

D. Bona fide Purchasers (#12.73):

Even if a sale is improper, a buyer who had no notice and paid value can keep the property. UPC § 3-714; *Restatement (Second) of Trusts* § 284 (1959).

1. ***Actual notice* (#12.74)**: Under *Restatement (Second) of Trusts* § 297 (1959), one who "knows *or should know* of the breach of trust" is not a bona fide purchaser. But Uniform Trustees' Powers Act § 7 protects any person who is "without actual knowledge that a trustee is exceeding his powers."

   a. The duty of inquiry imposed by the *Restatement* makes it harder for trustees to sell property, since purchasers are reluctant to incur the risk of not getting title.

2. ***Earmarking* (#12.75)**: At common law trustees had to have property "designated as property of the trust," *Restatement (Second) of Trusts* § 179 (1959), so purchasers would know that they were dealing with a trustee. Many trust instruments and statutes today allow trustees to hold securities without such disclosure in order to facilitate sales. Uniform Trustees' Powers Act § 3(16).

INVESTMENTS

VII. INVESTMENTS

A. Prudent Person Rule (#12.76):

Trustees must "make such investments [of trust funds] as a prudent man would make of his own property." *Restatement (Second) of Trusts* § 227 (1959). More recent versions of the rule refer to a "prudent person."

1. ***Other fiduciaries* (#12.77):** Similar language is used to describe the duty of custodians under Uniform Transfers to Minors Act § 12(b). It has also been applied to conservators and personal representatives. *E.g., Matter of Guardianship of Connor,* 525 N.E.2d 214 (Ill. App. 1988) (guardian surcharged for imprudence in selling ward's home).

2. ***Legal lists* (#12.78)**: Many states once had legal lists of proper investments for trustees. These tended to be conservative, *e.g.,* they did not allow investment in common stocks. Experience has proved that the more flexible standard of prudence produces better results.

   a. Some states retain a legal list for guardians. *E.g.,* Tex. Prob. Code § 389. Under UPC § 5-423, however, a conservator has the same investment powers as a trustee.

   b. Some states restrict personal representatives to a legal list, Ohio Rev. Code § 2109.37, but UPC § 3-715(5) applies the prudent person standard to personal representatives.

3. ***Professional fiduciaries* (#12.79):** A higher standard is imposed on professional trustees. "If the trustee has special skills or is named trustee on the basis of representations of special skills or expertise, he is under a duty to use those skills." UPC § 7-302.

   a. However, even an nonprofessional fiduciary serving without compensation can be surcharged for imprudent investments. *Buder v. Sartore*, 774 P.2d 1383 (Colo. 1989) (father acting as custodian under UTMA surcharged for speculative investments).

4. ***Speculation* (#12.80)**: Fiduciaries may not make "speculative" investments.

   a. New companies without a "track record" are considered too speculative. *First Ala. Bank v. Martin*, 425 So.2d 415 (Ala. 1982).

   b. Common stocks in companies that have paid regular dividends are today regarded as a prudent investment. *Restatement (Second) of Trusts* § 227, comment m (1959). A few states limit the percentage of assets which can be invested in common stocks.

   c. Continuing to operate a testator's business may be imprudent, particularly if the business is unincorporated and thus may incur liabilities which deplete the whole estate. Under UPC § 3-715(24), personal representatives can continue to operate an unincorporated business for only four months without court approval.

5. ***Diversification* (#12.81)**: Prudence requires that investments be diversified.

a. It is difficult to diversify a small portfolio. Therefore, many banks maintain "common trust funds" for pooling investments of small trusts and estates. Individual trustees can diversify by investing in mutual funds.

b. Many commentators argue that fiduciaries should not attempt to select investments but should invest in a "market portfolio" with holdings which match the market as a whole, including "speculative" investments.

c. Traditionally trustees were surcharged for a "bad" investment even though the portfolio as a whole did well. This is inconsistent with modern portfolio theory which is adopted by some statutes and in the *Restatement (Third) of Trusts* § 227 (1990).

6. ***Retention*** **(#12.82)**: Many statutes allow fiduciaries to retain an investment even if it would not have been suitable for purchase. *E.g.,* UPC § 3-715(1). However, a fiduciary may be surcharged for retaining securities which were properly acquired if prudence dictated that they should be sold.

   Example: Executors were surcharged for losses incurred on stock which they retained in a declining market. They were imprudent in failing to review the portfolio. *Matter of Estate of Donner,* 626 N.E.2d 922 (N.Y. 1993).

7. ***Production of income*** **(#12.83):** An investment which fails to produce income is ordinarily improper. Thus trustees were surcharged for leaving large sums in checking accounts for a long period. *Maryland Nat'l Bank v. Cummins*, 588 A.2d 1205 (Md. 1991).

   a. Traditionally personal representatives had lesser investment responsibilities than trustees, since they typically hold assets for only a short period. Under UPC § 3-715(5) they can only invest funds "not needed to meet debts and expenses currently payable and...not immediately distributable."

B. **Language of the Instrument (#12.84):** A will or trust may either restrict or expand the investments allowed for a fiduciary.

   Example: Trustees of a pension fund were surcharged for losses incurred when they invested over 50% of the funds in equities, contrary to a restriction in the agreement under which they operated. They were liable even though the investments were otherwise prudent. *Dardaganis v. Grace Capital Inc.*, 889 F.2d 1237 (2d Cir. 1989).

   1. ***Interpretation*** **(#12.85)**: Broad authority to invest does not necessarily allow investments which are imprudent. Also, suggestions must be distinguished from binding directions.

Example: A will "requested" a trustee to retain certain stock which the trustee nevertheless sold. This was held to be proper because the "request" was only precatory. *Stevens v. National City Bank*, 544 N.E.2d 612 (Ohio 1989)

2. ***Deviations* (#12.86)**: Courts sometimes allow trustees to deviate from a restriction because of a change in circumstances.

   Example: A trust created in 1936 limited investments to mortgages on land. In 1956 a court expanded this to allow up to two-thirds of the investments in equity securities. Now this limitation was removed. Inflation has caused prudent investors to switch to equities. *Steel v. Wellcome Trustees Ltd.* [1988] 1 W.L.R. (Ch. D. 1988).

VIII. SELF-DEALING

SELF-DEALING

A. Prohibition (#12.87): Fiduciaries are not allowed to engage in transactions which involve a conflict of interest, such as selling their own property to a trust or buying trust property for themselves. Even if the price is fair, the possibilities of abuse require the bar against self-dealing.

Example: A will named the testator's son and another as executors. They sold property of the estate to the son. The sale was set aside, even though the price was fair and the disinterested co-executor had approved the sale. *Matter of Garwood's Estate*, 400 N.E.2d 758 (Ind. 1980).

1. ***Relatives* (#12.88)**: When the transaction involves a relative of the fiduciary, the rule is less clear. In *Matter of Estate of Hawley*, 538 N.E.2d 1220 (Ill. App. 1989), a trustee was removed for selling trust property to his son. *But see In re Estate of Hughes,* 641 N.E.2d 248 (Ohio App. 1994) (allowing sale by an executor to his daughter).

2. ***Corporations* (#12.89)**: A conflict of interest also arises if a fiduciary is a director or officer of a company in which a trust or estate holds stock.

   Example: A trustee was surcharged for investing trust money in two companies of which he was the president. *Wheeler v. Mann,* 763 P.2d 758 (Utah 1988).

3. ***Attorneys* (#12.90):** Attorneys who engage in self-dealing as fiduciaries or advisors to fiduciaries may be disciplined.

   Example: An attorney for an estate lent money of the estate to a person for whom the attorney had guaranteed a loan. He was suspended from practice for violating DR 5-101(A) of the Code of Professional Responsibility. *In re Gordon*, 524 N.E.2d 547 (Ill. 1988).

B. **Exceptions (#12.91):** The prohibition against self-dealing often creates difficulties, *e.g.,* if stock in an estate must be sold and the only potential buyers are the executors. Therefore, exceptions to the prohibition have been created.

1. ***Authorization in instrument*** **(#12.92)**: UPC § 3-713 allows self-dealing if "the will...expressly authorized the transaction." The fiduciary must pay a fair price (unless the instrument expressly allows a sale at a bargain).

   a. Such authorization is sometimes inferred. For example, when a settlor made his brother trustee knowing that he had an interest in a company in which the trust held stock, he was deemed to have impliedly authorized a sale of stock by the trust to the company. *Huntington Nat'l Bank v. Wolfe*, 651 N.E.2d 458 (Ohio App. 1994).

12

2. ***Authorization by court*** **(#12.93)**: UPC § 3-713 also allows self-dealing if "the transaction is approved by the Court after notice to interested persons." Uniform Trustees' Powers Act § 5 is similar.

3. ***Self-deposit of funds*** **(#12.94)**: Many statutes allow commercial banks that act as trustees or personal representatives to deposit funds of the trust or estate in their own institution.

4. ***Retention*** **(#12.95)**: A conflict of interest also arises when a corporate trustee holds its own stock in an estate or trust, since the managers may use the stock to prevent a hostile takeover. *Restatement (Second) of Trusts* § 170, comment n (1959), prohibits a corporate trustee from either purchasing or retaining its own shares, but Uniform Trustees' Powers Act § 3(c) allows trustees to "retain trust assets received from a trustor" in which the trustee is personally interested. UPC 3-715(1) is similar.

5. ***Trustee of two trusts*** **(#12.96):** Some statutes allow a trustee who administers two trusts to sell property from one to the other if the sale is "fair and reasonable." Cal. Prob. Code § 16002. But Uniform Trustees' Powers Act § 5(b) requires court approval for such a sale.

C. **Transactions between Fiduciary and Beneficiary (#12.97):** Transactions between a fiduciary and a beneficiary are not *ipso facto* voidable, but courts scrutinize them for unfairness since fiduciaries commonly are more sophisticated than beneficiaries.

Example: A bank trustee had acquired a tavern as a result of a mortgage foreclosure which it had unsuccessfully tried to sell for $85,000. It sold the tavern to the beneficiary of a trust for $200,000. The beneficiary was allowed to set the sale aside. "Transactions with a beneficiary in which the trustee receives a benefit are presumed fraudulent; this presumption may be overcome [only] by clear and convincing evidence of fairness to the beneficiary." *Smith v. First Nat. Bank*, 624 N.E.2d 899 (Ill. App. 1993).

IX. REMEDIES AGAINST FIDUCIARIES

REMEDIES AGAINST FIDUCIARIES

A. Specific Relief (#12.98): Fiduciaries are sometimes enjoined from improper conduct. If the transaction has already taken place it may be subject to rescission.

Example: Land was conveyed to a city "for park purposes." The city conveyed the land to a developer. The court rescinded the conveyance, saying that the land was held in trust. *Cohen v. City of Lynn,* 598 N.E.2d 682 (Mass. App. 1992). Such relief would not have been available if the transferee had been a bona fide purchaser. *See* #12.73, *supra.*

B. Monetary Relief (#12.99): Often the relief awarded consists of an award of money.

1. ***Reimbursement of losses*** **(#12.100):** The money may be designed to reimburse the estate or trust for losses caused by the fiduciary's breach.

   Example: Trustees made an improper investment which became worthless. The beneficiaries were awarded the amount of the investment with interest. The court declined to add profits which might have been made on a proper investment because this was "too speculative." *Gillespie v. Seattle-First Nat. Bank*, 855 P.2d 680 (Wash. App. 1993).

   a. Where trustees improperly sold property of a trust, the court awarded damages based on the present value of the property, less the sale proceeds received. *Progressive Land Developers v. Exchange National Bank*, 641 N.E.2d 608 (Ill. App. 1994).

   b. In both of the foregoing cases the beneficiaries of the trust could have elected to affirm the improper transaction, and presumably would have done so if the investment or sale had proved to be advantageous.

2. ***Recovery of trustee's profit*** **(#12.101):** Sometimes the recovery is designed to wrest a profit made by the fiduciary on an improper transaction, even if it caused no loss.

   Example: A personal representative who borrowed money from the estate was charged with the profit he made with the money, even though he had repaid the loan with interest. *In re Estate of Stowell*, 595 A.2d 1022 (Me. 1991).

3. ***Equitable relief*** **(#12.102):** Even if a monetary recovery is sought, relief against a fiduciary is normally regarded as equitable, and so there is no right to jury trial. *Estate of Grove v. Selken*, 820 P.2d 895 (Or. App. 1991) (surcharge of an executor). *But see Levinson v. Citizens Nat. Bank,* 644 N.E.2d 1264 (Ind. App. 1994) (right to jury trial in suit for damages against a trustee).

a. Trial courts have discretion on such questions as the amount of prejudgment interest awarded and whether or not the interest is compounded.

b. Traditionally courts refused to award punitive damages because of the equitable nature of the litigation. *Kohler v. Fletcher*, 442 N.W.2d 169 (Minn. App. 1989). Some more recent cases, however, award punitive damages. *Gillespie v. Seymour*, 877 P.2d 409 (Kan. 1994).

C. Defenses

1. ***Exculpatory provision* (#12.103):** A provision in a will or trust relieving an executor or trustee from liability is effective unless the fiduciary acts in "bad faith" or profits from the breach. *Restatement (Second) of Trusts* § 222 (1959).

   Examples: A trustee was held liable despite an exculpatory clause for selling land to an affiliated company for less than its appraised value. *Lincoln Nat. Bank v. Shriners Hospitals*, 588 N.E.2d 597 (Ind. App. 1992). But a court refused to surcharge a trustee under the prudent man standard where the instrument relieved the trustee of liabilityso long as she acted in good faith. *Kerper v. Kerper,* 780 P.2d 923 (Wyo. 1989).

2. ***Consent of beneficiaries* (#12.104):** A beneficiary who consents to a breach of trust may not thereafter attack it, unless the beneficiary lacked capacity or "did not know of his rights and of the material facts." *Restatement (Second) of Trusts* § 216 (1959).

   Examples: A beneficiary who urged a trustee to lend trust funds to the beneficiary's nephew could not surcharge the trustee when the loan went sour. *Mahle v. First Nat. Bank*, 610 N.E.2d 115 (Ill. App. 1993). But beneficiaries who consented to an improper distribution by a trustee were not precluded from suing since they had not known that they had a right to all the property under a proper distribution. *Stowers v. Northwest Bank Indiana,* N.A., 624 N.E.2d 485 (Ind. App. 1993). Compare UPC § 3-713 (consent "after fair disclosure" may validate transaction by personal representative).

   a. Normally consent by one beneficiary does not bar the others, but some trust instruments allow adult beneficiaries to consent on behalf of others in order to facilitate transactions. *See Beyer v. First Nat. Bank,* 843 P.2d 53 (Colo. App. 1992) (trustee not liable for speculative investments where parents consented for themselves and their children as authorized by the trust).

   b. A beneficiary may also be barred by a release given after a breach by a trustee.

3. ***Laches* (#12.105):** A beneficiary who knows or has reason to know of a breach of trust and delays acting may be barred by laches. Since

beneficiaries can elect to affirm an improper transaction, delay in choosing to disaffirm might allow them to speculate unfairly.

a. Many states have statutes of limitations which may protect trustees. However, these generally do not start to run until the beneficiary knows of the breach, and this is construed favorably to unsophisticated beneficiaries.

Example: A trustee made a bad investment in 1985. The beneficiaries brought suit in 1989. The trustee relied on a statute which required suit within three years of discovery of the breach. The court allowed the suit. Even though the beneficiaries knew the investment was losing money, they did not understand the full extent of their claim. *Gillespie v. Seattle-First Nat. Bank*, 855 P.2d 680 (Wash. App. 1993).

4. ***Court approval* (#12.106):** A fiduciary may be protected if the transaction was approved by a court or was covered by a court-approved accounting.

a. An accounting may protect a fiduciary even as to claims which were not raised when the account was approved. But approval of an account does not preclude a later claim if the fiduciary was guilty of misrepresentation or concealment in presenting the account. *Cf. Coster v. Crookham,* 468 N.W.2d 802 (Iowa 1991) (court approval of loan by trustee not res judicata where court was not informed of trustee's interest in the transaction).

b. A beneficiary who does not get notice of proceedings is not bound by them, but beneficiaries may be bound by representation.

Example: Court approval of an executor's sale was not subject to collateral attack for failure to notify beneficiaries of a trust created by the will; notice to the trustee was sufficient. *Estate of Jones*, 770 P.2d 1100 (Wyo. 1989).

c. The UPC allows personal representatives to close an estate administration without court approval of their accounts. If they file a final account and send a copy to interested parties, they are protected against any claims not asserted within six months. UPC § 3-1005.

5. ***Advice from others* (#12.107):** Fiduciaries are not allowed to delegate their responsibilities to others. Nevertheless, in some cases they can use another's advice as a defense.

Example: An executor was not liable when an estate failed to get an available estate tax deduction because it "had a right to hire an attorney to handle the legal affairs of the estate and...to rely on the attorney's advice." *Jewish Hospital v. Boatmen's Bank*, 633 N.E.2d 1267 (Ill. App. 1994). See also UPC § 3-715(22) (personal representative may act "without independent investigation" on recommendations of attorneys, investment advisors, etc.); Uniform Trustees' Powers Act § 3(24) (same).

a. Fiduciaries are responsible for the acts of an agent when they have improperly delegated responsibility.

Example: A trustee was held liable for funds he had entrusted to an investment advisor who lost them. A trustee must supervise the agent, and the defendant had failed to do this. *Whitfield v. Cohen*, 682 F. Supp. 188 (S.D.N.Y. 1988).

D. **Cofiduciaries (#12.108):** A cofiduciary cannot escape responsibility by turning over management to the others; each fiduciary must use reasonable care to prevent or redress breaches by the others. *Restatement (Second) of Trusts* § 184, 224(2) (1959).

1. ***Contribution and indemnification* (#12.109):** A cofiduciary who is held liable may get contribution or even indemnification from the others if they were equally or more at fault. *Restatement (Second) of Trusts* § 258 (1959).

   a. Cofiduciaries are jointly liable for a breach so that if one is insolvent, the other must pay the whole liability. *In re Estate of Chrisman*, 746 S.W.2d 131 (Mo. App. 1988).

2. ***Participation by nonfiduciaries* (#12.110):** Persons who are not fiduciaries may be liable for participating in a breach of trust. *Restatement (Second) of Trusts* § 326 (1959); *Gillespie v. Seymour*, 796 P.2d 1060 (Kan. App. 1990) (accountant who overcharged a trust).

   a. However, the modern tendency is to protect third parties in order to facilitate administration.

   Example: A bank was not liable for allowing an agent to withdraw money from an account which she later embezzled. The bank had no duty to investigate the principal's capacity at the time she executed the power of attorney. *Bank IV, Olathe v. Capitol Federal S. & L.*, 828 P.2d 355 (Kan. 1992). *See also* UPC § 5-505(protecting persons who rely on durable powers). As to bona fide purchasers, *see* #12.73, *supra.*

ALLOCATIONS BETWEEN PRINCIPLE AND INCOME

X. ALLOCATIONS BETWEEN PRINCIPAL AND INCOME

A. **Governing Law (#12.111):** Most trusts call for the distribution of "income" to certain beneficiaries and "principal" to others. Therefore, trustees must know how to allocate receipts and expenses between principal and income.

1. ***Uniform Acts* (#12.112):** Most states have adopted one of two Uniform Principal and Income Acts (UPIA). The 1962 version differs somewhat from the 1931 version, and there are variants in some of the adopting states.

2. ***Contrary intent* (#12.113):** The rules of allocation are superseded if the will or trust manifests a different intent.

   Example: A trust provided that the settlor's widow should receive the income and that if property was sold, the proceeds "shall become part of the trust property and not income." This made the proceeds of sale of timber principal, even though by statute part of them would be income. *See* #12.121, *infra*. *Hardin v. McPhearson,* 569 So.2d 319 (Ala. 1990).

B. **Proceeds of Sale (#12.114):** When property is sold, the proceeds are principal even if they include a capital gain which is "income" for tax purposes.

1. ***Underproductive property* (#12.115):** However, if the property had not been producing sufficient income, some of the proceeds go to the income beneficiary to make up for this.

   Example: A farm which was worth $1.5 million had been producing income of less than $1,300 a year. The trustee was ordered to sell it and allocate part of the proceeds to the income beneficiary as "delayed income" under a formula in the UPIA. *Sturgis v. Stinson*, 404 S.E.2d 56 (Va. 1991).

C. **Corporate Distributions (#12.116):** In most states, the allocation of corporate distributions usually depends on whether they are paid in cash or in stock.

1. ***Dividends* (#12.117):** Dividends which a company pays in cash are usually income, but distributions of stock of the distributing company are principal. A few states allocate small stock dividends to income. N.Y.E.P.T.L. § 11-2.1(e)(2) (6% or less).

2. ***Bonds* (#12.118):** Interest paid on bonds is income. Money paid to redeem them is principal, except for United States Series E bonds which nominally pay no interest. 1962 UPIA § 7.

D. **Wasting Assets (#12.119):** Certain assets, like oil wells, lose value over time as the oil is depleted. If all the revenue is allocated to income, there may be nothing left for the remaindermen.

1. ***Common law* (#12.120):** Under the common-law "open-mines" doctrine, if a mine was already open when a life estate was created, the life tenant took all the revenue, but a life tenant could not open new mines.

2. ***1962 UPIA* (#12.121):** Section 9 apportions revenues from natural resources between income and principal.

3. ***Depreciation* (#12.122):** At common law, the "income" derived from renting a building was not reduced by any reserve for depreciation. But the 1962 UPIA § 13 requires trustees to make "a reasonable allowance for depreciation."

E. Apportionment (#12.123): When an income beneficiary dies, his estate is entitled to part of the income not yet distributed.

Example: When an income beneficiary died, the trustee had collected some income but not yet distributed it. Also there was interest not yet due to the trust and a dividend which had been declared but not paid. The court awarded all these to the income beneficiary's estate, including interest accrued up to the income beneficiary's date of death. *Hedrick v. West One Bank*, 853 P.2d 548 (Idaho 1993). *See also* UPIA (1962) § 4(d).

F. Income of an Estate (#12.124): Allocation issues also arise regarding income earned by an estate during administration. These are covered by UPIA 1962 § 5.

1. ***Specific devises*** **(#12.125):** Specific devises carry with them the income earned by the devised property during administration. *Matter of Estate of Niehenke*, 818 P.2d 1324 (Wash. 1991) (specific devisee of farm gets crops growing at testator's death).

2. ***Pecuniary devises*** **(#12.126):** The rest of the estate income goes to the other devisees pro rata, except that pecuniary devises (unless in trust) do not share. But in most states pecuniary devises earn interest starting a year after administration begins. UPC § 3-904.

DISTRIBUTION

XI. DISTRIBUTION

A. Liability for Improper Distribution

1. ***Fiduciary*** **(#12.127):** Fiduciaries are liable for making distribution to the wrong person, even when they act in good faith.

   Example: A trust gave the settlor's wife the income as long as she remained unmarried. She remarried without telling the trustee, who continued to pay her the income. The trustee was liable to the person who should have received the income. *National Academy of Sciences v. Cambridge Trust Co.*, 346 N.E.2d 879 (Mass. 1976).

   a. In some states, the trustee would have been protected if it had exercised "reasonable care." Wash. Rev. Code § 11.98.100. But *Restatement (Second) of Trusts* § 226, comment b (1959), says trustees should be liable despite a "reasonable mistake" because in case of doubt they can apply to a court for instructions.

2. ***Liability of distributee*** **(#12.128):** Anyone to whom property is improperly distributed is liable to return it or its value, unless he is protected by a statute of limitations or estoppel. UPC § 3-909; *Restatement (Second) of Trusts* § 254 (1959).

   Example: A personal representative who had distributed property and then had to pay estate taxes could claim reimbursement from the distributee. Laches was not a defense since the defendant suffered no prejudice from the delay. *Quintana v. Quintana*, 802 P.2d 488 (Idaho App. 1990).

B. **Distributions to Incompetents (#12.129):** If a distributee lacks the capacity to give a release, it may be necessary to appoint a guardian or conservator to take distribution. In order to avoid this expense, many wills and trusts allow distribution to someone who is connected with the beneficiary.

1. ***Custodians* (#12.130):** Uniform Transfer to Minors Act § 6 allows a personal representative or trustee to distribute property for a minor to a custodian, but court approval is required if the amount exceeds $10,000.

C. **Distribution in Kind (#12.131):** Often even pecuniary devises are satisfied by distributing property of the estate rather than cash. For this purpose, the property should be valued at the date of distribution. UPC § 3-906. This means that any appreciation of the estate during administration inures to the benefit of the residuary devisees.

Example: A will leaves $10,000 to my sister, the residue to my wife. The estate is worth $100,000 when the testator dies, but $150,000 when it is distributed. The sister will get only $10,000, whether her devise is satisfied in cash or in kind. The wife will get assets worth $140,000.

1. ***Pro-rata distributions* (#12.132):** Under UPC § 3-906 each residuary beneficiary is entitled to a "proportionate share of each asset," but some statutes and wills allow fiduciaries to make non-pro-rata distributions.

   Example: A widow and a child were each entitled to 1/2 an estate. It was proper to distribute all the estate to the widow and order her to pay the child cash for her share. *In re Estate of Meyer*, 802 P.2d 148 (Wash. App. 1990).

Notes

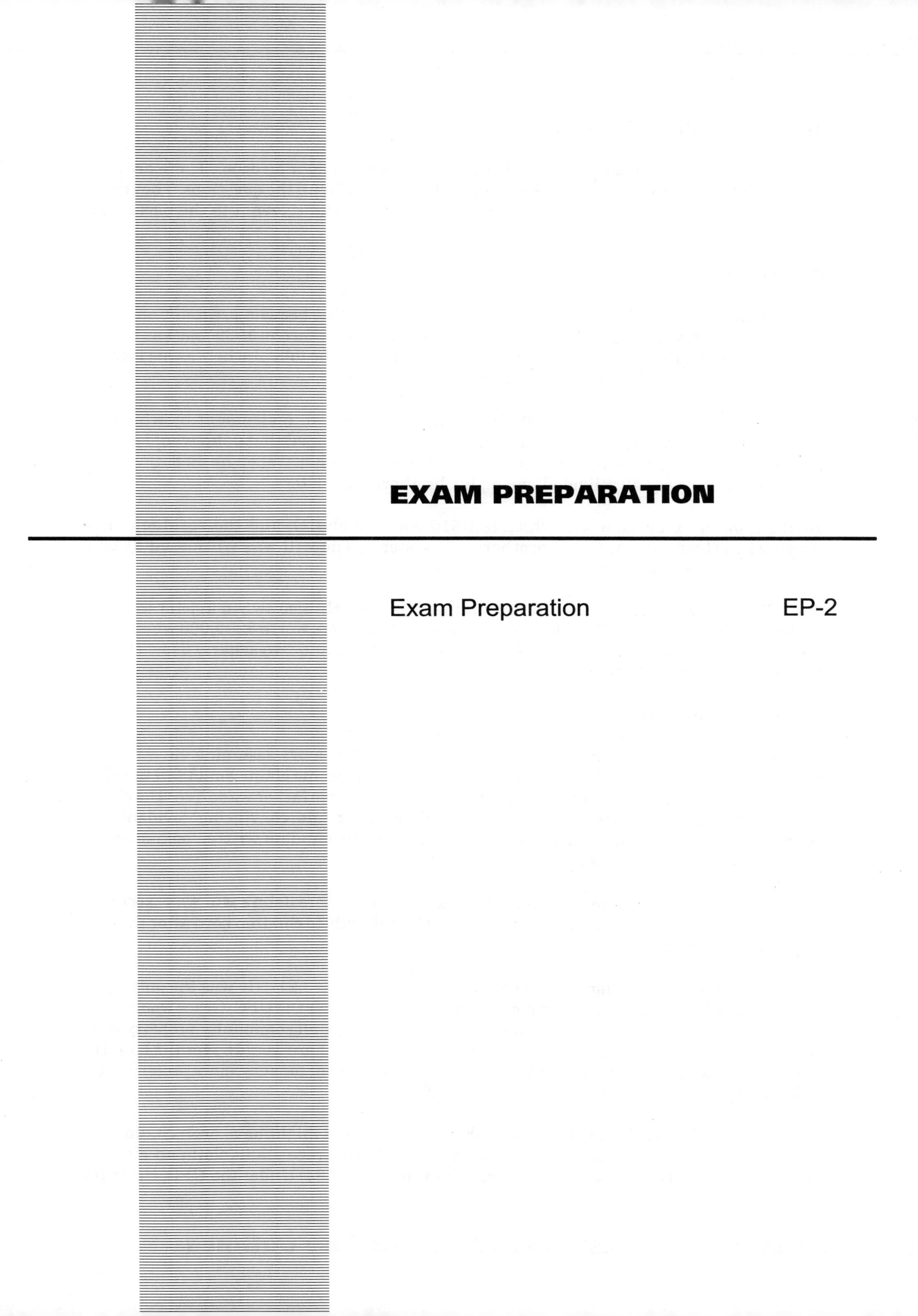

EXAM PREPARATION

Exam Preparation EP-2

MODEL EXAMINATION QUESTIONS

There are four essay questions. You should spend about an hour on each. There are also twenty-two true/false questions. There are model answers for all the questions. They refer to specific sections of this outline to help you review material relevant to the particular question.

Question 1

In 1961, John Moore lived next door to Ernestine. Ernestine became pregnant and told her mother that John was the father. The child, Richard, was born in 1962 and was raised by his maternal grandparents. In 1979, Richard met John who told him he was his father, but there was no further communication between the two.

John Moore married Grace in 1980. In 1984, he executed an instrument by which he declared himself trustee of certain property. The trust provided that John would get all the income for life and he reserved the right to revoke the trust. When he died, the trust assets were to be equally divided among his brothers and sisters.

In 1994, John executed a will which left $10,000 to a church and the residue of his estate ½ to Grace and ½ to his brothers and sisters. The will was witnessed by one of John's brothers and by two friends of John.

John died in 1996. His probate estate contained $50,000. He also owned in joint tenancy with Grace a house worth $50,000. The assets in the trust were worth $200,000 when John died. John was survived by Grace, Richard, two brothers, and two sisters. How should his property be distributed?

Answer to Question I

In some states, Richard might claim as a pretermitted heir, assuming he was not mentioned in John's will. Since he was born out of wedlock, his claim would fail in some states because there was no adjudication of paternity while his father was alive. His claim might even fail in a state which simply required "clear and convincing" evidence of paternity since there was so little contact between the two and no written acknowledgment of paternity. (#2.34-.35)

In many states, his claim would fail because he was born before John's will was executed. Many pretermitted heir statutes, such as the UPC, apply only to children born after the will was executed. (#3.17)

If his claim succeeds, Richard would get his intestate share. (#3.21) He was the only child and would take everything that did not pass to Grace. But under the UPC, Grace would take all of the estate. (#1.12) In many community property states, all community property goes to the other spouse in case of intestacy, so Richard's intestate share would be zero. (#1.14) He would not get a share of the assets in the trust or the house in joint tenancy, since pretermitted heirs only get a share of the probate estate. (#3.22)

The trust is valid even though it is revocable. At one time it might have been challenged as "testamentary," but this is likely to fail today. (#4.66) Grace might claim an elective share. Some courts would say the transfer was illusory. (#3.34) Under the UPC, the trust would be included in John's augmented estate. (#3.33) The augmented estate would amount to $300,000: the $200,000 trust, plus the $50,000 house, plus the $50,000 probate estate. Since they were married for over fifteen years, her share would be 50%. But the UPC would take into account Grace's property, including the $50,000 house, the assets she will get under the will, and any other property she may own, such as savings from employment and inheritance. The question provides no information as to the latter. If she had no assets other than the house and the $20,000 she takes under John's will ($50,000 minus $10,000, divided by two), she can claim the difference between that and 1/2 of the augmented estate ($150,000 minus $70,000). This $80,000 would be taken pro rata from the other beneficiaries of the augmented estate, the charity and John's siblings. (#9.22)

In some states, Grace's elective share would extend only to assets in the probate estate. (#3.32) She was already getting 40% of that under the will, so it would not be advantageous for her to elect against the will if her elective share is only 1/3, as it is in many states.

In a community property state, Grace's rights to the trust would turn on whether it was funded with community property. This seems unlikely since it was created so soon after John married, but there is a presumption that everything is community property. (##3.49-.51)

In some states, the brother who witnessed the will might lose his share as an interested witness. But there were two disinterested witnesses, and most states only require two witnesses to a will and do not disqualify an interested witness if he is an extra. Under the UPC, interested witnesses do not lose their legacies even if there are no disinterested witnesses. (#4.12) If the brother lost his share, it would go to the other brother and sisters since this was a class gift. (#2.13)

Since the will was executed so long before John died, there is no problem with the bequest to the church, even in those few states which still have mortmain statutes. (#3.86)

Question 2

In 1975, Frank Brown created a trust for his wife, Ann. The First National Bank was designated as trustee. The trust provided that:

> The trustee shall pay all the income to my wife, Ann, for her life, and such amounts of principal as are necessary for her support. Upon her death, it shall distribute the assets to me if living, if not, to my heirs in equal shares.

Frank has two daughters, Dorothy and Ellen, by a prior marriage.

1. Can Frank and Ann terminate the trust if they wish to do so?

2. John Smith has a claim against Ann arising from an automobile accident. Can he reach the assets of the trust to satisfy his claim?

Answer to Question 2

1. The trust could be terminated if it was revocable. In some states, trusts are presumed to be revocable, but in most states they are presumed to be irrevocable. (#5.25)

   Even if the trust was irrevocable, if Frank and Ann were the only beneficiaries, they could terminate it. The *Claflin* rule poses no problem when the settlor consents to termination. The Bank's interest in earning trustee fees would not be a reason for refusing termination. (#10.54)

   The consent of all the beneficiaries would be necessary, however. Frank's "heirs" cannot be ascertained until he dies. Some states would presume that Frank did not intend to give them an interest but rather to leave a reversion in himself. (#10.47)

   If the heirs do have an interest, a guardian might be appointed for them to consent to termination. Guardians have a fiduciary obligation to protect the wards' property, but the interest of the heirs here has limited value because they get nothing if Frank survives his wife. A few states allow a guardian to consent to termination of a trust if this will benefit the family. (#10.48)

2. John can reach Ann's income interest in the trust. No spendthrift provision is indicated in the exam question. In any event, in the opinion of many commentators, tort claimants should be immune from such provisions because they did not extend credit voluntarily. (#11.35)

   A court might order the income to be paid to John until his claim was paid, or Ann's income interest could be sold and the proceeds given to John (to the extent of his claim). (#11.18)

   As to the corpus, even tort victims can't reach property which doesn't belong to the tortfeasor, and Ann has no interest in the corpus unless the trustee decides to exercise its discretion to pay it to her. But a court might order the trustee to pay John in case the trustee decides to exercise its discretion in Ann's favor. (#11.19)

   Ann might be treated as a settlor of the trust if it was funded with community property. If so, the creation of the trust might be challenged as a fraudulent conveyance if creation of the trust left her insolvent. (# 11.1) Also, a creditor can reach the maximum amount which the trustee in its discretion could pay to the settlor, which would presumably be the entire trust. (#11.15)

Question 3

Clara Mayo was married to James Mayo from 1963 to 1988. On February 2, 1981, Clara executed a trust agreement which named John Hill as trustee. At the same time, she designated the trust as the beneficiary of an insurance policy and of the death benefit under a pension plan of her employer. The trust was revocable by its terms. It provided that when Clara died, the trustee should pay the income to James for life. When James died, the trustee was to distribute the assets to "the niece and nephews of the settlor." On the same day, Clara also executed a will which left her estate to the trustee of the trust which she had just executed "to be held under the terms of the trust as they exist at the time of my death."

In 1988 Clara and James were divorced. They executed a property settlement in which James received certain assets and waived any claim "to Clara's property." Clara changed the beneficiary of her insurance policy to Marianne, a friend, but she made no changes in her will, the trust, or the pension plan.

Clara died in 1995, survived by James, her parents and one brother. She never had any niece or nephews. James had two nephews and a niece, with whom Clara was very friendly, even after the divorce. Marianne predeceased Clara.

How should Clara's estate, the insurance policy, and the death benefits under the pension plan be distributed?

EP

Answer to Question 3

In most states, a divorce revokes a bequest to the testator's spouse. (#5.19) This might not apply in this case because the bequest is to a trust, and the spouse is not identified as a beneficiary of the trust in the will. Under the theory of incorporation by reference, the terms of the trust would become part of the will, but most states validate pour-over wills without relying on the doctrine of incorporation by reference. (#6.30)

Even if the statute was held to cover the pour-over will, it would probably not apply to the pension benefit, which would not be part of Clara's probate estate. James's agreement to waive any claims against Clara's property might be construed to bar him, but this is not clear, since the agreement did not specifically refer to the pension. (##5.48, 3.78) The waiver might also be challenged for lack of fair disclosure, but this is more likely to happen when the waiver is part of an antenuptial agreement signed without independent counsel. Usually in a divorce, each spouse has counsel, and there is less likelihood of an improvident contract. (*Cf.* ##3.80-.84)

Arguably, the gift to the niece and nephews of the settlor failed because she had none. However, a mistake in drafting could be corrected by reformation if there was clear evidence that she intended to say "the settlor's husband," since this was a living trust, as distinguished from a will. (#6.39) Even in a will, a devise to a legatee who does not exist may be regarded as a latent ambiguity which can be "explained" by extrinsic evidence. (#6.9) Courts are more willing to admit evidence of the circumstances, like Clara's close relationship with her husband's niece and nephews, than evidence of declarations by a testator. (#6.12) On the other hand, ordinarily a gift to "children" does not include children of a spouse, unless they have been adopted. (#2.67)

If the gift to the niece and nephews fails, Clara's estate may go intestate. In most states, her parents would be her heirs, but in some they would share the estate with her brother. (#1.23)

If the trust had said "the niece and nephews of my husband," the interest would not be affected by the divorce in most states, but they would be excluded under the UPC. (#5.19) Most insurance policies require the designated beneficiary to survive the insured. Since Marianne died before Clara, if no alternate beneficiary was named, the proceeds would be paid to Clara's probate estate. The antilapse statute does not apply to insurance policies in many states. It also does not apply to nonrelatives of the testator, so it is unlikely that the proceeds would go to any children of Marianne. (##2.7, 2.17)

Question 4

Victor Nichols owned a majority of the stock in the Nichols Company. His will named Frederick Wright, the vice-president of Nichols Company, as executor of his estate. The will directed that the Nichols Company stock "be distributed to my heirs at law." When Victor died, he was survived by a wife, Minnie, a brother, Thomas, and three nieces and nephews, who were the children of a deceased sister. Victor never had any children. During the administration of the estate, the Nichols Company bought Victor's stock from the estate, with the consent of the executor, Minnie, and Thomas. The stock is now worth much more than what the company paid for it.

1. What remedies, if any, are available to the parties?

2. How could the drafting of Victor's will be improved?

Answer 4

1. To determine the remedies available to the parties, we must first decide who Victor's heirs were. Normally, the word "heirs" refers to the intestacy statutes, and so we must ask who would get the stock if Victor died intestate. Since the stock was personal property, the law of the state of Victor's domicile would control. (#1.3) In some states, his wife would take all his estate, since he had no issue. In a community property state, the surviving spouse usually gets all of the community property on intestacy. In some states she would share with Victor's brother, nieces and nephews. (##1.14, 1.16) The nieces and nephews would take by representation the share the sister would have received if she had survived Victor. (Even states which limit representation by collateral relatives allow it for the children of brothers and sisters). (#1.26)

Did the executor have a power of sale? Under the UPC, such a power is implied, but in some states a sale by an executor may require court approval. (#12.67) Was the sale necessary for some purpose, like raising money to pay taxes? If not, the sale might be challenged because the direction in the will that the stock be distributed suggests that the testator did not contemplate a sale. (##12.68-.69)

Even if the executor had a power of sale, the sale might be voidable for self-dealing, since the executor was also the company vice-president and thus had an interest in buying the stock at a low price. (#12.89) Also, if the executor sold the stock at less than its current value, this was a breach of his fiduciary duties. (#12.72) However, the only remedy might be to surcharge him for the difference between the price paid by the company and the value of the stock, particularly if the stock had passed into the hands of a bona fide purchaser. (#12.73)

Since Minnie and Thomas consented to the sale, they might be barred from suing. If Minnie was the only heir, that would mean no one would have a remedy. However, if she was not the only heir, her consent would not bar the others. (#12.104) Even Minnie and Thomas might have a claim despite their consent if the transaction was very unfair and there was no full disclosure of the facts, *e.g.,* if the executor got them to agree without revealing the true value of the stock. Courts closely scrutinize transactions between fiduciaries and beneficiaries for unfairness. (#12.97)

2. The will should have made it clear whether or not the executor had power to sell the stock. If Victor did not want the stock to be sold, he should have said so explicitly. However, he should also have realized that the estate might need to sell the stock to meet expenses. Also, if Victor had several heirs, dividing the stock among them might dilute its value, since the recipients would no longer own a majority interest. Selling the stock as a block might produce a larger sum for the heirs. (#12.69).

If a sale was contemplated, a sale to the company might be the only practical alternative, since interests in small companies are often hard to market. Any sale to the company raises a problem when a company officer is named executor. Therefore, an express authorization of a sale to the company might be a good idea. Self-dealing is allowed when it is expressly authorized in the will. (#12.92) Including a formula for arriving at a fair price in the will could avoid later claims that the sale price was too low.

There are also problems if the stock is not sold. Retaining stock in a small company may be an imprudent investment, particularly if the stock constitutes a large portion of the estate, or fails to pay dividends. (##12.81-.83) Therefore, the will should expressly authorize retention of the stock if this is what Victor wants. A bequest to "heirs" raises a potential problem as to which law should be used to determine them. This can be avoided by specifying a state and a time, such as "under the law of Alabama as of the date of my death."(#1.5) The heirs, or some of them, might turn out to be minors for whom a guardian would have to be appointed. Victor might provide a contingent trust to cover this possibility. (#1.42) Also, the heirs might include very remote relatives in case the closer relatives all predeceased Victor; he might prefer that his property go to a friend or to a charity if this happened. (#1.44)

True/False Questions

Fact Pattern

Tom Testator duly executed a will in 1988, which provided as follows:

1. I bequeath my fifty shares of General American stock to my sister Alice.
2. I devise my summer house in Wisconsin to my sisters, Barbara and Catherine.
3. I devise the building I own at 547 Main Street to my brother David.
4. I bequeath $10,000 to the American Cancer Society, to be used for research into the causes of cancer.
5. I devise and bequeath the residue of my estate to my brothers Edward and Frank, share and share alike.
6. I intentionally make no provision for my sister Guenivere.

In 1990, Tom sold the building on Main Street for $500,000. The contract of sale provided for a down payment of $50,000, the balance to be paid in monthly installments.

In 1991, when General American paid a 100% stock dividend, Tom received an additional fifty shares. Also in 1991, Edward died, survived by a widow, to whom he left his estate, and her three children, whom Edward had adopted.

In 1992, Tom died. He had never changed his will. He was survived by Alice, Barbara, Catherine, David, Frank, Guenivere, Edward's widow, and her three children. At the time of his death, Tom owned 100 shares of General American stock, and $350,000 was still due to him for the building on Main Street.

Questions

Answer each one True or False and give a brief reason for your answer. A statement is false if it gives the correct result for the wrong reason. Unless otherwise indicated, assume that the UPC governs.

1. Alice will receive 100 shares of General American stock.
2. If Tom had sold the stock after executing his will, Alice would still get fifty shares because this was a general devise.
3. David is entitled to $500,000, the amount for which the Main Street property was sold.
4. If the summer house was destroyed by a fire after the will was executed but before Tom died, Barbara and Catherine would be entitled to any insurance proceeds that were still identifiable among Tom's assets.

5. If the summer house is mortgaged, Barbara and Catherine will take subject to the mortgage and cannot have it exonerated from Tom's other assets.

6. In all states, if Barbara dies after Tom, Catherine will take the summer house by right of survivorship.

7. In many states, Barbara and Catherine would hold as tenants by the entirety, and neither of them could sever the tenancy.

8. Edward's three children would each take 1/6 of the residue.

9. Edward's adopted children cannot inherit from their biological father because they have been adopted by Edward and this would give them a double inheritance.

10. If Edward had died without issue, Frank would take all the residue under the UPC.

11. If Alice and Tom died simultaneously in a plane crash and she had no issue, the General American stock would pass under the residuary clause, but if Alice survived Tom by thirty minutes, the stock would go to her estate.

12. Guenivere has standing to contest the will, but Frank's children do not.

13. If Edward's children successfully contest the will on the ground that Tom lacked testamentary capacity, they will each take 1/9 of the estate.

14. If Alice was a lawyer and had drafted the will for Tom, she would have the burden of showing that the devise to her was not the product of undue influence.

15. Alice's drafting the will for Tom would violate the Model Rules of Professional Conduct.

16. If the General American stock had been left in trust to pay the income to Alice for her life, remainder to her issue, stock dividends paid during Alice's life after Tom died would go to her as income.

17. Under the facts supposed in 16, if the stock paid no dividends, the trustee would have a duty to sell it, and some of the sale proceeds would be allocated to Alice.

18. All the devisees except the American Cancer Society will have to contribute pro rata to the payment of any estate taxes on Tom's estate.

19. If the American Cancer Society is not in existence when Tom dies, the $10,000 will pass under the residuary clause.

20. The American Cancer Society is free to use the $10,000 as it wishes, so long as it is used for charitable purposes.

21. Evidence that Tom really intended the $10,000 to go to St. Joseph's Hospital would be inadmissible.

22. If an authorized representative of the American Cancer Society had promised Tom that it would share the bequest with St. Joseph's, this promise would be enforceable only if it was in writing.

True/False Answers

1. True. UPC § 2-605 gives the devisee additional securities owned by the testator as a result of action initiated by the entity. (#9.8)

2. False. The word "my" indicates that the bequest is specific. (#9.3)

3. False. He is only entitled to the balance of the price which is still owed at death, absent a showing that there was no intent to adeem. (#9.4)

4. False. UPC § 2-606 does not give the insurance proceeds to the devisee if they are paid to the testator before he dies. (#9.9)

5. True. UPC § 2-607 changes the common law rule on exoneration. (#9.20)

6. False. Many states have abolished the common law presumption of joint tenancy, so they would hold as tenants in common. (#4.77)

7. False. Tenancy by the entirety only applies when the tenants are husband and wife. (#5.42)

8. True. They are covered by the antilapse provision, even if this is viewed as a class gift. This is true even though they are adopted. They would divide their father's share, which would not pass under his will. (##2.7, 2.10, 2.55).

9. False. Adoption does not sever the tie between the child and her biological parents when the adoption is by a stepparent. UPC § 2-114 only bars the adopted child from inheriting twice from the same decedent. (##2.60, 2.62)

10. True, even though this is not a class gift. (#2.15)

11. False. UPC § 2-702 requires a devisee to survive by 120 hours. The first part of the sentence is correct: if Alice had no issue, her devise would lapse and go into the residue. (##2.15, 2.24)

12. True. Frank's children could not inherit while he was alive, and normally only heirs (and devisees under another will) can contest a will. (##1.18, 12.10)

13. False. They would only take their father's share by representation and this would amount to 1/21, since Tom had seven siblings. (#1.19)

14. True. A rebuttable presumption of undue influence would arise because of the attorney-client relationship, though not because of the brother-sister relationship. However, the devise might still be upheld if it seemed natural. (##7.16-.21)

15. False. Model Rule 1.8 makes an exception "where the client is related to the donee." (#7.32)

16. False. In most states, stock dividends are allocated to principal. (#12.117)

17. True. A trustee has a duty to sell property which produces no income. Ordinarily, sales proceeds are principal, but not when the property sold has failed to produce income. (##12.83, 12.115)

18. True. UPC § 3-916. The Cancer Society is exempt because its devise qualifies for the charitable deduction. (##9.26, 9.30)

19. False. The money will probably be applied *cy pres* to another organization engaged in cancer research, assuming Tom had a "general charitable intent."(#10.71)

20. False. Restrictions in charitable gifts are enforceable. (#10.70).

21. True. Most cases hold that an unambiguous will cannot be reformed for mistake. (##6.4-.6)

22. False. A constructive trust would be imposed to prevent unjust enrichment even if the promise was simply inferred from silence. (#6.16)

Notes

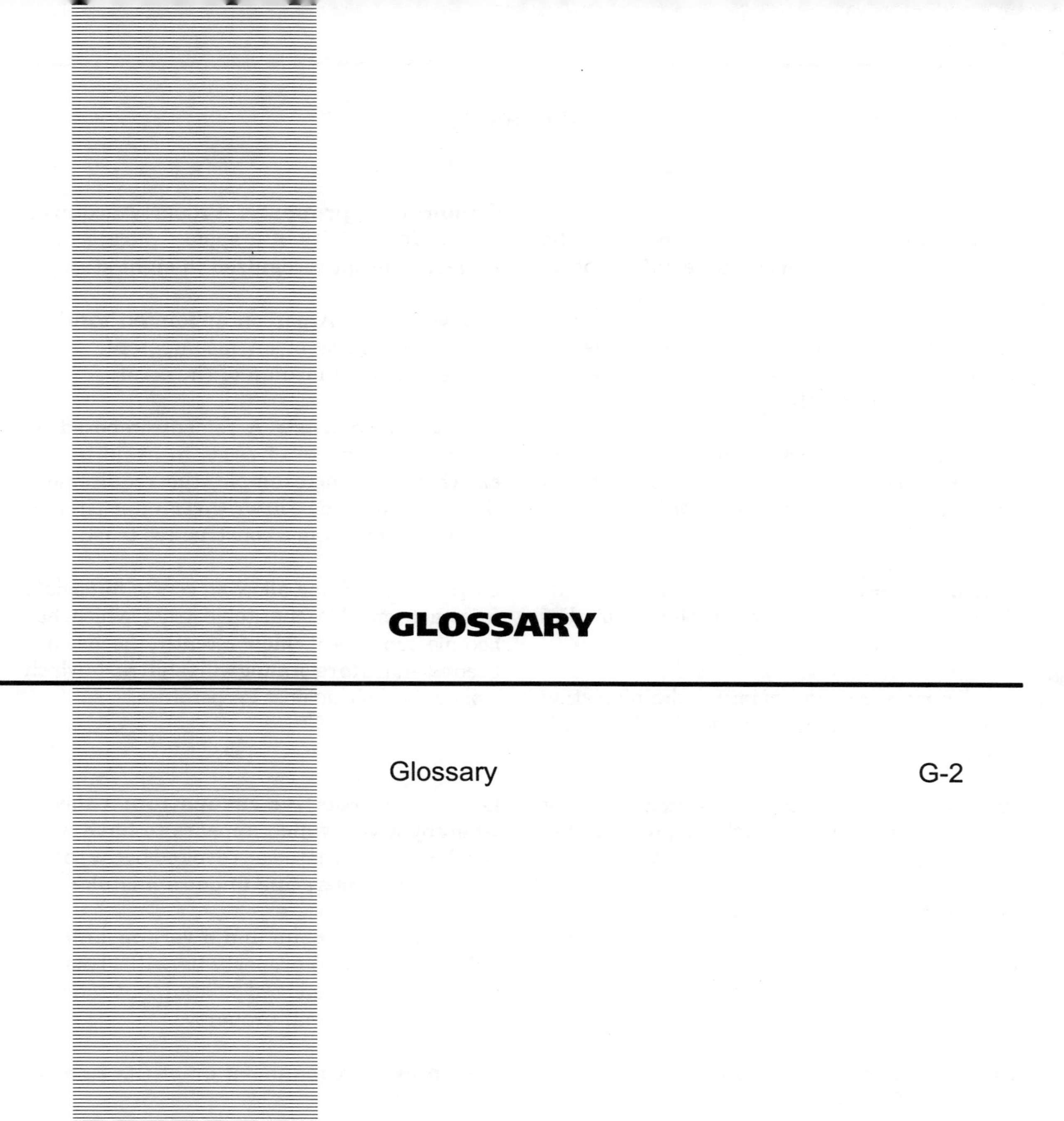

GLOSSARY

Glossary G-2

GLOSSARY

A

Abatement: The process of reducing the devises in a will because the testator's property is insufficient to satisfy them all.

Ademption: Failure of a specific devise because the property is no longer owned by the testator at death.

Administrator: Person who administers an estate; distinguished from an executor only by the fact that an administrator is not designated in a will.

Advancement: A gift to an heir that is deducted from her share when the donor dies intestate.

Ancillary administration: Administration of property in a state outside the decedent's domicile.

Antilapse statute: Statute designed to prevent a devise from lapsing; usually it provides that property shall go to the issue of the devisee.

Attestation clause: A clause signed by the witnesses to a will certifying that it was duly executed.

B

Bequest: A gift of personal property in a will. See **Devise.**

C

***Claflin rule*:** A rule, named after the leading case which held that a trust could not be terminated even with the consent of all the beneficiaries, so long as the settlor's purposes had not been fulfilled.

Class gift: A gift in a will or trust to a group, such as "my children."

Codicil: A document making minor changes in a previous will.

Community property: Property acquired by gainful activity of a spouse during marriage; a concept recognized in eight states.

Conservator: A person appointed to manage the property of an incompetent; sometimes called a guardian of the estate.

Constructive trust: A remedy imposed by courts in a variety of cases to avoid unjust enrichment. For example, the requirement that trusts of land be in writing is often circumvented by imposing a constructive trust.

***Cy pres*:** A doctrine allowing courts to deviate from a term of a charitable trust which has become impractical. More recently, the idea has been extended to reforming wills and trusts which violate the Rule against Perpetuities.

D

Dependant relative revocation: A theory whereby a will which appears to have been revoked is not treated as revoked because the testator was operating under a mistake.

Devise: Both a noun and a verb meaning a gift of (or to give) property by will. Historically this word referred to land, but today it also covers personal property.

Disclaimer: A renunciation of the right to take property.

E

Executor: A person named in a will to carry out (execute) its provisions.

Elective share: A share of an estate given in most states to a surviving spouse to protect against disinheritance by the decedent's will.

F

Family allowance: An allowance awarded to a spouse and children of a decedent for their support while the estate is being administered.

G

General devise: A devise not referring to specific property, such as, "I leave $10,000 to Mary." When the devise is of money, it is also referred to as pecuniary.

Gross estate: A tax concept which includes all items subject to an estate tax, including many assets not in the "probate estate."

Guardian of the estate: A person appointed to manage the property of a minor. Not to be confused with the guardian of the person who has the responsibilities of a parent toward the child. See also **Conservator.**

H

Heirs: The persons who take property by intestate succession. Historically it referred to those who succeeded to land, but today it also covers personal property also. It does *not* mean those who take by will; such persons are properly called devisees or legatees.

Holographic: A will entirely in the testator's handwriting. Holographic wills do not require witnesses in many states.

Honorary trust: A trust which is not charitable and has no beneficiary with standing to enforce it, such as a trust to care for a pet.

I

Intestate: A person who dies without a valid will.

J

Joint tenancy: A form of holding property whereby the surviving tenant succeeds to ownership of the whole, in contrast to tenancy in common.

Joint will: A will executed by two persons which disposes of the property of both.

L

Lapse: Failure of a devise, usually because the devisee dies before the testator.

Legatee: The person who receives a gift of personal property by will. Today commonly called a devisee.

Living trust: A trust created while the settlor is alive, as distinguished from a testamentary trust which is created by will. Living trusts are often called *inter vivos,* from the Latin "between the living."

M

Mortmain: The name given to statutes in a few states which restrict devises to charity.

N

Nonclaim statute: Statutes which require that claims against an estate be filed shortly after administration begins.

P

Personal representative: A generic term covering both executors and administrators who are so called because they represent the decedent.

Per stirpes: Dividing property by representation. See **Representation.**

Pourover: A devise to a trust, the terms of which are not set forth in the will.

Precatory: Words like "wish" added to a devise which were not intended to impose an enforceable obligation on the devisee.

Pretermitted heir: Heirs not mentioned in a will who, in many states, can get an intestate share on the theory that they were overlooked by the testator.

Probate: The process for proving the validity of a will. Also, the name given in most states to the court which deals with probate and administration of estates.

Publication: A declaration by the testator to the witnesses that the document is his will.

Purchase money resulting trust: When one person pays for land and another takes title, it is presumed that it was their intention that the person taking title hold in trust for the payor.

R

Representation: The right of children of a deceased relative to take the share their parent would have inherited if she had been alive.

Republication: A reference to a will in a codicil which causes it to be treated as if it had been executed when the codicil was executed.

Resulting trust: An interest in a trust which "results" (i.e., reverts) to the settlor, often because a situation occurs for which the trust makes no provision. See also **Purchase money resulting trust.**

Revival: A theory allowing a revoked will to be probated because the revoking will was itself revoked.

S

Secret trust: A trust which does not appear on the face of a will where the devisee has orally promised the testator to use the property for another person. If the trust, but not the designated beneficiary is disclosed, it is called a "semi-secret trust."

Settlor: The person who creates a trust.

Specific devise: A devise of specified property, such as "my home."

Spendthrift trust: A trust which provides that creditors of a beneficiary cannot reach his interest.

Statute of Frauds: An English statute of 1676 which has been widely copied in American law. It imposed more stringent formal requirements for wills and required that trusts of land be in writing, with certain exceptions.

T

Tenancy by entireties: A form of joint tenancy between spouses which exists in some states. Unlike ordinary joint tenancy, it cannot be severed.

Tenancy in common: A form of co-ownership in which the share a deceased tenant passes into his estate at death. Compare **Joint tenancy.**

Testament: The Latin word for will, sometimes doubled as in the phrase "last will and testament."

Testamentary: A trust created by will is "testamentary." The word is also applied to other transfers which have some of the characteristics of wills and which should therefore (arguably) be subject to the same requirements.

***Totten trust*:** An informal trust of a bank account, so called from a leading case which upheld them.

W

Wills Act: An English statute of 1837 which regulated the formalities for wills. Many American statutes are modeled on it. Often the term is used generally to refer to the local statute specifying the requirements for a will.

TABLE OF AUTHORITIES

Table of Cases TA-2

Statutes, Provisions and Other Authorities TA-9

TABLE OF CASES

Ablamis v. Roper .... #3.66
Abney v. Western Res.
Mutual Cas. Co. .... #4.39
Adoption of Kesey .... #2.46
Akers v. Hodel .... #7.9
Albertson v. Ryder .... #11.33
Alburn's Estate .... #5.17
Aldridge v. Mims .... #2.59
Allard v. Frech .... #3.58
Allen v. Amaco Production Co. .... #12.22
Allen, In re Estate of .... #11.51
Allen v. Storer .... #2.75
Allen, Estate of .... #11.51
Ambrose Succession v. Ambrose ...... #3.7
Amendaris Water Dev. Co.
v. Rainwater .... #6.64
Andrews v. Troy Bank
and Trust Co. .... #4.39
Arch Ltd. v. Yu .... #3.57
Armstrong v. Bray .... #2.89
Artope, In re Will of .... #6.19
Artz, Estate of v. Artz .... #2.85
Ascherl, Matter of Estate of .... #3.81
Ashe, Matter of Estate of .... #4.79
Atkinson, Matter of Estate of .... #9.31
Ausley, Matter of
Estate of .... ##5.1, 5.5, 5.16
Austin v. U.S. Bank
of Washington .... #10.36
Ayala v. Marinez .... #12.34
Azunce v. Estate of Azunce .... #3.17
Baker v. Leonard .... #6.35
Baker v. Mohr .... #8.6
Bancker, Estate of .... #5.3
Bank IV, Olathe
v. Capitol Federal S. & L.. .... #12.109
Barber v. Barber .... #10.48
Barrett's Estate .... #5.15
Barshak v. Buccheri .... #7.25
Bartell, Matter of Estate of .... #3.73
Barthelmess, Estate of .... #12.68
Bartlett v. Commissioner .... #8.18
Bassett v. Bassett .... #6.55
Batcheldor v. Boyd .... #2.42
Bearbower, Matter of Estate of .... #4.14
Beatty v. Beatty .... #3.80
Beck, In re Estate of ..... ##6.9, 6.11, 10.71
Bedree v. Bedree .... #7.24
Beesley, Matter of Estate of .... #3.76
Belgard, Matter of Trust
Created by .... #2.58
Bergen v. Travelers Insurance Co. .. #5.34
Berger v. United States .... #5.28
Berry, Estate of .... #7.7
Beyer v. First National Bank .... #12.103
Binns v. Vick .... ##4.72, 4.74
Black v. Unknown Creditors .... #2.27
Blackmon v. Estate of Battock .... #8.16
Bland v. Graves .... #7.2
Boatmen's Trust Co. v. Conklin .... #2.58
Boatwright v. Perkins .... #6.52
Bob Jones Univ. v. United States .. #10.60
Boehm v. Allen .... #7.11
Bol, Matter of Estate of .... #5.30
Bonner v. Arnold .... #9.20
Bonney v. Granger .... #2.28
Bookasta, In re
Conservatorship of .... #12.1
Boright, Matter of .... #10.49
Bosone v. Bosone .... #3.57
Brent v. St. Cent. Collection Unit .. #11.30
Brosamer v. Mark .... #11.29
Brown, Matter of Estate of .... #9.2
Boyle v. Schmitt .... #8.9
Bozell, Estate of .... #3.45
Branigan, Matter of Estate of .... #6.6
Brannan, Estate of
v. LaSalle State Bank ...... ##9.16, 9.34
Breckner v. Prestwood .... #6.11
Brickhouse v. Brickhouse .... #4.12
Briley, Matter of Estate of .... #9.10
Bronston, Estate of .... #7.29
Brown, Matter of Estate of .... #12.9
Brown v. Metz .... #4.46
Brunel, In re Estate of .... #1.31
Buder v. Sartore .... #12.78
Burcham, Matter of Estate of .... #2.7
Burns v. Adamson .... #4.4
Butler v. Halstead .... #1.39
Button v. Elmhurst
National Bank .... #2.86
Button by Curio v. Elmhurst
National Bank .... ##2.86, 11.19
Button, Matter of Estate of .... #2.100
Calcutt, Estate of v. Calcutt .... #3.76
Campbell, Matter of Estate of .... #12.13

TA

Cardiovascular & Thoracic Surgery v. DiMazzio .... #11.1
Carr v. Carr .... #2.78
Carrol, In re Estate of .... #4.19
Carter v. Carter .... #7.13
Carter v. United Methodist Church #5.16
Casey, Estate of .... #7.29
Casey, Estate of v. Commissioner .. #10.32
Casey, In re Estate of .... #8.9
Central Trust Bank v. Stout .... #1.18
Certain Scholarship Funds, In re .. #10.60
Chaitlen, Estate of .... #4.62
Chaney, Matter of Adoption of .... #2.57
Chapman v. Chapman .... #9.10
Chase, Matter of Estate of .... #2.68
Chenot v. Bordelau .... #11.19
Chesnin v. Fischler .... #3.59
Chiesi v. First Citizens Bank .... ##2.87, 11.9
Chichton, Estate of .... ##3.60, 3.62
Chrisman, In re Estate of .... #12.108
Christensen v. Sabad .... #5.46
Citizens Action League v. Kitzer ... #11.5
Citizens National Bank v. Stasell .... #5.43
Claflin v. Claflin .... #10.51
Clark v. Greenhalge .... #6.24
Clark v. Jeter .... #2.43
Clark, Matter of .... #9.11
Clark v. Studenwalt .... #4.9
Clark v. Unknown Creditors .... #12.19
Cleveland Bar Association v. Kelley .... #7.32
Clymer v. Mayo .... ##2.66, 5.48
Cohen v. City of Lynn .... #12.97
Cohn v. Heymann .... #3.8
Cole v. Guy .... #4.38
Colgan v. Sisters of St. Joseph .... #10.71
Conkle v. Walker .... #5.7
Connecticut National Bank & Trust Co. v. Chadwick .... #6.10
Connol v. Francisco .... #2.76
Continental Bank, N.A. v. Herguth . #2.37
Cook v. Holland .... #11.62
Cooper v. Trust Co. Bank .. ##10.45, 10.47
Coster v. Crookham .... #12.105
Council v. Owens .... #11.31
Courtney v. Lawson .... #12.27
Cousee v. Estate of Efston .... #12.9
Craig, Matter of Estate of .... #10.71
Creed's Estate .... #9.5
Crump's Estate v. Freeman .... #3.18
Curry v. Williman .... #1.25
Dalia v. Lawrence .... ##3.32, 3.33
Dalton, In re Estate of .... #2.79
Damon, Matter of .... #10.41
Daniels, Matter of Will of .... #6.29
Dankbar, Estate of .... #7.13
Dardaganis v. Grace Capital, Inc. . #12.83
Dawson v. Yucus .... #2.13
Dauer v. Butera .... ##2.20, 2.21
Dean v. Johnson .... #11.10
DeLuca v. Bancohio National Bank, Inc. .... #4.39
Dethorne, Matter of Estate of .... #4.8
Dewire v. Haveles .... #2.27
Dickie v. Dickie .... #8.12
Dire, Matter of Estate of .... #11.50
Dittus, Matter of Estate of .... #4.36
Dock v. Tuchman .... #11.7
Doe v. Colligan .... #11.45
Dollar Savings v. Turner .... #2.17
Donner, Matter of Estate of .... #12.81
Ducey, Matter of Estate of .... #3.64
Duggan v. Keto .... ##4.63, 12.57
Dulles, Estate of .... #2.48
DuPont v. Southern National Bank #5.28
Durwood v. Nelson .... #6.52
Dwan, Matter of Trusts under Will of .... #12.51
Dwyer v. Allyn .... #4.64
Eastman, Estate of v. Eastman .... #5.4
Edwards, Estate of .... #6.15
Efird v. Efird .... #3.38
Elam, Estate of .... #7.7
Ellis National Bank v. Irving Trust Co. .... #11.35
Erickson, Matter of Estate of .... #4.9
Ernst v. Shaw .... #2.107
Eschler v. Eschler .... #5.34
Evans v. Abney .... #10.67
Evans v. Newton .... #10.60
Eyerman v. Mercantile Trust Co. .... #3.86
Farkas v. Williams .... #4.67
Federal Kemper Life Assurance v. Eichwedel .... #2.87
Felonenko v. Siomka .... #6.40
Fenzel v. Floyd .... #6.8

TA

Fifth Third Bank v. Fifth Third Bank ... #12.15
First Alabama Bank v. Martin ... #12.79
First Interstate Bank v. First Wyoming Bank ... #7.25
First Interstate Bank v. Lindberg ... #5.19
First Interstate Bank v. Young ... #6.4
First National Bank v. Anthony ... #2.16
First National Bank v. King ... #2.56
First National Bank v. Singer ... #2.28
First Union Bank v. Cisa ... #10.41
Fitzgerald, Estate of ... #4.31
Fleischman, Estate Of ... #9.29
Foley v. Evans ... #2.56
Foran, Matter of Marriage of ... #3.79
Ford v. Peoples Trust and Savings Bank ... #12.46
Forsyth v. Rowe ... #11.17
Fox Valley v. Brown ... #5.47
Francoeur, Estate of ... #5.12
Froman, Matter of Estate of ... #3.35
Gagnier, In re Estate of ... #3.81
Garwood's Estate, Matter of ... #12.86
Gaspelin, In re Estate of ... #3.72
Getty, Matter of Estate of ... #12.10
Geyer, In re Estate of ... #3.80
Gibbs, Matter of Estate of ... #2.85
Gillespie v. Davis ... #4.64
Gillespie v. Seattle First National Bank ... ##12.99, 12.104
Gillespie v. Seymour (877 P.2d 409 [Kan. 1994]) ... #12.101
Gillespie v. Seymour (796 P.2d 1060 [Kan. App. 1990]) ... #12.109
Gillingham, Discipline Proceeding against ... #7.31
Gonzales, Matter of ... #10.71
Goodman v. Zimmerman ... #7.10
Gordon, In re ... #12.89
Gorham State Bank v. Seliens ... #11.53
Gould's Will, In re ... #12.70
Graham v. Graham ... #6.58
Granado v. Granado ... ##6.59, 6.62
Greenfield, Estate of ... #6.8
Greening, Donald v. Oklahoma Wire Rope Prod. ... #11.40
Gregory v. Estate of Gregory ... #8.17
Griffin, Matter of Estate of ... #2.103
Grimes v. Commissioner ... #8.18
Gross v. Gross ... #4.50
Grove, Estate of v. Selken ... #12.101
Groves, Matter of Estate of ... #3.69
Guaranty Bank & Trust Co., Ex parte ... #12.69
Gruen v. Gruen ... #4.43
Guardianship of Connor, Matter of ... #12.76
Guidry v. Sheet Metal Workers National Pen. Fund ... #11.37
Gulf Nat'l Bank v. Sturtevant ... #10.39
Gustie, In re ... ##4.54, 4.55
Hagaman v. Morgan ... ##2.55, 2.58
Hale, Matter of Estate of ... #9.17
Hall v. Eaton ... ##3.87, 12.9
Hall v. Nelson ... ##2.77, 7.30
Hall v. Vallandingham ... #2.59
Hamilton v. Hamilton ... #2.78
Hamilton, In re ... #2.85
Hamilton, Matter of Estate of ... ##3.12, 9.28
Hamiter, Succession of ... #7.6
Hanau, Estate of v. Hanau ... #3.51
Hancock v. Krause ... ##5.10, 6.14
Hannah v. Hannah ... #3.39
Hannan, In re Estate of ... #1.4
Hansen, In re Estate of ... #3.54
Harbaugh's Estate, Matter of ... #10.53
Hardins v. McPhearson ... #12.112
Harris, Estate of ... #2.81
Harrison, Estate of ... #4.12
Hartsfield v. Lescher ... #11.17
Hawley, Matter of Estate of ... #12.87
Haynes v. Williams ... #2.10
Heater, Estate of v. Illinois Dept. of Public Aid ... #2.106
Hedrick v. West One Bank ... #12.122
Heggstead, Estate of ... ##3.68, 4.57
Heinbach, Matter of Estate of ... #3.15
Heins, Matter of ... #11.11
Hendrickson, Matter of Estate of ... #2.77
Henkle v. Henkle ... #6.41
Herron v. Underwood ... #4.44
Herz, Matter of Estate of ... #9.35
Higgs v. Estate of Higgs ... #7.21
Hilliard v. Hilliard ... #6.53
Hinson v. Hinson ... #6.42
Hocks v. Jeremiah ... ##4.37, 4.41
Hoffman v. Kohns ... #7.30

TA

Hoover v. Smith .... #4.77
Howard v. Reynolds .... #1.3
Hoyle, Matter of Estate of .... #4.40
Hughes, In re Estate of.................. #12.87
Hull v. Williams .... #3.50
Huntington Nat'l Bank
v. Wolfe .... #12.91
Hutchinson Nat'l Bank &
Trust Co. v. Brown .... #11.5
Huxtable Living Trust,
Matter of .... #6.38
Hyman v. Glover .... #2.55
Ioupe, Estate of .... #7.3
Jackson v. Phillips .... #10.71
Jewish Hospital v. Boatmen's
Bank ....#12.106
Johnson v. Farmers & Merchants
Bank .... #3.34
Johnson by and through Lackey
v. Schick .... #4.48
Johnson, In re Estate of................... #8.9
Johnson, Matter of Estate of .... #2.24
Johnson v. Ramsey .... #6.44
Jones, Estate of ....#12.105
Jones, Estate of, v. Jones .... #3.20, 7.19
Jones, In re .... #2.57
Jones, Matter of............................... #7.28
Juran v. Epstein .... #8.8
Kalk v. Security Pacific Bank
Washington .... #11.5
Kalouse, Estate of .... #2.10, 2.13
Kaplan, In re Estate of .... #8.3
Kasper, Matter of Estate of .... #5.6
Katleman, Estate of .... #3.71
Katze-Miller, Matter of Estate of..... #1.32
Kauzlarich v. Landrum .... #6.16, 6.17
Kavanaugh v. Estate of
Dobrowolski .... #4.62
Keegan v. Estate of Keegan............. #2.25
Keener v. Archibald .... #4.9
Kegel v. State .... #11.17
Kemper v. Kemper, ... #12.29
Kerper v. Kerper ....#12.102
Kerr, In re Estate of......................... #5.19
Kesterson v. Cronan .... #4.44
Kirkendall, Matter of Estate of........ #2.15
Kleefeld, Estate of .... #5.7
Klein, Matter of Estate of................ #6.15
Knight v. Knight .... #11.41
Kohler v. Fletcher ....#12.101
Kolbinger, Estate of .... #9.9
Kolkovich v. Tosolin .... #6.39
Korten v. Chicago City Bank
and Trust Co. .... #10.46
Kreitman's Estate, In re .... #2.99
Krokowsky, Matter of Estate of .... #3.88
Krotz, Estate of .... #4.65
Laas, Estate of .... #10.66
Lalli v. Lalli .... #2.35
Lane, Estate of .... #7.12
Lane, In re Trust of........................ #10.53
Langley, Matter of Estate of............ #4.83
Larabee v. Booth .... #4.48
Latham v. Father Devine .... #6.20
Lauga, Succession of .... #3.7
Lawson v. Atwood .... #2.64
Lealaimatafoa v. Woodward-Clyde
Consl. .... #2.76
Leatherwood v. Meisch .... #3.20
Leaver v. McBride .... #9.3
Lehman v. Irving Trust Co. .... #12.52
Leone, Matter of Estate of .... #7.28
Lettergraver, Matter of
Estate of .... #3.30, 3.40
Levin v. Smith .... #6.57
Levinson v. Citizens National
Bank ....#12.101
Lille, Estate of .... #10.42
Lincoln National Bank
v. Shriners Hopsitals ....#12.102
Lindgren, Matter of Estate of......... #10.38
Lineback v. Stout .... #10.38
Lollis v. Lollis .... #6.52
Lucero v. Lucero .... #7.6
Lundsford v. Western States
Life Ins. .... #2.90
Lynch v. Lynch .... #3.55
Lynch, Estate of v. .... #3.43
Lynchburg College
v. Central Fidelity Bank............ #9.29
MacDonald, In re Estate of .... #3.75
Maestas v. Martinez .... #2.99
Mahan v. Mahan .... #10.53
Maher, Estate of.............................. #8.4
Maheras, Matter of
Estate of............................ #7.14, 7.18
Mahoney v. Leddy .... #4.63
Mahle v. First National Bank ....#12.103

TA

Maier v. Henning .... #12.68
Main v. Howard .... #5.38
Mak-M v. SM .... #2.43
Malmquist v. Malmquist .... #3.53
Martin v. Gerdes .... #6.10, 6.14
Martinson v. Holso .... #4.87
Maryland National Bank v.
Cummins .... #12.82
Mattes v. Olearain .... #6.48
Maurice F. Jones Trust
v. Barnett Bank......................... #9.33
May v. Estate of McCormick .... #5.14
Mayberry, Estate of
v. Mayberry .... #9.1, 9.5
McClintock v. Scahill, ...#2.106
McCool, In re Estate of .... #12.68
McFayden, In re Estate of .... #2.99
McGahee, In re Estate of .... #6.21
McGill v. Johnson .... #2.12, 2.13
McGill v. Lazzaro .... #12.18
McIntyre v. Raukhorst..................... #5.24
McKenzie v. Francis .... #5.2
McKim, Matter of
Estate of...................................... #6.48
McLane v. Russell .... #5.44
McNicholas, Estate of v. State ....#2.109
Mebust, Matter of Estate of .... #1.27
Mest v. Dugan .... #12.71
Metropolitan Life Ins. Co.
v. Hanslip .... #5.48
Meyer, In re Estate of ....#12.131
Miller v. Estate of Miller ..... ##2.81, 12.23
Miller v. Todd .... #12.10
Mitchell, Estate of........................... #9.12
Mocny, In re Estate of...................... #3.35
Mongold v. Mayle .... #3.70
Montoya v, New Mexico Human
Services Dept............................. #4.38
Moore v. Livingston.......................... #1.4
Morice v. Bishop of Durham........... #10.63
Morse v. Volz .... ##7.5, 7.19
Mothershed v. Schrimsher .... #2.89
Muder, Estate of.............................. #4.27
Munford v. Maclellan .... #12.37
Murdock, Matter of Estate of .... #10.71
National Academy of Sciences
v. Cambridge Trust Co. ....#12.126
National Home Life Ins. Co.
v. Patterson .... #2.66
Nationsbank of Virginia
v. Estate of Grandy ...... ##10.37, 10.38
Nessralla v. Peck .... #6.47
Newick v. Mason .... #10.64
Newton, In re Estate of.................... #2.79
Niehenke, Matter of Estate of ....#12.124
Nielson, Estate of .... #5.10
Noble v. McNerny .... #3.73
Norton, Matter of Estate of .... #6.23
O'Brien v. Dudenhoeffer .... #7.23
O'Hara v. Public Employees
Retirement Board .... #3.57
O'Keefe v. State Department of
Revenue .... #1.36
Oliver v. Estate of Oliver .... #2.80
Opperman v. Anderson .... #9.7
Overt, Estate of .... #4.17
Papale-Keefe v. Altomare .... #4.58
Parham v. Hughes............................ #2.46
Parker v. Kokot .... #5.38
Pascale v. Pascale .... #10.24
Pate v. Ford ....#2.108
Paul, Matter of .... #2.57
Pedersen v. Bibioff .... #6.43
Peffley-Warner v. Bowen .... #2.76
Penn Mutual Life Ins. Co.
v. Abramson .... #3.22
Perino v. Eldert .... #8.11
Perkins v. Stuemke .... #11.10
Pessein v. Pessein .... #3.9
Petty's Estate, Matter of.................. #4.20
Phillips, Estate of .... #9.31
Pickrell, Matter of Estate of .... #9.29
Pilafas, Matter of Estate of .... #5.29
Pogue v. Pogue .... #1.38
Powell v. American Charter
Fed. S&L .... #8.16
Powers v. Steele .... #2.51
Powers v. Wilkinson .... #2.49
Price, In re Estate of .... #4.17
Progressive Land Developers v.
Exchange National Bank .... #12.99
Putnam v. Via .... #8.17
Quintana v. Quintana ....#12.127
Ramage v. Ramage .... #4.53
Ramirez, Matter of Estate of........... #4.25
Ranney, Matter of Will of .... #4.4
Raulston, Matter of Estate of.......... #2.42
Rayman, Matter of Estate of........... #5.19

Record, Estate of .... #7.2
Redfern v. Ford .... #3.57
Reed v. Campbell .... ##2.39, 2.50
Reed, Estate of .... #12.6
Reeves, In re .... #5.19
Reiman's Estate, Matter of .... #6.17
Remax of Blue Springs
v. Vajda & Co., Inc. .... #11.3
Restaino v. Vannah .... #8.15
Reynolds v. City of Los Angeles .... #2.64
Richter, Estate of .... #12.14
Roe, Matter of Estate of .... #9.29
Ross, Estate of v. Ross .... #4.45
Ross, Matter of Estate of .... #2.7
Rosser v. Prem .... #10.59
Rothenberg, Estate of .... #7.15
Rothko, In re Estate of .... #9.11
Rowland v. Rowland .... #3.81
Royal, Matter of Estate of .... #4.16
Rozell, Matter of Estate of .... #12.71
Ruehl, Estate of v. Ruehl .... #11.56
Ruel v. Hardy .... #5.5
Russell, Estate of .... #2.15
Ryan v. Ryan .... #4.33
Sander, Matter of Estate of .... #5.49
Sauter's Estate .... #12.34
Savage, Matter of Estate of .... #6.33
Schafroth, In re Estate of .... #12.3
Schildberg v. Schildberg .... #12.34
Schimke v. Karlstad .... #5.41
Schroll, Matter of .... #10.48
Schulz v. Miller .... #5.39
Seegers, Estate of .... #7.36
Seidlitz v. Eames .... #2.87
Seradell v. Hartford Accident and
Indemnity Co. .... #2.70
Shannon, Estate of .... #3.73
Shannon, In re Marriage of .... #3.54
Shaw, Estate of .... #5.5
Shaw, In re .... #10.59
Shriners Hospital v. Zrillic .... #3.84
Siegel Mobile Home Group
v. Bowen .... #4.49
Simpson, Matter of .... #2.102
Simpson, Matter of Estate of .... #2.8
Simpson v. Calvert .... #4.33
Sims v. Cox .... #3.15
Sisters of Mercy Health
v. First Bank .... #11.34
Slawsby v. Slawsby .... #8.8
Smelzer, Matter of Estate of .... #6.5
Smith v. First National Bank .... #12.96
Smith v. Smith .... #3.53
Smith, Matter of .... #7.33
Smith, Matter of Will of .... #4.25
Snyder, Matter of Estate of .... #4.78
Snyder v. Peterson .... #6.39
Soles' Estate .... #9.3
Speelman v. Pascal .... #4.48
Spivey v. Pulley .... #4.33
Spruance v. Northway .... #7.8
Stallworth v. Hicks .... #2.50
Stasis, Estate of .... #4.9
State v. Hawes .... #11.15
Steel v. Wellcome Trustees Ltd. .... #12.85
Sterling v. Wilson .... #3.25
Stevens v. National City Bank .... #12.84
Stokes v. Stokes .... #1.10
Story v. Hargrave .... #8.15
Stowell, In re Estate of .... #12.100
Stowers, Estate of
v. Northwest Bank Indiana .... #2.2
Stowers v. Northwest
Bank Indiana .... #12.103
Sturgis v. Stinson .... #12.114
Sturm, Estate of .... #11.60
Sullivan v. Sullivan .... #2.13
Sundin v. Klein .... #2.88
S.V. v. Estate of Bellamy .... #2.43
Sykes v. Propane Power Co. .... #2.76
Takabuk v. Ching .... #10.68
Talbot, Succession of .... #5.5
Talley v. Succession of Stuckey .... #3.19
Tarbox v. Palmer .... #9.32
Task, In re Estate of .... #1.26
Tate v. Kennedy .... #2.22
Territorial Sav. & Loan Ass'n
v. Baird .... #11.13
Thomas v. Reid .... #6.42
Thomas v. Sullivan .... #2.72
Thomas v. Thomas .... #2.96
Tierce v. Macedonia United
Methodist Church .... #6.24
Tolin, In re Estate of .... #5.5
Totten, In re .... #4.68
Tovrea, Estate of v. Nolan .... #9.29
Traders Travel Int'l, Inc.
v. Howser .... #11.2

TA

Trim v. Daniels .... #4.7
Triable v. Gordon .... #2.33
Trout v. Parker .... #5.24
Tsilidis v. Pedakis .... #2.67
Tulsa Professional Collection
Services, Inc. v. Pope .... #11.5
United States v. Chandler .... #4.39
United States v. Irvine .... #2.104
Utterback, Estate of .... #6.12
Vadman v. American Cancer Society #6.9
Venturi v. Taylor .... #11.50
Vick, Matter of Estate of.................. #6.2
Village of Mount Prospect,
Matter of .... #10.69
Villwock, Matter of Estate of........... #2.24
Vitacco v. Eckberg .... #5.35
Waits v. Hamlin .... #12.35
Wales, Estate of, ... #9.3
Wallace, In re Estate of .... #12.47
Walsh v. Walsh, ... #6.49
Walton v. Walton .... #8.14
Warner, Estate of .... #5.49
Warner, Matter of Estate of .... #12.4
Warren-Boynton State Bank
v. Wallbaum .... #2.22
Wasserman v. Cohen .... #9.2
Watkins v. Watkins .... #6.54
Watson v. Santalucia .... #9.8
Webb, Matter of Estate of
(863 P.2d 1116 [Okl. 1993]) .... #7.11
Webb, Matter of Estate of (832 P.2d 27
[Okl. App. 1994]) .... #12.42
Webster, Matter of Estate .... #4.12
West v. White .... #12.4
Wheeler v. Mann .... #12.88
Whitfield v. Cohen .... #12.106
Whorton v. Dillingham .... #2.76
Whyte, Estate of v. Whyte .... #2.73
Wich v. Fleming .... #4.21
Widmeyer, Matter of Estate of .... #12.21
Wier v. Howard Hughes
Medical Institute .... #10.67
Wilcox v. Gentry .... #11.19
Wilhelm, Estate of .... #3.10
Williams v. Faucett .... #9.16
Wilmington Trust Co. v. Amian .... #2.49
Wilson v. Dixon .... #11.39
Wilson v. Flowers .... #10.63
Wilson, Matter of Estate of .... #12.9
Witt v. Rosen .... #6.1
Woelke v. Calfee .... #8.7
Wolfe v. Wolfe .... #4.25
Wolfinger, Estate of
v. Wolfinger .... #5.37
Worthley, Estate of .... #4.71
Wood v. Bettis .... #7.2
Woods v. Harris .... #2.43
Woodward, Matter of Estate of .... #3.20
Wrage, Estate of .... #4.80
Wright, Matter of Estate of .... #3.8
Wright v. Union Nat. Bank ... ##4.83, 9.29
Yakima Adjustment Service, Inc.
v. Durand .... #11.2
Zahn's Estate .... #10.60
Zoglauer, Estate of .... #5.40
Zuckerman, In re Estate of.............. #4.56

TABLE OF STATUTES, CODES AND OTHER AUTHORITIES

Restatement (Second) of Property (Donative Transfers)

§ 18.6 .... # 2.8
§ 25.1 .... # 2.4
§ 25.3 .... # 2.44
§ 25.5 .... # 2.60
§ 25.8 .... # 2.4
§ 28.2 .... ## 2.1, 2.3, 2.30
§ 29.6 .... # 2.31
§ 31.1 .... # 4.42
§ 34.4 .... # 7.26
§ 34.7 .... # 6.6

Restatement (Second) of Trusts

§ 44 .... # 6.46
§ 45 .... # 6.46
§ 47 .... # 4.53
§ 55 .... ## 6.16, 6.17, 6.18
§ 57 .... # 4.66
§ 58 .... # 5.26
§ 106 .... # 12.38
§ 108 .... ## 12.29, 12.41
§ 122 .... # 4.73
§ 124 .... # 10.65
§ 127 .... # 10.47
§ 152 .... # 11.43
§ 153 .... # 11.26
§ 155 .... # 11.19
§ 156 .... # 11.39
§ 157 .... ## 11.32, 11.34, 11.38
§ 162 .... # 11.18
§ 170 .... # 12.94
§ 179 .... # 12.74
§ 184 .... # 12.107
§ 185 .... # 10.40
§ 188 .... # 12.54
§ 190 .... # 12.68
§ 194 .... # 12.44
§ 196 .... # 12.42
§ 216 .... # 12.103
§ 222 .... # 12.102
§ 224 .... # 12.107
§ 226 .... # 12.126
§ 227 .... ## 12.75, 12.79
§ 254 .... # 12.127
§ 257 .... # 11.36
§ 258 .... # 12.108
§ 268 .... # 11.62
§ 275 .... # 11.64
§ 276 .... # 11.64
§ 284 .... ## 6.63, 12.72
§ 292 .... # 6.63
§ 297 .... # 12.73
§ 313 .... # 6.64
§ 326 .... # 12.109
§ 330 .... ## 5.25, 11.16
§ 332 .... # 5.27
§ 333 .... # 6.40
§ 340 .... # 10.46
§ 348 .... # 10.70
§ 368 .... # 10.58
§ 374 .... # 10.61
§ 376 .... # 10.62
§ 391 .... # 10.69
§ 399 .... # 10.71
§ 415 .... # 4.75
§ 440 .... # 6.50
§ 442 .... # 6.52
§ 443 .... # 6.53
§ 444 .... # 6.60

TABLE OF STATUTES

Employee Retirement Income Security Act (ERISA)

.......................## 3.66, 3.82, 5.48, 11.28

Internal Revenue Code

§ 1 .... # 10.16
§ 678 .... ## 10.18, 10.43, 12.44
§ 2036 .... # 10.23
§ 2038 .... # 10.23
§ 2041 .... # 10.42
§ 2055 .... # 9.30
§ 2056 .... # 9.30
§ 2206 .... # 9.25
§ 2207 .... ## 9.25, 9.33
§ 2207B .... # 9.25
§ 2518 .... ## 2.101, 2.104

Uniform Commercial Code

.... # 4.39

Uniform Disposition of Community Property Rights at Death Act

.... # 3.63

Uniform Fraudulent Transfer Act

.... # 11.1

Uniform Marriage and Divorce Act

.... ## 2.71, 3.9

Uniform Parentage Act

.... ## 2.38, 2.39, 2.40, 2.41, 2.42, 2.43, 2.44

Uniform Premarital Agreement Act

.... # 3.78

Uniform Principal and Income Acts (1931, 1962)

In general .... # 12.111

Uniform Principal and Income Act (1962)

§ 2 .... # 12.114
§ 4 .... # 12.122
§ 5 .... # 12.123
§ 7 .... # 12.117
§ 9 .... # 12.120
§ 13 .... # 12.121

Uniform Probate Code

§ 1-102 .... # 1.12
§ 1-107 .... # 2.26
§ 1-201 .... ## 2.47, 2.65
§ 1-306 .... # 12.11
§ 2-101 .... # 3.89
§ 2-102 .... ## 1.10, 1.12, 1.16
§ 2-102A .... # 1.14
§ 2-103 ...... ## 1.17, 1.23, 1.24, 1.26, 1.29
§ 2-104 .... # 2.24
§ 2-106 .... ## 1.20, 1.21, 1.22, 1.27
§ 2-112 .... # 1.25
§ 2-107 ...... ## 2.91, 2.93, 2.94, 2.95, 2.97
§ 2-110 .... # 1.19
§ 2-112 .... # 3.26
§ 2-113 .... # 2.61
§ 2-114 ...... ## 2.38, 2.46, 2.54, 2.59, 2.62
§ 2-202 .... ## 3.28, 3.61
§ 2-203 .... ## 3.30, 3.31, 12.27
§ 2-204 .... # 3.31
§ 2-205 ...... ## 3.33, 3.34, 3.35, 3.36, 3.38
§ 2-207 .... # 3.30
§ 2-208 .... ## 3.37, 3.74

TA

§ 2-209 .... ## 3.30, 3.39, 3.40, 9.22
§ 2-211 .... # 3.41
§ 2-212 .... ## 3.44, 3.45
§ 2-213 .... ## 3.76, 5.19
§ 2-301 .... ## 3.67, 3.68, 3.69, 3.70, 3.72, 3.73
§ 2-302 ...... ## 3.16, 3.17, 3.18, 3.21, 9.21
§ 2-402 .... ## 3.15, 3.39
§ 2-403 .... # 3.39
§ 2-404 .... ## 3.10, 3.11, 3.39
§ 2-405 .... # 3.12
§ 2-501 .... # 7.1
§ 2-502 .... ## 4.8, 4.13, 4.16, 4.26
§ 2-503 .... ## 4.4, 4.23
§ 2-504 .... ## 4.9, 4.20
§ 2-505 .... # 4.12
§ 2-506 .... ## 4.30, 4.31
§ 2-507 .... ## 5.1, 5.3, 5.4, 5.12
§ 2-509 .... # 5.14
§ 2-510 .... ## 6.23, 6.24
§ 2-511 .... ## 6.26, 6.29
§ 2-512 .... # 6.31
§ 2-513 .... # 6.25
§ 2-514 .... ## 8.2, 8.3, 8.5, 8.8
§ 2-515 .... # 5.8
§ 2-601 .... # 6.6
§ 2-603 .... ## 2.6, 2.7, 2.8, 2.10
§ 2-604 .... # 2.15
§ 2-605 .... ## 9.7, 9.8
§ 2-606 .... ## 9.2, 9.4, 9.7, 9.9, 9.10
§ 2-607 .... # 9.20
§ 2-608 .... # 9.10
§ 2-609 .... # 2.99
§ 2-701 .... # 2.55
§ 2-702 .... ## 2.24, 2.25
§ 2-703 .... # 3.64
§ 2-706 .... # 2.17
§ 2-707 .... # 2.21
§ 2-711 .... ## 2.22, 2.31
§ 2-705 .... ## 2.47, 2.55, 2.58, 2.60
§ 2-708 .... # 2.30
§ 2-709 .... # 2.28
§ 2-801 .... ## 11.49, 11.50
§ 2-803 .... ## 11.50, 11.51, 11.55, 11.58
§ 2-804 .... ## 5.19, 5.48, 5.49
§ 3-907 .... # 10.65
§ 2-1009 .... # 4.11
§ 3-108 .... # 12.3
§ 3-201 .... # 12.4
§ 3-203 .... ## 12.27, 12.33
§ 3-306 .... # 12.7
§ 3-312 .... # 11.66
§ 3-401 .... # 12.8
§ 3-406 .... # 4.22
§ 3-407 .... ## 7.4, 7.16
§ 3-408 .... # 12.6
§ 3-707 .... ## 12.7, 12.64
§ 3-713 .... ## 12.91, 12.92
§ 3-714 .... # 12.72
§ 3-715 .... ## 11.61, 12.55, 12.65
§ 3-716 .... # 2.42
§ 3-718 .... # 12.40
§ 3-719 .... ## 12.45, 12.52
§ 3-801 .... ## 11.49, 11.50
§ 3-802 .... # 11.48
§ 3-803 ...... ## 11.50, 11.51, 11.55, 11.58
§ 3-804 .... # 11.51
§ 3-805 .... ## 11.47, 12.17
§ 3-807 .... # 11.60
§ 3-808 .... # 11.63
§ 3-810 .... # 11.58
§ 3-814 .... # 9.20
§ 3-902 .... ## 9.15, 9.17, 9.18, 9.19
§ 3-903 .... # 2.100
§ 3-905 .... # 12.13
§ 3-906 .... # 12.68, 12.130, 12.131
§ 3-909 .... # 12.127
§ 3-916 .... # 9.26, 9.28, 9.29, 9.30
§ 3-1101 .... # 10.55, 12.15
§ 3-1201 .... # 12.19
§ 3-1202 .... # 12.19
§ 4-205 .... # 12.22
§ 5-401 .... # 12.30
§ 5-407 .... # 2.106, 7.27, 7.28
§ 5-419 .... # 7.23
§ 5-423 .... # 12.77

§ 5-424 .... # 7.28
§ 5-426 .... # 9.10
§ 5-428 .... # 11.63
§ 5-501 .... # 7.29, 10.32
§ 5-505 .... # 12.109
§ 6-201 .... # 4.79, 4.84, 4.87
§ 6-204 .... # 4.79
§ 6-211 .... # 5.35, 5.36, 5.38, 11.2
§ 6-212 .... # 2.16, 4.76, 4.79, 4.85, 6.33
§ 6-213 .... # 5.30, 5.33, 5.37, 5.46
§ 6-215 .... # 9.23, 10.7, 11.6
§ 6-222 .... # 5.35
§ 6-226 .... # 5.35
§ 7-302 .... # 12.78
§ 7-304 .... # 12.62
§ 7-306 .... # 11.63
§ 6-307 .... # 4.86
§ 8-101 .... # 1.7

Uniform Simultaneous Death Act

.... # 2.23, 2.24, 2.25

Uniform Testamentary Additions to Trusts Act

.... # 6.26

Uniform Transfers to Minors Act

.... # 4.45, 4.59, 4.60, 4.61, 10.31, 12.62, 12.76, 12.129

Uniform Trustees' Powers Act

§ 3 ... # 12.54, 12.65, 12.74, 12.94, 12.106
§ 5 .... # 12.92
§ 6 .... # 12.40, 12.44
§ 7 .... # 12.73

Uniform Statutory Will Act

.... # 10.35
§ 6 .... # 10.35, 10.38, 10.42
§ 8A .... # 10.35

Married Women's Property Acts

.... # 1.9, 3.3, 10.2

Uniform Determination of Death Act

.... # 2.26

Uniform Management of Institutional Funds Act

.... # 10.71

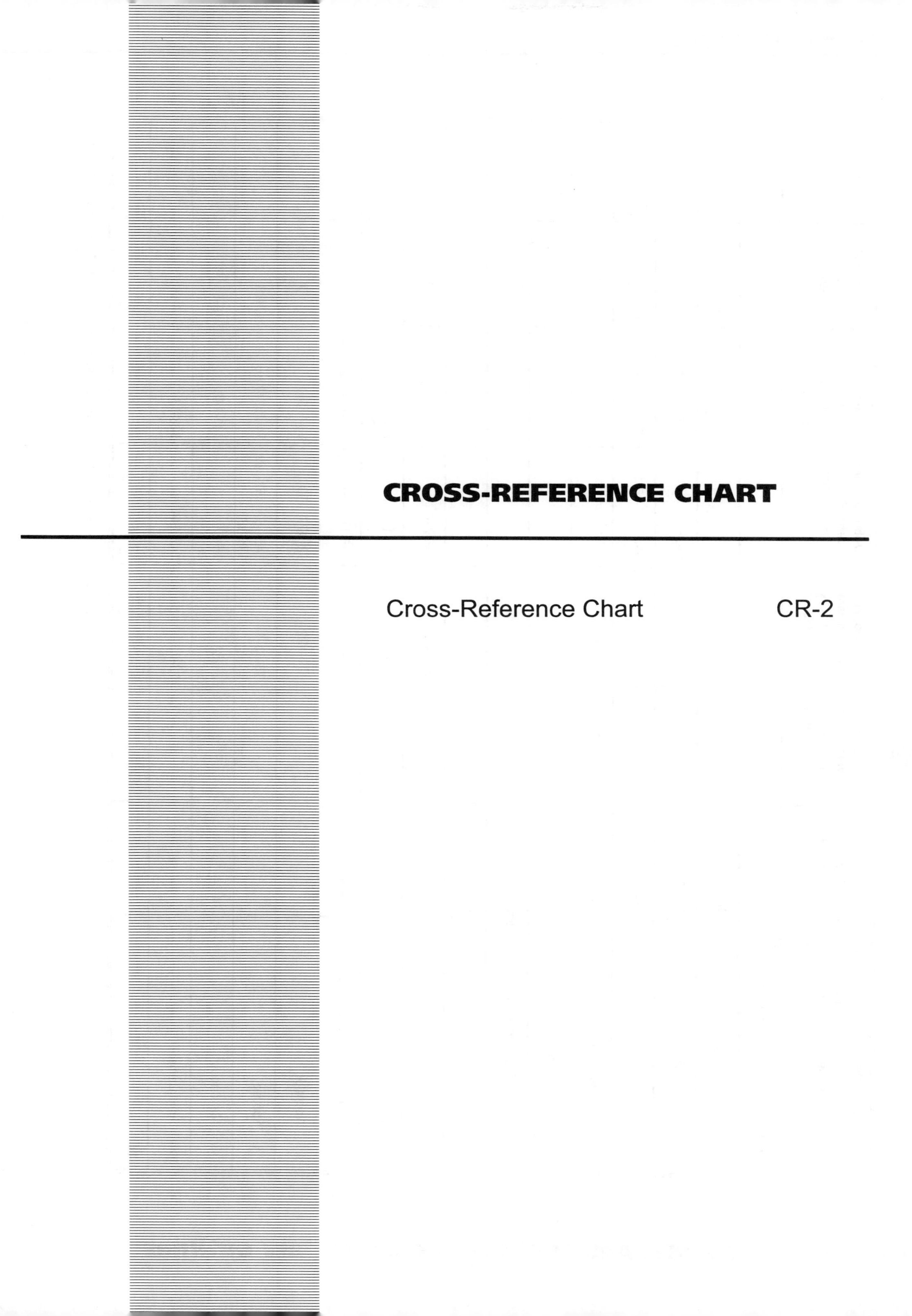

CROSS-REFERENCE CHART

Cross-Reference Chart CR-2

CR

WILLS, TRUSTS AND ESTATES Casenote Law Outline Cross-Reference Chart	Scoles *Trusts & Estates* 5th ed. 1993	Bittker *Federal Estate & Gift Taxation* 7th ed. 1996	Waggoner & Wellman *Family Property Law* 2nd ed.	Dobris & Sterk *Estates & Trusts* 1st Ed. 1998	Dukeminier *Wills, Trusts & Estates* 6th ed. 2000	Mechem *Wills* 5th ed.	Bogert *Law of Trusts* 6th ed.
CHAPTER 1: Intestate Succession							
I. Choice of Law	48-50		71-72		72-78, 392-395, 521-530	34-37	
II. Surviving Spouse	50-52		36-43, 80-112	70-78	74-75, 507-513, 521-525	17-18	
III. Relatives	55-58		44-62, 113-165	78-82, 83-96, 87-125	73-74, 90-101	34-77	
IV. Wrongful Death	74-84		462-470			530-535	
V. Disadvantages of Intestacy			29-35				
CHAPTER 2: Common Problems of Intestacy							
I. Claims by Remote Issue	55-58		61-62	63			
II. Lapse			345-360	266-270		408-412	
III. Shares	52-55		44-52	152-175	72-75, 86-97, 98-130		
IV. Children Born out of Wedlock	68-74		127-147	106-119, 730	115-117, 122-124	63	
V. Adoption			114-122	92, 427, 730	98-113	47-50	
VI. Spouses			36-62	145-152, 161-169, 175-181	74-75, 471	17-18	
VII. Misconduct	74-84		81-82	16-27	141-148	78-84	
VIII. Advancements			73-76	142-144	128-132	64-69	
IX. Disclaimer			65-71	132-142	148-157	70-77	

Please visit **www.casenotes.com** for the latest version of the cross-reference chart.

Please visit **www.casenotes.com** for the latest version of the cross-reference chart.

WILLS, TRUSTS AND ESTATES Casenote Law Outline Cross-Reference Chart	**Scoles** *Trusts & Estates* **5th ed. 1993**	**Bittker** *Federal Estate & Gift Taxation* **7th ed. 1996**	**Waggoner & Wellman** *Family Property Law* **2nd ed.**	**Dobris & Sterk** *Estates & Trusts* **1st Ed. 1998**	**Dukeminier** *Wills, Trusts & Estates* **6th ed. 2000**	**Mechem** *Wills* **5th ed.**	**Bogert** *Law of Trusts* **6th ed.**
CHAPTER 3: Limitations on the Right of Disposition							
I. Protection of Children	112-118		579-584	181-192	90, 536-551	54-63	
II. Protection of the Spouse	91-112		585-586	145, 161-169, 175-179	74-77, 471-480	19-33	
III. Elective Share	94-107	494-495 502-505	516-575	145-175	480-512	19-33	
IV. Community Property	109-112	220-223, 535-539	518-523	179-181	521-536		
V. Choice of Law			522-523		526-530	17-18	
VI. Omitted Spouse			585-586	177-179	530-536		
VII. Waiver			520-522	169-175			
CHAPTER 4: Formal Requirements							
I. Wills	137-148		167-212	193-202	35-38, 233-236, 242-247, 301-323	138-175	
II. Gifts	251-267		415-416	45-50	578, 1029-1032		
III. Trusts	320-349		671-746	465-472	581, 597, 750-775		123-132
IV. Joint Tenancy		223-233, 247-48	381-382	50, 843	350-351	244-251	
V. Payable-on-Death Contracts			416-417	56	331-344		
CHAPTER 5: REVOCATION							
I. Wills	137-148		259-315	317-323, 330-345	276-298	280-344	
II. Gifts	251-267		421-424	50			
III. Trusts	320-350		412, 425-437	560-567	351-371		
IV. Insurance	390-395	369-407	421-422				
V. Joint Tenancy		231-233	381-382, 422-424	843			

CR

CR

WILLS, TRUSTS AND ESTATES Casenote Law Outline Cross-Reference Chart	Scoles *Trusts & Estates* 5th ed. 1993	Bittker *Federal Estate & Gift Taxation* 7th ed. 1996	Waggoner & Wellman *Family Property Law* 2nd ed.	Dobris & Sterk *Estates & Trusts* 1st Ed. 1998	Dukeminier *Wills, Trusts & Estates* 6th ed. 2000	Mechem *Wills* 5th ed.	Bogert *Law of Trusts* 6th ed.
VI. Change of Circumstances			290-291	327-330, 487-488		54-57	
CHAPTER 6: Extrinsic Evidence							
I. Mistake of Fact	171-185		615-622	296-302		112-116 131-135	
II. Mistake as to Contents			638-647	309-315	427-438	118-131	
III. Ambiguity			622-636	291-309	424-427	117, 118	
IV. Constructive Trusts	306-308		239-244	408-409	584-589, 614-617	131-135	
V. Incorporation by Reference and Pour-over Wills	411-419		246-251, 458-460	226-239, 241-245	303-312, 371-373	192-199	
VI. Bank Accounts	387-390		417-421	55-56, 478-479, 843	344-350		
VII. Other *Inter vivos* Transfers			415-424	530, 543-549	557-562, 654		
CHAPTER 7: Incapacity and Undue Influence							
I. Incapacity	634-652		220-226	843-845	163-175, 388, 396		
II. Undue Influence	652-672		226-238	379-404	175-213	97-108	
III. *Inter vivos* Transfers				543-549			
IV. Ethical Problems			231-239	202, 380-394, 512-513, 863-874, 940-995	187, 211-213, 628	253-255	
CHAPTER 8: Contracts to Make Wills							
I. Formal Requirements	218-220		589-613	343-352	318-329	345-358	
II. Remedies			589-613			351	
III. Disadvantages of Contractual Wills			594-595				
CHAPTER 9: Ademption and Abatement							
I. Ademption	953-969		319-333	254-266	459	359-392	

Please visit **www.casenotes.com** for the latest version of the cross-reference chart.

Please visit **www.casenotes.com** for the latest version of the cross-reference chart.

WILLS, TRUSTS AND ESTATES Casenote Law Outline Cross-Reference Chart	**Scoles** ***Trusts & Estates*** **5th ed. 1993**	**Bittker** ***Federal Estate & Gift Taxation*** **7th ed. 1996**	**Waggoner & Wellman** ***Family Property Law*** **2nd ed.**	**Dobris & Sterk** ***Estates & Trusts*** **1st Ed. 1998**	**Dukeminier** ***Wills, Trusts & Estates*** **6th ed. 2000**	**Mechem** ***Wills*** **5th ed.**	**Bogert** ***Law of Trusts*** **6th ed.**
II. Abatement	969-971		340-342	246-254	468	392-415	
III. Payment of Taxes			363-402	430-444, 543-560, 579			
CHAPTER 10: Purposes of Trusts							
I. Historical Uses of Trusts	314-319		672-677		553-567		
II. Avoiding Probate	600-608		677-679	43-45, 58-60, 472-479, 496, 896	44-49		
III. Tax Advantages of Trusts	600-608		677-679	473, 543-549, 559-560			
IV. Management of Property			687-694	989-990, 456-460			
V. Discretionary Trusts	426-436		774-777	496-508	617-631		193-196
VI. Modification of Trusts	472-506		793-816	560-580, 995-1001	869-883		546-5,73
VIII. Charitable Trusts	514-523		825-884	579-589, 589-610, 772-776	883-901		200-238
CHAPTER 11: Rights of Creditors: Spendthrift Trusts							
I. Fraudulent Conveyances	443-462		414-415	153-156		537-540	
II. Joint Tenancy			69-70				
III. Insurance			760				
IV. Trusts			414-415, 1301-1303	905-939			171-199
V. Spendthrift Provisions			750-793	513-527	631-646		171-199
VI. Claims against Probate Estate			1210-1213	528-530			

WILLS, TRUSTS AND ESTATES Casenote Law Outline Cross-Reference Chart	Scoles *Trusts & Estates* 5th ed. 1993	Bittker *Federal Estate & Gift Taxation* 7th ed. 1996	Waggoner & Wellman *Family Property Law* 2nd ed.	Dobris & Sterk *Estates & Trusts* 1st Ed. 1998	Dukeminier *Wills, Trusts & Estates* 6th ed. 2000	Mechem *Wills* 5th ed.	Bogert *Law of Trusts* 6th ed.
VII. Liability of Beneficiaries, Heirs and Devisees							
CHAPTER 12: Probate and Administration							
I. Probate	617-620		19-21, 168-169	43-45, 357, 903-904	34-49	425-446	
II. Necessity for Administration	558-582		168-169	896-898	44	447-472	
III. Ancillary Administration	613-615			899-900	391		
IV. Choice of Fiduciary	679-89 324-325		19-21	900-903			46-74
V. Fees and Other Costs			1289-1301	918-919			539-545
VI. Sales by Fiduciaries			1216-1234			510-573	522-545
VII. Investments	807-860		1234-1262	968-988	954-974	573-579	328-361
VIII. Self-dealing	707-728		1224-1225	942-952, 961-963	903-904	553-563	411-438
IX. Remedies against Fiduciaries	748-780		412-413, 1234-1264	900-902		563-570	598-619
X. Allocations between Principal and Income	426-436 507-511		1271-1276		971-974		479-522
XI. Distribution			1279-1289	989			388-392

Please visit **www.casenotes.com** for the latest version of the cross-reference chart.

Notes

Notes

Index ID-2

INDEX

A

Abatement ## 9.14 - 9.23
- Classifications of devises # 9.16
- Contrary intent # 9.17
- Hierarchy of devises # 9.15
- Legatee # 9.19
- Nonprobate assets # 9.23
- Taxes ## 9.24 - 9.36
- Type of property # 9.18

Ademption ## 9.1 - 9.13
- Casualty # 9.9
- Change of form # 9.5
- Classification of bequests # 9.3
- Intent # 9.2
- Involuntary transfers ## 9.6 - 9.10
- Sale by conservator # 9.10
- Sale on credit # 9.4
- Stock splits # 9.8

Administration
- Avoiding ## 12.19 - 20
- Purpose of ## 12.16 - 18

Administrators
- Choice of # 12.27

Adoption ## 2.52 - 2.67
- Adults # 2.57
- Biological relatives ## 2.59 - 2.62
- Choice of law # 2.67
- Class gifts # 2.60
- Equitable ## 2.63 - 2.64
- Intestate succession # 2.54

Advancements ## 2.91 - 2.100
- Death before donor # 2.95
- Effect of # 2.91
- Proof of # 2.97
- Valuation # 2.93
- Wills # 2.98

Agency # 10.32

Agents
- Liability for acts of # 12.106
- Power to make gifts # 7.29
- Reimbursement for cost of . # 12.54

Alimony ## 11.31 - 11.33

Ambiguity
- Circumstances # 6.12
- Class gifts # 6.10
- Latent ## 6.7 - 6.10
- Patent # 6.11

Ancillary administration ## 12.21 - 12.24

Antilapse statutes # 2.17

Apportionment of taxes ## 9.24 - 9.36
- Appraisal of estate # 12.63
- Contrary intent ## 9.29, 9.31
- Internal Revenue Code # 9.25
- Marital and charitable devises # 9.30
- State apportionment statutes # 9.26
- State inheritance taxes # 9.35

Artificial insemination # 2.44

Assignment by beneficiary ## 11.41 - 11.43

Attestation clauses # 4.18

Attorney
- *See also* Ethical problems, Malpractice, Computation of fees ## 12.56 - 12.59

Augmented estate # 3.33

B

Beneficiary
- Consent to breach # 12.103
- Failure to designate # 4.72
- Liability of # 11.64
- Transaction with fiduciary .. # 12.96

Bona fide purchaser # 12.72

Bond # 12.60

Bypass trusts # 10.25

C

Capacity
- Adjudication of competence ## 7.2, 7.23
- Age # 7.1
- Burden of proof # 7.4
- Insane delusion # 7.8
- Testimony as to # 7.6
- Wills ## 7.1 - 7.10

Charitable trusts
- Benevolence # 10.63
- *Cy pres* # 10.71
- Definition of # 10.58
- Racial restrictions # 10.60
- Restrictions in gift to charity # 10.70
- Standing to enforce ## 10.66 - 10.69

Tax deduction .... ## 9.30, 10.57
Children born out of wedlock
.... ## 2.32 - 2.51
Choice of law .... # 2.49
Constitution .... # 2.33
Construction of gifts to "children"
.... ## 2.47 - 2.48
History .... # 2.32
Inheritance .... ## 2.45 - 2.46
Invalid marriage .... # 2.39
Parentage .... # 2.38
Proof of paternity .... # 2.34
Class gifts
Adoption .... # 2.55
Ambiguity .... # 6.10
Antilapse statutes .... # 2.6
What constitutes .... # 2.13
Codicil .... # 5.15
Cohabitants .... ## 2.72 - 2.76
Common law marriage .... # 2.75
Community property
Choice of law .... # 3.60
Classification .... # 3.49
Differences from elective share
.... ## 3.56 - 3.59
Intestate succession .... # 1.14
Transmutation of .... # 3.75
Confidential relationship
Presumption of undue influence
.... ## 7.18 - 7.21
Statute of Frauds .... # 6.48
Conflict of interest
Discretionary trust .... # 10.41
Drafting a will .... ## 7.31 - 7.35
Conservator
Definition of .... # 12.30
Sale by .... # 9.10
Consideration
Contract to make wills .... # 8.10
Disclaimer .... # 2.103
Gift .... ## 4.47 - 4.48
Trust .... # 4.62
Constructive trust ... ## 4.55, 6.16 - 6.20
Confidential relationship ...... # 6.48
Deeds .... ## 6.45 - 6.49
Force and fraud .... # 6.20
Homicide .... ## 2.83 - 2.90
Promise by devisee ..... ## 6.16 - 6.19
Contracts to make wills ..... ## 8.1 - 8.20
Anticipatory breach .... # 8.12
Consideration .... # 8.10
Disadvantages of .... ## 8.18 - 8.20
Executory contracts .... # 8.9
Inter vivos transfers .... # 8.16
Jurisdiction to enforce .... # 8.11
Part performance .... ## 8.7 - 8.9
Remedies for breach .. ## 8.11 - 8.17
Statute of frauds .... ## 8.1 - 8.7
Statute of limitations .... # 8.13
Third parties .... ## 8.16 - 8.17
Cotrustee
Contribution .... # 12.108
Liability for .... ## 12.107 - 12.108
Standing to sue .... # 10.66
Creditors
Disclaimer .... # 2.102
Of beneficiary
.... ## 11.11, 11.18 - 11.20
Of settlor .... ## 11.13 - 11.17
Of trustee .... # 6.64
Curtesy .... ## 3.24 - 3.26
Custodianship .... # 4.59
Cy pres .... # 10.71

D

Demonstrative bequests .... # 9.3
Delivery
See Gifts
Dependent relative revocation
.... # 5.16-.18
Desertion by spouse .... # 2.80
Disclaimer .... ## 2.101 - 2.109
By fiduciaries .... ## 2.105 - 2.106
Creditors .... # 2.102
Effect of .... # 2.107
Formal requirements .... # 2.103
Spendthrift provisions .... # 11.42
Tax avoidance .... # 2.101
Time limits .... # 2.104
Discretionary trusts
.... ## 10.34 - 10.43, 11.19
Conflict of interest .... # 10.41
Judicial review of ... ## 10.36 - 10.40
Other resources of beneficiary
.... # 10.38
Rights of creditors .... # 11.19
Station in life .... # 10.39
Tax consequences ... ## 10.42 - 10.43
Distribution
In kind .... # 12.130
Liability for improper
.... ## 12.126 -12.127

ID

To incompetents .... # 12.128
Divorce
Effect on will .... # 5.19
Nonprobate assets ...... ## 5.46 - 5.49
Domicile
Choice of law
.... ## 1.3, 3.62 - 3.63, 4.30
Dower .... ## 3.24 - 3.26
Durable powers of attorney .... # 10.32

E

Earmarking of assets .... # 12.74
Election .... # 5.43
Elective share
Abatement to satisfy .... # 9.22
By guardian .... # 3.43
Claims, subject to .... # 3.31
Contribution to taxes .... # 9.32
Death of spouse .... # 3.45
Nonprobate assets ...... ## 3.32 - 3.38
Other benefits .... ## 3.39 - 3.40
Size .... # 3.27
Time for .... # 3.41
Equitable conversion .... # 1.4
ERISA .... ## 3.66, 3.82, 5.48, 11.28
Escheat .... # 1.36
Estate tax
See also Bypass trusts, Marital deduction
Irrevocable trusts ... ## 10.20 - 10.23
Power to distribute to self ... # 10.43
Savings .... # 10.20
Ethical problems .... ## 7.31 - 7.36
Conflict of interest ..... ## 7.31 - 7.35
Lawyer as witness .... # 7.36
Exculpatory provisions .... # 12.102
Executors
See also Personal representatives, Fiduciaries
Choice of .... # 12.26
Exoneration .... # 9.20
Expectancy .... ## 2.103, 4.48
Extrinsic evidence .... ## 6.1 - 6.65

F

Facts of independent significance
.... # 6.31
Family allowance .... # 3.10
Fees of fiduciaries .... # 10.4
Contract .... # 12.52
Personal representatives ..... # 12.45
Trustees .... # 12.50
Waiver of .... # 12.53
Fiduciary
Administrators .... # 12.27
Agents .... # 12.31
Choice of .... ## 12.25 - 12.44
Custodians .... # 12.32
Executors .... # 12.26
Guardians/conservators .... # 12.30
Personal representatives ..... # 12.28
Professional .... # 12.78
Removal .... ## 12.33 - 12.37
Resignation .... # 12.38
Successors .... ## 12.40 - 12.44
Trustees .... # 12.29
Types .... # 12.25
Forfeiture clauses .... # 12.12
Formal requirements
Choice of law .... ## 4.29 - 4.31
Gifts .... ## 4.35 - 4.50
Trusts .... ## 4.51 - 4.75
Wills .... ## 4.1 - 4.34
Fraud
Basis for attack on will .... # 6.3
Constructive trusts ..... ## 6.20, 6.47
Fraudulent conveyance .... # 11.1

G

General bequests .... # 9.3
Generation skipping tax .... # 10.6
Gift tax
Annual exemption .... # 10.21
Contract to make a will .... # 8.18
Valuation .... # 10.22
Gifts
By guardians and agents
.... ## 7.27 - 7.29
Causa Mortis .... # 5.23
Consideration .... # 4.47
Delivery .... # 4.40
Recording .... # 4.49
Revocation .... ## 5.21 - 5.24
Testamentary .... # 4.36
Writing .... # 4.38
Guardianship
Compared with trust .... # 10.31
Definition of .... # 10.30
Elective share .... # 3.43
Power to make gifts, disclaim
.... ## 2.105, 7.27 - 7.28, 10.32
Termination of trusts .... # 10.44

ID

H

Heirs
- Definition of .... # 2.22
- Devise to .... # 2.31
- Gift to in trust .... # 10.47
- Liability of .... ## 11.64 - 11.66
- Standing to contest will .... # 12.10

Holographic wills .... # 4.23
- Date .... # 4.26
- Printed matter .... # 4.27
- Testamentary intent .... # 4.25

Homestead .... ## 3.10, 3.15

Homicide .... ## 2.83 - 2.90
- Degree of crime .... # 2.85
- Disqualification .... # 2.87
- History .... # 2.83
- Joint tenancy .... # 2.88
- Proof of crime .... # 2.86
- Statutes .... # 2.84

Honorary trusts .... # 10.65

I

Illusory transfers .... # 3.34

Incapacity .... ## 7.1 - 7.10
- Mental capacity .... # 7.2
- Conservatorship .... # 7.3
- Evidence .... ## 7.4 - 7.7
- Insane delusion .... # 7.8

Income tax
- Advantages of trust .... ## 10.14 - 10.28
- Basis .... # 10.6
- Power to distribute to self .... # 10.43

Incorporation by reference .... ## 6.21 - 6.25
- Future documents .... # 6.24
- Tangible personalty .... # 6.25

Inheritance tax .... # 9.35

Insane delusion .... ## 7.8 - 7.10

Insolvent estates .... # 11.47

Insurance .... # 4.28
- *See also* Life insurance

Insurance creditors .... ## 11.7 - 11.12

Integration of wills .... # 6.22

Intent .... ## 3.72, 6.12, 9.2

Inter vivos transfers .... ## 6.38 - 6.55, 7.22 - 7.30, 8.16

Intestate succession
- Choice of law .... ## 1.1 - 1.7
- Disadvantages of .... ## 1.40 - 1.44
- Half blood .... # 1.35
- In general .... ## 1.1 - 1.46
- Laughing heirs .... # 1.30
- Maternal/paternal kindred .... # 1.29
- Parents .... # 1.23
- Remoter issue .... # 1.18
- Representation .... ## 1.19, 1.26
- Shares .... ## 1.20 - 1.22, 1.27
- Source of property .... # 1.35
- Spouse .... ## 1.11 - 1.16
- Spouse's relatives .... # 1.33

Investments by fiduciaries
- Diversification .... # 12.80
- Language of instrument .... # 12.83
- Legal lists .... # 12.77
- Nonproductive assets .... # 12.82
- Prudent person rule .... # 12.75
- Retention of assets .... # 12.81

Irrevocable trusts
- Risks .... # 10.24
- Tax advantages .... ## 10.14 - 10.28

Issue, devise to .... ## 2.1, 2.30

J

Joint bank accounts
- Contributions test .... ## 5.35 - 5.37
- Creditors rights .... ## 11.2 , 11.6
- Extrinsic evidence .... ## 6.33 - 6.36

Joint wills .... # 8.3

Joint tenancy
- Alteration by will .... ## 5.42 - 5.44
- Compared to trust .... ## 10.10 - 10.13
- Creditors .... ## 11.2 - 11.6
- Delivery .... ## 4.81 - 4.82
- Disclaimer .... ## 2.103 - 2.104
- Formal requirements .... ## 4.76 - 4.83
- Homicide .... # 2.88
- Land .... ## 5.39 - 5.41
- Language needed .... # 4.77
- Safe deposit box .... # 4.83
- Severance of .... # 5.40
- Testamentary nature .... # 4.76
- Writing .... # 4.80

L

Laches .... # 12.104

Lapse
- Antilapse statutes .... ## 2.6 - 2.10
- Class gifts .... ## 2.10, 2.13
- Contracts to make wills .... # 8.18
- Nonprobate property .... ## 2.16 - 2.18
- Residuary gifts .... # 2.15

ID

Legal life estate .... # 10.6
Legitime .... # 3.6
Life Insurance
  Change of beneficiary .... # 5.31
  Community property .... # 3.50
  Designation of beneficiary ..... # 4.84
  Creditors rights .... ## 11.7 - 11.11
  Homicide .... ## 2.83 - 2.90
  Insurance trusts .... # 4.69
  Options .... # 10.33
  Spouse's claims .... # 3.36
  Survival .... # 2.16
Lost wills .... # 5.7

M

Malpractice .... ## 4.32, 5.44
  Liability for mistake in will .. # 4.33
  Privity .... # 4.33
Marital deduction
  Allocation of taxes .... # 9.30
  Bypass trusts .... # 10.25
  Contractual will .... # 8.18
  Discretionary trust .... # 10.34
Marriage
  See also Common law marriage, Putative spouse
  Capacity .... ## 2.70, 7.30
  Misconduct .... ## 2.80 - 2.90
  Revocation of will by .... # 3.69
Married Women's Property Acts
  .... ## 1.9, 3.3, 10.2
Mistake
  As to contents .... ## 6.4 - 6.6
  Of fact .... ## 6.1 - 6.3
  Reformation .... # 6.4
Mixed trusts .... # 10.64
Mortmain .... # 3.84
Multiple fiduciaries
  Fees .... # 12.45
  Tax advantages .... # 12.44
  Unanimity .... # 12.44
Mutual wills .... # 8.4

N

Nonclaim statutes .... ## 11.49 - 11.58
Nonresident fiduciaries .... # 12.37

O

Omitted spouse .... ## 3.67 - 3.7
Oral wills .... # 4.28

P

Parol evidence rule .... # 6.38
Participation in breach of trust
  .... # 12.109
Payable on death contracts .... # 4.84
Pensions
  Creditors rights .... # 11.28
  Death benefits .... # 4.84
  Spouse's claims .... # 3.36
Per stirpes vs. *Per capita*
  .... ## 1.27, 2.2 - 2.3
Personal representative
  See also Sales by fiduciaries, Investments by fiduciaries
  Bond .... # 12.60
  Definition .... # 12.28
  Fees .... # 12.45
  Liability for improper payment
  .... # 11.59
  Liability for torts/contracts
  .... ## 11.62 - 11.63
Pour-over wills .... ## 6.26 - 6.32
Precatory language .... # 4.64
Pretermitted heirs ... ## 3.16 - 3.22, 9.21
  Children vs. grandchildren ... # 3.18
  Contrary intent .... # 3.20
  Existing vs. afterborns .... # 3.17
  Share .... # 3.21
Principal and Income
  Apportionment .... # 12.122
  Corporate distributions .... # 12.125
  Depreciation .... # 12.121
  Income of an estate .... # 12.123
  Proceeds of sale .... # 12.113
  Uniform acts .... # 12.111
  Wasting assets .... # 12.118
Probate
  Advantages of .... # 10.8
  Ante-mortem .... # 12.1
  Avoidance of .... ## 10.3, 10.10
  Notice .... # 12.7
  Time limits .... # 12.3
Protective trusts .... # 11.23
Prudent person rule .... # 12.75
Publication .... # 4.14
Public policy .... # 3.86
Purchase money resulting trust
  Clean hands .... # 6.60
  In general .... # 6.50
  Partial payment .... # 6.55
  Presumption of gift .... # 6.52

Sale on credit .... # 6.54
Statute of limitations .... # 6.59
Third persons .... # 6.63
Putative spouse .... # 2.71

Q

QTIP trusts .... # 9.33

R

Recording .... # 4.49
Reformation
Mistake of fact .... # 6.42
Mutuality of mistake .... # 6.40
Negligence .... # 6.41
Of deeds .... # 6.39
Of trusts .... # 5.27
Of wills .... # 6.4
Remedies against fiduciaries
Defenses .... ## 12.102 - 12.106
Monetary relief .... ## 12.98 - 12.101
Specific relief .... # 12.97
Removal of fiduciaries
.... ## 12.33 - 12.37
Republication by codicil .... # 5.15
Resignation of fiduciaries
.... ## 12.38 - 12.39
Resulting trust
See Purchase money resulting trust
Revival .... ## 5.14 - 5.15
Revocable trusts
Elective share .... ## 3.33 - 3.34
Rights of creditors .... # 11.16
Validity of .... # 4.66
Revocation
Change of circumstances
.... ## 5.19 - 5.20
Gifts .... ## 5.21 - 5.24
Insurance .... ## 5.31 - 5.34
Intents .... # 5.2
Partial .... # 5.4
Physical act .... ## 5.1 - 5.8
Presumption of .... ## 5.5 - 5.6
Subsequent will .... ## 5.9 - 5.13
Trusts .... ## 5.25 - 5.30
Rule against perpetuities
.... ## 5.17, 10.65

S

Sales by fiduciaries
Credit .... # 12.70
In general .... ## 12.65 - 12.74
Price .... # 12.71
Prohibition on .... # 12.69
Purpose of .... # 12.68
Satisfaction of devises .... # 2.99
Secret trusts .... # 6.17
Self-dealing
Authorized by court .... # 12.92
Authorized in instrument .... # 12.91
Prohibition of .... # 12.86
Retention .... # 12.94
Self-deposit .... # 12.93
Transaction between fiduciary and beneficiary .... # 12.96
Trustee of two trusts .... # 12.95
Self-proved wills .... # 4.20
Severance .... # 5.40
Shares
"Equally" .... # 2.27
"Heirs" .... # 2.31
Intestate succession ..... ## 1.1 - 1.44
"Issue" .... # 2.30
"*Per stirpes*" .... # 2.28
Signature
Mark as .... # 4.7
Of testator .... ## 4.6 - 4.9
Of witnesses .... ## 4.16 - 4.17
Place of .... # 4.9
Proxy .... # 4.8
Simultaneous death .... # 2.23
Social security .... # 11.28
Specific devises
See also Ademption, Abatement
Definition .... # 9.3
Construction problems .... # 9.11
Income during administration
.... # 12.124
Spendthrift trusts .... ## 11.21 - 11.43
Alimony .... # 11.31
Bankruptcy .... # 11.25
Necessaries .... # 11.34
Self-settled trusts .... # 11.39
Statutory limits on .... # 11.24
Taxes .... # 11.38
Tort claims .... # 11.35
Validity of .... # 11.21
Voluntary transfers .... # 11.41
Sprinkling trusts .... # 10.18
Spouses
Bigamy .... # 2.71
Capacity .... # 2.77
Common law .... # 2.74

ID

Divorce .... # 2.78
Importance .... # 2.69
In general............................ # 10.18
Statute of Frauds
Contracts to make wills
.... ## 8.1, 8.7
Transfers of land .... # 4.38
Trusts .... ## 4.52 - 4.56
Wills .... # 4.1
Statute of limitations
Effect of death on .... # 11.48
Statute of Uses .... # 3.2
Statute of Wills.................... ## 3.2, 4.1
Stepchildren...................... ## 2.65 - 2.66
Stock splits.................................. # 9.8
Substituted judgment .... # 7.28
Successor fiduciaries .... ## 12.40 - 12.44
Support
Survival of duty .... # 3.9
Trusts for .... ## 10.39 - 10.40
Survival of claims .... ## 11.44 - 11.46

T

Tenancy by the entirety .... # 5.41
Testamentary gifts .... ## 4.36, 4.66
Totten trusts .... ## 4.68, 5.30
Condition of survival .... # 2.16
Revocation of .... # 5.30
Rights of creditors .... # 11.16
Trustees
Appointment of.................... # 12.29
Bond .... # 12.62
Failure to designate .... # 4.71
Fees .... # 12.50
Trusts
Consideration .... # 4.62
Creditors .... ## 11.13 - 11.20
Delivery .... # 4.57
Honorary .... # 10.65
Insurance .... # 4.69
Language .... # 4.63
Purposes of .... ## 10.1 - 10.28
Resulting..................... ## 6.50 - 6.63
Revocation of .... ## 5.25 - 5.30
Tax advantages ...... ## 10.14 - 10.28
Testamentary .... # 4.66
Writing .... # 4.52

U

Undue Influence
Bona fide purchasers .... # 7.25
Character of influence .... # 7.13
Circumstantial evidence........ # 7.17
Influence by others .... # 7.14
Inter vivos transfers... ## 7.22 - 7.30
Naturalness of will................ # 7.15
Presumption of .... ## 7.18 - 7.24
Ratification .... # 7.26
Wills .... ## 7.11 - 7.21
Uniform acts
See Table of Authorities

W

Waiver
Defenses to .... ## 3.78 - 3.82
Fees .... # 12.53
Joinder in conveyance .... # 3.74
Property settlement .... # 5.47
Statute of Frauds .... # 4.54
Will contests
Jury trial .... # 12.11
Standing.............................. # 12.10
Time limits .... ## 10.9, 12.9
Wills
History .... # 4.1
Policy .... # 4.3
Substantial compliance .... # 4.4
Signatures .... ## 4.6 - 4.17
Holographic .... # 4.23
Oral .... # 4.28
Witnesses .... ## 4.10 - 4.22
Competency .... # 4.11
Interested .... # 4.12
Lawyer as .... # 7.36
Number .... # 4.10
Present at same time .... # 4.15
Signature by .... ## 4.16 - 4.17
Unavailability of .... # 4.22
Wrongful death .... ## 1.37 - 1.39

Notes

Notes

Notes

NOTES

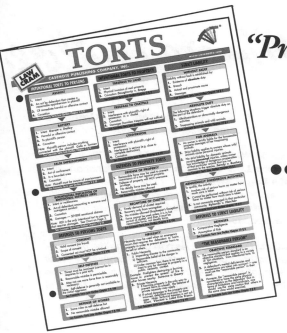

the Ultimate Outline

➤ *RENOWNED AUTHORS: Every **Casenote Law Outline** is written by highly respected, nationally recognized professors.*

➤ *KEYED TO **CASENOTE LEGAL BRIEF** BOOKS: In most cases, **Casenote Law Outlines** work in conjunction with the **Casenote Legal Briefs** so that you can see how each case in your textbook relates to the entire subject area. In addition, **Casenote Law Outlines** are cross-referenced to most major casebooks.*

➤ *FREE SUPPLEMENT SERVICE: As part of being the most up-to-date legal outline on the market, whenever a new supplement is published, the corresponding outline can be updated for free using the supplement request form found in this book.*

ADMINISTRATIVE LAW (1999) **$21.95**
Charles H. Koch, Jr., Dudley W. Woodbridge Professor of Law, College of William and Mary
Sidney A. Shapiro, John M. Rounds Professor of Law, University of Kansas

CIVIL PROCEDURE (1999) **$22.95**
John B. Oakley, Professor of Law, University of California, Davis School of Law
Rex R. Perschbacher, Professor and Dean of University of California, Davis School of Law

COMMERCIAL LAW (see SALES ● SECURED TRANSACTIONS ● NEGOTIABLE INSTRUMENTS & PAYMENT SYSTEMS)

CONFLICT OF LAWS (1996) **$21.95**
Luther L. McDougal, III, W.R. Irby Professor of Law, Tulane University
Robert L. Felix, James P. Mozingo, III, Professor of Law, University of South Carolina

CONSTITUTIONAL LAW (1997) **$24.95**
Gary Goodpaster, Professor of Law, University of California, Davis School of Law

CONTRACTS (1999) **$21.95**
Daniel Wm. Fessler, Professor of Law, University of California, Davis School of Law

CORPORATIONS (2000) **$24.95**
Lewis D. Solomon, Arthur Selwin Miller Research Professor of Law, George Washington University
Daniel Wm. Fessler, Professor of Law, University of California, Davis School of Law
Arthur E. Wilmarth, Jr., Associate Professor of Law, George Washington University

CRIMINAL LAW (1999) **$21.95**
Joshua Dressler, Professor of Law, McGeorge School of Law

CRIMINAL PROCEDURE (1999) **$20.95**
Joshua Dressler, Professor of Law, McGeorge School of Law

ESTATE & GIFT TAX (2000) **$22.95**
Joseph M. Dodge, W.H. Francis Professor of Law, University of Texas at Austin

EVIDENCE (1996) **$23.95**
Kenneth Graham, Jr., Professor of Law, University of California, Los Angeles School of Law

FEDERAL COURTS (1997) **$22.95**
Howard P. Fink, Isadore and Ida Topper Professor of Law, Ohio State University
Linda S. Mullenix, Bernard J. Ward Centennial Professor of Law, University of Texas

FEDERAL INCOME TAXATION (1998) **$22.95**
Joseph M. Dodge, W.H. Francis Professor of Law, University of Texas at Austin

LEGAL RESEARCH (1996) **$21.95**
Nancy L. Schultz, Professor of Law, Chapman University
Louis J. Sirico, Jr., Professor of Law, Villanova University

NEGOTIABLE INSTRUMENTS & PAYMENT SYSTEMS (1995) **$22.95**
Donald B. King, Professor of Law, Saint Louis University
Peter Winship, James Cleo Thompson, Sr. Trustee Professor, SMU

PROPERTY (1999) **$22.95**
Sheldon F. Kurtz, Percy Bordwell Professor of Law, University of Iowa
Patricia Cain, Professor of Law, University of Iowa

SALES (2000) **$22.95**
Robert E. Scott, Dean and Lewis F. Powell, Jr. Professor of Law, University of Virginia
Donald B. King, Professor of Law, Saint Louis University

SECURED TRANSACTIONS (1995 w/ '96 supp.) **$20.95**
Donald B. King, Professor of Law, Saint Louis University

TORTS (1999) **$22.95**
George C. Christie, James B. Duke Professor of Law, Duke University
Jerry J. Phillips, W.P. Toms Professor of Law, University of Tennessee

WILLS, TRUSTS, & ESTATES (1996) **$22.95**
William M. McGovern, Professor of Law, University of California, Los Angeles School of Law

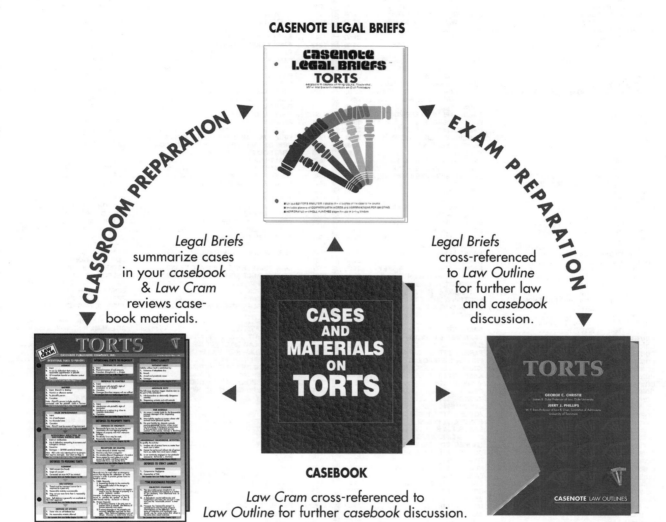

CASENOTE LEGAL BRIEFS

PRICE LIST — EFFECTIVE JULY 1, 2000 ● PRICES SUBJECT TO CHANGE WITHOUT NOTICE

Ref. No.	Course	Adaptable to Courses Utilizing	Retail Price
1265	ADMINISTRATIVE LAW	ASIMOW, BONFIELD & LEVIN	21.00
1263	ADMINISTRATIVE LAW	BREYER, STEWART & SUNSTEIN	22.00
1266	ADMINISTRATIVE LAW	CASS, DIVER & BEERMAN	20.00
1260	ADMINISTRATIVE LAW	GELLHORN, B., S., R. & F.	20.00
1268	ADMINISTRATIVE LAW	FUNK, SHAPIRO & WEAVER	22.00
1264	ADMINISTRATIVE LAW	MASHAW, MERRILL & SHANE	21.50
1267	ADMINISTRATIVE LAW	REESE	20.00
1262	ADMINISTRATIVE LAW	SCHWARTZ	21.00
1350	AGENCY & PARTNERSHIP (ENT.ORG)	CONARD, KNAUSS & SIEGEL	24.00
1351	AGENCY & PARTNERSHIP	HYNES	24.00
1281	ANTITRUST (TRADE REGULATION)	HANDLER, P., G. & W.	20.50
1283	ANTITRUST	SULLIVAN & HOVENKAMP	21.00
1611	BANKING LAW	MACEY & MILLER	20.00
1305	BANKRUPTCY	JORDAN, WARREN & BUSSELL	20.00
1058	BUSINESS ASSOCIATIONS (CORPORATIONS)	KLEIN, RAMSEYER & BAINBRIDGE	22.00
1059	BUSINESS ORGANIZATIONS (CORPORATIONS)	SODERQUIST, S., C., & S.	24.00
1040	CIVIL PROCEDURE	COUND, F., M. & S	21.00
1043	CIVIL PROCEDURE	FIELD, KAPLAN & CLERMONT	23.00
1049	CIVIL PROCEDURE	FREER & PERDUE	19.00
1041	CIVIL PROCEDURE	HAZARD, TAIT & FLETCHER	22.00
1047	CIVIL PROCEDURE	MARCUS, REDISH & SHERMAN	22.00
1044	CIVIL PROCEDURE	ROSENBERG, S. & D.	23.00
1046	CIVIL PROCEDURE	YEAZELL	20.00
1311	COMM'L LAW	FARNSWORTH, H., R., H. & M.	22.00
1312	COMM'L LAW	JORDAN, WARREN & WALT	22.00
1310	COMM'L LAW (SALES/SEC.TR./PAY.LAW [Sys.])	SPEIDEL, SUMMERS & WHITE	24.00
1313	COMM'L LAW (SALES/SEC.TR./PAY.LAW)	WHALEY	23.00
1314	COMMERCIAL TRANSACTIONS	LOPUKI, W., K. & M.	22.00
1320	COMMUNITY PROPERTY	BIRD	20.50
1630	COMPARATIVE LAW	SCHLESINGER, B., D., H.& W.	19.00
1048	COMPLEX LITIGATION	MARCUS & SHERMAN	20.00
1072	CONFLICTS	BRILMAYER	20.00
1071	CONFLICTS	CRAMTON, C. K., & K.	20.00
1070	CONFLICTS	HAY, WEINTRAUB & BORCHER	23.00
1073	CONFLICTS	SYMEONIDES, P., & M.	23.00
1086	CONSTITUTIONAL LAW	BREST, LEVINSON, B.& A.	21.00
1082	CONSTITUTIONAL LAW	COHEN & VARAT	24.00
1088	CONSTITUTIONAL LAW	FARBER, ESKRIDGE & FRICKEY	21.00
1080	CONSTITUTIONAL LAW	GUNTHER & SULLIVAN	21.00
1081	CONSTITUTIONAL LAW	LOCKHART, K., C., S. & F.	21.00
1085	CONSTITUTIONAL LAW	ROTUNDA	23.00
1089	CONSTITUTIONAL LAW (FIRST AMENDMENT)	SHIFFRIN & CHOPER	18.00
1087	CONSTITUTIONAL LAW	STONE, S., S. & T.	22.00
1103	CONTRACTS	BARNETT	24.00
1102	CONTRACTS	BURTON	23.00
1017	CONTRACTS	CALAMARI, PERILLO & BENDER	26.00
1101	CONTRACTS	CRANDALL & WHALEY	23.00
1014	CONTRACTS	DAWSON, HARVEY & H.	22.00
1010	CONTRACTS	FARNSWORTH & YOUNG	20.00
1011	CONTRACTS	FULLER & EISENBERG	24.00
1013	CONTRACTS	KESSLER, GILMORE & KRONMAN	26.00
1016	CONTRACTS	KNAPP & CRYSTAL	23.50
1012	CONTRACTS	MURPHY & SPEIDEL	25.00
1015	CONTRACTS	ROSETT	24.00
1019	CONTRACTS	VERNON	23.00
1502	COPYRIGHT	GOLDSTEIN	21.00
1504	COPYRIGHT	JOYCE, PETRY, L. & J.	20.00
1501	COPYRIGHT	NIMMER, M., M. & N.	22.50
1218	CORPORATE TAXATION	LIND, S. L. & R	17.00
1050	CORPORATIONS	CARY & EISENBERG	22.00
1054	CORPORATIONS	CHOPER, COFFEE, & GILSON	24.50
1350	CORPORATIONS (ENTERPRISE ORG.)	CONARD, KNAUSS & SIEGEL	24.00
1053	CORPORATIONS	HAMILTON	22.00
1058	CORPORATIONS (BUSINESS ASSOCIATIONS	KLEIN, RAMSEYER & BAINBRIDGE	22.00
1057	CORPORATIONS	O'KELLEY & THOMPSON	21.00
1059	CORPORATIONS (BUSINESS ORG.)	SODERQUIST, S., C. & S.	24.00
1056	CORPORATIONS	SOLOMON, S., B. & W.	22.00
1052	CORPORATIONS	VAGTS	21.00
1300	CREDITOR'S RIGHTS (DEBTOR-CREDITOR)	RIESENFELD	24.00
1550	CRIMINAL JUSTICE	WEINREB	21.00
1029	CRIMINAL LAW	BONNIE, C., J. & L.	20.00
1020	CRIMINAL LAW	BOYCE & PERKINS	25.00
1028	CRIMINAL LAW	DRESSLER	24.00
1027	CRIMINAL LAW	JOHNSON	22.00
1021	CRIMINAL LAW	KADISH & SCHULHOFER	22.00
1026	CRIMINAL LAW	KAPLAN, WEISBERG & BINDER	21.00
1205	CRIMINAL PROCEDURE	ALLEN, KUHNS & STUNTZ	20.00
1206	CRIMINAL PROCEDURE	DRESSLER & THOMAS	25.00
1202	CRIMINAL PROCEDURE	HADDAD, Z., S. & B.	23.00
1200	CRIMINAL PROCEDURE	KAMISAR, LAFAVE & ISRAEL	22.00
1204	CRIMINAL PROCEDURE	SALTZBURG & CAPRA	20.00
1300	DEBTOR-CREDITOR (CREDITORS RIGHTS)	RIESENFELD	24.00
1304	DEBTOR-CREDITOR	WARREN & WESTBROOK	22.00
1224	DECEDENTS ESTATES (TRUSTS)	RITCHIE, A, & E.(DOBRIS/STERK).	24.00
1222	DECEDENTS ESTATES	SCOLES, HALBACH, L. & R.	24.50
	DOMESTIC RELATIONS (*see* FAMILY LAW)		
3000	EDUCATION LAW (COURSE OUTLINE)	AQUILA & PETZKE	28.50
1670	EMPLOYMENT DISCRIMINATION	FRIEDMAN & STRICKLER	20.00
1671	EMPLOYMENT DISCRIMINATION	ZIMMER, SULLIVAN, R. & C.	21.00
1660	EMPLOYMENT LAW	ROTHSTEIN, KNAPP & LIEBMAN	22.50
1342	ENVIRONMENTAL LAW	ANDERSON, MANDELKER & T.	19.00
1341	ENVIRONMENTAL LAW	FINDLEY & FARBER	21.00
1345	ENVIRONMENTAL LAW	MENELL & STEWART	20.00
1344	ENVIRONMENTAL LAW	PERCIVAL, MILLER, S. & L.	21.00
1343	ENVIRONMENTAL LAW	PLATER, A., G. & G.	20.00
1217	ESTATE & GIFT TAXATION	BITTKER, CLARK & McCOUCH	18.00
	ETHICS (*see* PROFESSIONAL RESPONSIBILITY)		
1063	EVIDENCE	LEMPERT, GROSS & LIEBMAN	TBA
1066	EVIDENCE	MUELLER & KIRKPATRICK	20.00
1064	EVIDENCE	STRONG, BROUN & M..	25.50
1062	EVIDENCE	WELLBORN	25.00
1061	EVIDENCE	WALTZ & PARK	21.00
1060	EVIDENCE	WEINSTEIN, M., A. & B.	25.50
1244	FAMILY LAW (DOMESTIC RELATIONS)	AREEN	25.00
1242	FAMILY LAW (DOMESTIC RELATIONS)	CLARK & ESTIN	22.00
1245	FAMILY LAW (DOMESTIC RELATIONS)	ELLMAN, KURTZ & BARTLETT	23.00
1246	FAMILY LAW (DOMESTIC RELATIONS)	HARRIS, T. & W.	22.00
1243	FAMILY LAW (DOMESTIC RELATIONS)	KRAUSE, O., E. & G.	27.00
1240	FAMILY LAW (DOMESTIC RELATIONS)	WADLINGTON & O'BRIEN	23.00
1247	FAMILY LAW (DOMESTIC RELATIONS)	WEISBERG & APPLETON	22.00
1360	FEDERAL COURTS	FALLON, M. & S. (HART & W.)	22.00
1360	FEDERAL COURTS	HART & WECHSLER (FALLON)	22.00
1363	FEDERAL COURTS	LOW & JEFFRIES	19.00
1361	FEDERAL COURTS	McCORMICK, C. & W.	23.00
1364	FEDERAL COURTS	REDISH & SHERRY	20.00
1690	FEDERAL INDIAN LAW	GETCHES, W. & W.	23.00
1089	FIRST AMENDMENT (CONSTITUTIONAL LAW)	SHIFFRIN & CHOPER	18.00
1700	GENDER AND LAW (SEX DISCRIMINATION)	BARTLETT & HARRIS	22.00
1510	GRATUITOUS TRANSFERS	CLARK, L., M., A., & M.	21.00
1651	HEALTH CARE LAW	CURRAN, H., B. & O.	24.00
1650	HEALTH LAW	FURROW, J., J. & S.	20.50
1640	IMMIGRATION LAW	ALEINIKOFF, MARTIN & M.	19.00
1641	IMMIGRATION LAW	LEGOMSKY	22.00
1690	INDIAN LAW	GETCHES, W. & W.	23.00
1373	INSURANCE LAW	ABRAHAM	23.00
1371	INSURANCE LAW	KEETON	24.00
1370	INSURANCE LAW	YOUNG & HOLMES	20.00
1503	INTELLECTUAL PROPERTY	MERGES, M.& J.	22.00
1394	INTERNATIONAL BUSINESS TRANSACTIONS	FOLSOM, GORDON & SPANOGLE	18.00
1393	INTERNATIONAL LAW	CARTER & TRIMBLE	19.00
1392	INTERNATIONAL LAW	HENKIN, P., S. & S.	20.00
1390	INTERNATIONAL LAW	OLIVER, F., B., S. & W.	25.00
1331	LABOR LAW	COX, BOK, GORMAN & FINKIN	22.00
1471	LAND FINANCE (REAL ESTATE TRANS.)	BERGER & JOHNSTONE	21.00
1620	LAND FINANCE (REAL ESTATE TRANS.)	NELSON & WHITMAN	21.00
1452	LAND USE	CALLIES, FREILICH & ROBERTS	20.00
1421	LEGISLATION	ESKRIDGE, FRICKEY & GARRETT	18.00
1480	MASS MEDIA	FRANKLIN & ANDERSON	18.00
1312	NEGOTIABLE INSTRUMENTS (COMM. LAW)	JORDAN, WARREN & WALT	22.00
1541	OIL & GAS	KUNTZ., L., A., S. & P..	21.00
1540	OIL & GAS	MAXWELL, WILLIAMS, M. & K.	21.00
1561	PATENT LAW	ADELMAN, R., T. & W.	25.00
1560	PATENT LAW	FRANCIS & COLLINS	26.00
1310	PAYMENT LAW [SYST.][COMM. LAW]	SPEIDEL, SUMMERS & WHITE	25.00
1313	PAYMENT LAW (COMM.LAW / NEG. INST.)	WHALEY	23.00
1431	PRODUCTS LIABILITY	OWEN, MONTGOMERY & K.	25.00
1091	PROF. RESPONSIBILITY (ETHICS)	GILLERS	16.00
1093	PROF. RESPONSIBILITY (ETHICS)	HAZARD, KONIAK, & CRAMTON	21.00
1092	PROF. RESPONSIBILITY (ETHICS)	MORGAN & ROTUNDA	16.00
1094	PROF. RESPONSIBILITY (ETHICS)	SCHWARTZ, W. & P.	16.00
1030	PROPERTY	CASNER & LEACH -(by F., K. & V.	24.00
1031	PROPERTY	CRIBBET, J., F. & S.	24.50
1037	PROPERTY	DONAHUE, KAUPER & MARTIN	21.00
1035	PROPERTY	DUKEMINIER & KRIER	20.00
1034	PROPERTY	HAAR & LIEBMAN	23.50
1036	PROPERTY	KURTZ & HOVENKAMP	21.00
1033	PROPERTY	NELSON, STOEBUCK, & W.	23.50
1032	PROPERTY	RABIN & KWALL	23.00
1038	PROPERTY	SINGER	21.50
1621	REAL ESTATE TRANSACTIONS	GOLDSTEIN & KORNGOLD	21.00
1471	REAL ESTATE TRANS. & FIN. (LAND FINANCE)	BERGER & JOHNSTONE	21.00
1620	REAL ESTATE TRANSFER & FINANCE	NELSON & WHITMAN	21.00
1254	REMEDIES (EQUITY)	LAYCOCK	23.00
1253	REMEDIES (EQUITY)	LEAVELL, L., N. & K-F.	24.00
1252	REMEDIES (EQUITY)	RE & RE	26.00
1255	REMEDIES (EQUITY)	SHOBEN & TABB	25.50
1250	REMEDIES (EQUITY)	RENDLEMAN	28.00
1310	SALES (COMM. LAW)	SPEIDEL, SUMMERS & WHITE	25.00
1313	SALES (COMM. LAW)	WHALEY	23.00
1312	SECURED TRANS. (COMMERICIAL LAW)	JORDAN, WARREN & WALT	22.00
1310	SECURED TRANS.	SPEIDEL, SUMMERS & WHITE	25.00
1313	SECURED TRANS. (COMMERCIAL LAW)	WHALEY	23.00
1272	SECURITIES REGULATION	COX, HILLMAN, LANGEVOORT	21.00
1270	SECURITIES REGULATION	JENNINGS, M., C. & S.	21.00
1680	SPORTS LAW	WEILER & ROBERTS	20.50
1217	TAXATION (ESTATE & GIFT)	BITTKER, CLARK & McCOUCH	18.00
1219	TAXATION (INDIV. INCOME)	BURKE & FRIEL	22.00
1212	TAXATION (FEDERAL INCOME)	FREELAND, L., S. & L.	21.00
1211	TAXATION (FEDERAL INCOME)	GRAETZ & SCHENK	20.00
1210	TAXATION (FEDERAL INCOME)	KLEIN, BANKMAN & SHAVIRO	21.00
1218	TAXATION (CORPORATE)	LIND, S., L. & R.	17.00
1006	TORTS	DOBBS	22.00
1003	TORTS	EPSTEIN	23.50
1004	TORTS	FRANKLIN & RABIN	20.50
1001	TORTS	HENDERSON, P. & S.	23.50
1000	TORTS	PROSSER, W., S., K. & P.	25.00
1005	TORTS	SHULMAN, JAMES & GRAY	25.00
1281	TRADE REGULATION (ANTITRUST)	HANDLER, P., G. & W.	20.50
1410	U.C.C.	EPSTEIN, MARTIN, H. & N.	18.00
1510	WILLS/TRUSTS (GRATUITOUS TRANSFER)	CLARK, L., M., A., & M.	21.00
1223	WILLS, TRUSTS & ESTATES	DUKEMINIER & JOHANSON	22.00
1220	WILLS	MECHEM & ATKINSON	23.00

CASENOTES PUBLISHING CO. INC. ● 1640 FIFTH STREET, SUITE 208 ● SANTA MONICA, CA 90401 ● (310) 395-6500

E-Mail Address - info@casenotes.com

Website - www: http://www.casenotes.com

PLEASE PURCHASE FROM YOUR LOCAL BOOKSTORE. IF UNAVAILABLE, YOU MAY ORDER DIRECT.*

4TH CLASS POSTAGE (ALLOW TWO WEEKS) $1.00 PER ORDER; 1ST CLASS POSTAGE $3.00 (ONE BOOK), $2.00 EACH (TWO OR MORE BOOKS)

*CALIF. RESIDENTS PLEASE ADD 8¼% SALES TAX